The Infinite Moment

The Infinite Moment
and Other Essays in
Robert Browning

BY

WILLIAM O. RAYMOND

UNIVERSITY OF TORONTO PRESS: 1950

*Copyright, Canada, 1950
University of Toronto Press
Printed in Canada
London: Geoffrey Cumberlege
Oxford University Press*

PR
4238
.R3

Preface

WITH THE EXCEPTION of the closing essay, the contents of this book represent a garnering of various articles on the poetry of Browning printed during the course of years in scholarly journals. Roughly they divide themselves into two classes: essays of a general character and articles of a more specialized nature. One or two of the latter I have hesitated to include, because their findings have been accepted in recent authoritative works on Browning. Since, however, the processes of investigation which led to their conclusions are of some interest, I have let them stand as they were written, with the addition of a few notes on subsequent confirmatory evidence. The essay on "The Forgeries of Thomas J. Wise and Their Aftermath" possibly breaks the unity of the book as a collection of Browning essays. Yet, as the defence of Sir Edmund Gosse against the charge of being implicated in the Wise forgeries, centres about the circumstances which led him to combine the story of Mrs. Browning's first showing the manuscript of *Sonnets from the Portuguese* to her husband with the fictitious tale of their printing in the Reading edition, I have felt that this essay has at least an indirect connection with the body of the book.

My thanks are due to the editors of the following journals who have very kindly allowed me to make use of material previously printed in these magazines: *Publications of the Modern Language Association of America; Studies in Philology; Modern Language Notes; The University of Toronto Quarterly; Journal of English and Germanic Philology; The Baylor Bulletin; Papers of the Michigan Academy of Science, Arts, and Letters.*

I should like to express my appreciation of financial assistance from the Humanities Research Council of Canada and the Publication Fund of the University of Toronto Press.

I am indebted to Miss F. G. Halpenny, Assistant Editor of the University of Toronto Press, for her careful and able editing of the text and notes of my manuscript.

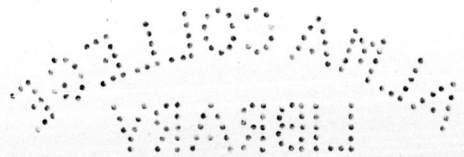

List of Abbreviations

THE following abbreviated forms of reference have been used:

Archiv   *Archiv für das Studium der neueren Sprachen*

AJT   *American Journal of Theology*

BJRL   *Bulletin of the John Rylands Library*

CJ   *Classical Journal*

Essays and Studies   *Essays and Studies by Members of the English Association*

ELH   *ELH: A Journal of English Literary History*

HSCP   *Harvard Studies in Classical Philology*

HTR   *Harvard Theological Review*

MLN   *Modern Language Notes*

MLR   *Modern Language Review*

PMLA   *Publications of the Modern Language Association of America*

QR   *Quarterly Review*

RSSCW   *Research Studies of the State College of Washington*

SP   *Studies in Philology*

UMS   *University of Missouri Studies*

Contents

1	The Infinite Moment	3
2	Browning and Higher Criticism	19
3	"Our Lady of Bellosguardo": A Pastel Portrait	52
4	New Light on the Genesis of *The Ring and the Book*	75
5	Browning's First Mention of the Documentary Sources of *The Ring and the Book*	89
6	Browning's Roman Murder Story as Recorded in a Hitherto Unknown Italian Contemporary Manuscript	95
7	Browning's Dark Mood: A Study of *Fifine at the Fair*	105
8	Browning's Casuists	129
9	Browning's Conception of Love as Represented in *Paracelsus*	156
10	The Forgeries of Thomas J. Wise and Their Aftermath	176
11	Browning Studies in England and America, 1910-1949	193
	Notes	232
	Index	245

The Infinite Moment

Oh moment, one and infinite!
—*By the Fire-side*

1

The Infinite Moment

THOUGH IT IS now sixty years since the death of Robert Browning, the time is yet unripe for a definitive estimate of his place amongst English men of letters. During his lifetime he experienced, perhaps to a greater extent than any of his contemporaries, the vicissitudes of a poet's lot. A long period of depreciation, in which his poetry was a byword for difficulty and obscurity, was followed by a sudden access of fame. From the time of the publication of *The Ring and the Book* in 1868-69 until his death in 1889, his niche beside Tennyson as one of the two master poets of the Victorian era was secure. Criticism was succeeded by panegyric, reaching its acme in the adulation of the Browning Society and its mushroom offshoots in England and America.

In the sixty years that have passed since Browning's death, his poetic reputation has varied as widely as in his lifetime. The pendulum of critical opinion has again swung violently from one extreme to the other. In particular, Browning has suffered, along with Tennyson, from the general reaction inimical to Victorianism and all its works which has characterized the opening decades of the twentieth century. There are signs that the nadir has been reached, and that a juster and truer appreciation of the Victorian epoch is at hand. But we are still in the wake of that inevitable shift of literary evaluation which marks the transition from one generation to the next. The baiting of Victorianism continues to be a favourite sport of modern writers; and prevailing currents of present-day historical and aesthetic criticism run counter to some of the cherished ideals and standards in life and art of our Victorian forerunners. Part of this censure is wholesome, part is regrettable, but the winnowing of our Victorian inheritance by the fan of time is as yet incomplete.

A tentative estimate, within brief compass, of Browning's place in English letters must strive for centrality of view. In reckoning with a poet of such far-ranging interests, it is important to insist that he be appraised first of all as an artist. However beguiling the bypaths of his work in literature may be, it is essential to keep steadily in sight the beaten highway, lit by the flash of his genius, where his powers are exhibited at full stretch.

Yet such an emphasis should not be inconsistent with a recognition of the composite nature of Browning's contribution to English poetry. In certain ways he is both an intellectual and a moralist, and the philosophical, ethical, and theological aspects of his writings are fruitful subjects of inquiry. Much has been said concerning the confinement of these elements of his work within a set Victorian mould. But in dealing with a mind of a rare order and a poet of genius, stress should be laid upon those gleams of intuition which break through the conventional Victorian framework with keen insight into the heart of life and the problems of man's destiny. Such a reverie as that of Pope Innocent XII, in *The Ring and the Book,* is no mere collection of theological platitudes. It is a definitive summing-up of Browning's philosophy of life, and a high watermark of metaphysical thought in nineteenth-century poetry, enriched by acute religious perception.

Nevertheless, it is inevitable that a study of the didactic interests of Browning often leads to the periphery rather than to the centre of his poetry. Within their sphere, prodigious mental energy or moral fervour tends to obscure the poet. There is in him a conflict between imagination and intellect, only resolved in the poems of happiest vein, written between 1840 and 1870, beginning with *Pippa Passes* and ending with *The Ring and the Book.* For the understanding of his view of life, the deep-seated opposition between faith and reason pivotal to his thought, his ethical outlook, his conception of the relation between God and man and of man's place in the universe, a consideration of the

The Infinite Moment

earlier and later poems lying outside his golden period of imaginative vision is indispensable. Nor can the depths of Browning's analysis of character be plumbed without a knowledge of those stages of his work which abound in subtle probing of impulse and motive, the incidents in the development of the soul underlying outward action.

In order to comprehend these varying interests, a student must toil through the labyrinth of *Sordello,* "a bewildering potpourri of poetry, psychology, love, romance, humanitarianism, philosophy, fiction, and history."[1] He must wrestle with poems which in the aggregate, at any rate, tax his patience and mental faculties even more than that "Giant Despair" of English letters. Some of the later writings of Browning, while they contain lines and passages of sheer poetic beauty, are jungles of involved argument. The mind reels amid the elusive, ever shifting sophistries of *Fifine at the Fair* and *Aristophanes' Apology,* or is repelled by the sordidness of *Red Cotton Night-Cap Country.* Though the poet tells us that a delectable ortolan is sandwiched between the plain bread of *Ferishtah's Fancies,* the appetite of the average reader is hardly reconciled to the crust he must crunch before reaching the toothsome bird.

Even the wit and dexterity of Browning's numerous studies in casuistry scarcely atone for their redundancy. We are dizzied by their juggling and wearied by their tortuousness. *Mr. Sludge, "the Medium," Bishop Blougram's Apology,* and *Prince Hohenstiel-Schwangau* are overweighted with ratiocination. The hair-splitting arguments of the lawyers in *The Ring and the Book* make gnarly and tiresome reading, and their crabbed forensic quibbles are only slightly enlivened by quaint Latin puns illustrating the humour of pedants. Whatever tribute is due to Browning's ingenuity in constructing these cumbersome leviathans of verse, the most ardent devotee of the poet, when caught in their toils, must compare his state of mind to that of Milton's spirits in torment, who "found no end in wandering mazes lost."

Happily for Browning's enduring fame as an artist, he has written a large body of fine poetry in which he was able to exorcize his intellectual devil. He cast it from him, even as the hero of one of his poems, in rollicking mockery of arid scholasticism, tossed the bulky tome of Sibrandus Schafnaburgensis into the crevice of a garden tree. "Plague take all your pedants, say I!" It is a pleasure to turn from the "grey argument" of tracts of his verse to the magic of such poetry as is garnered in *Dramatic Romances* and *Men and Women*. Here imagination has not been supplanted by dialectic; and passion and intuition are enlisted in the depicting of character and situation with swift and brilliant portraiture. The sweep and vivacity of Browning's humanism are a perpetual source of delight. As a humanist he is of the lineage of Chaucer and Shakespeare, a poet of whose work it may be said, "here is God's plenty." Above all other Victorian writers, he has that spaciousness of mind we are wont to link with the Elizabethans. Spiritually a disciple of the Renaissance, he is akin to that great age in his zest of life, *élan* of temperament, overflowing curiosity regarding the ways and works of man. His creative genius has many facets and in richness and versatility is unsurpassed in nineteenth-century English literature. How far flung is his poetic net and what treasure trove he brings to land! Strange fish sometimes, but all

> Live whelks, each lip's beard dripping fresh,
> As if they still the water's lisp heard
> Through foam the rock-weeds thresh.

I intend to centre my estimate of Browning on his artistic quality. This, in itself, has various aspects, and many of them must be left untouched. His dramatic gift, its capacity and limitation, is a fascinating theme, but it has been exhaustively written on from various points of view. The style and diction of his verse have been the subject of a number of technical treatises. I have in mind, rather, to dwell on what may be called the elemental spirit of Browning's art. This choice is in part due to a wish to take issue with what I conceive to be the general drift of Browning criticism at present. If I interpret this rightly,

The Infinite Moment

its quarrel is with the whole tone and temper of the poet's work, not with this or that specific weakness.

An initial definition is, therefore, necessary. What is the basic element which inhabits and glints through the body of Browning's verse as its pervasive and animating soul? Can we in reading his numerous poems, so diverse in theme and setting, "loose their subtle spirit" in a cruce, like the Arab sage of *In a Gondola*?

Writing to Elizabeth Barrett in 1845,[2] Browning spoke of his poetry as momentary escapes of a bright and alive inner power and (in a figure of speech) compared it to flashes of light he had seen at sea leaping out at intervals from a narrow chink in a Mediterranean pharos. The vehemence and impulsiveness of Browning's verse have been universally recognized. Both the form and the content of his poetry are vividly impressionistic. His favourite medium is the dramatic monologue, which in his best work is the distillation of a crucial moment of human experience. Light is focused at one point in a white heat of concentration and intensity. In the revelation of the significance of the precipitous moment, vivacity and turbulence are outstanding attributes of his poetic diction and spirit.

Yet the general recognition of the flair or impetuosity of Browning's poetry has by no means been accompanied by unanimity of opinion concerning its merit. Differing judgments of this essential quality have led to a battle of controversy, dividing the poet's admirers and detractors into hostile camps. Before singling it out for praise, it is, therefore, well to glance at some of the criticism it has provoked. "Cockney Sublime, Cockney Energy," was FitzGerald's jaundiced comment.[3] In our own day, Mr. Santayana, in an essay "The Poetry of Barbarism," has scored the work of Browning as that of "a thought and an art inchoate and ill-digested, of a volcanic eruption that tosses itself quite blindly and ineffectually into the sky."[4] Santayana likens Browning to Whitman, and in this comparison has been followed by T. S. Eliot.

The germ of that approach to Browning's writings which

emphasizes their so-called barbaric, Gothic, ultra-romantic elements, may be found back in 1864, in Bagehot's "Wordsworth, Tennyson, and Browning, or, Pure, Ornate, and Grotesque Art in English Poetry." It is a conception that was taken up and enlarged upon by Chesterton in his arresting but untrustworthy biography of the poet. Of late it has been made a formidable weapon of attack in the hands of a school of aesthetic thought which extols classical standards and is deeply distrustful of romanticism. F. L. Lucas has given recent expression to this neo-classicist credo in *The Decline and Fall of the Romantic Ideal*. Our appraisal of it will depend on whether we regard romanticism as abnormal and pathological, or as rooted in an experience of life as normative and intrinsic as that on which the classic tradition is based. It is important to recognize that criticism of Browning as voiced by Irving Babbitt, Santayana, F. L. Lucas, and T. S. Eliot is an offshoot of a general neo-classicist position.

Viewed as a whole, the modern indictment of the energy of Browning's poetry seems a weighty one. At present, the moral, intellectual, and aesthetic aspects of his outlook on life are all suspect. To Santayana, the poet's vagrancy of impulse is indicative of the barbarity of his genius, the essence of which lies in the fact that to him "life is an adventure, not a discipline; that the exercise of energy is the absolute good, irrespective of motives or of consequences."[5] To Babbitt, Browning's unrestrained emotion is an example of those centrifugal and neurotic tendencies that, from the standpoint of neo-classicism, are regarded as evidence of a decadent romanticism. Passion and sensation, we are told, run riot in his poetry, and there is an utter lack of classical decorum, balance, and repose. To Mr. Lucas, there is a trace of a bouncing vulgarity in Browning's energetic verse, which smacks too much of the hearty hail-fellow-well-met manner of a Philistine. Metaphorically speaking, the unfastidious poet slaps his readers on the back. His "stamping and shouting," the jarring dissonances of his verse, "his hastily scribbled poems as fuzzy and prickly and tangled as a furze-bush"[6] are at once excesses of his temperament and an undisciplined romanticism. Such comments are reminiscent of an earlier criticism that all of Browning's poetry is summed up in the line, "*Bang-whang-whang* goes the drum, *tootle-te-tootle* the fife."[7]

Although, in justice to Mr. Lucas, it should be noted that he does recognize the vitality of Browning's dramatic portrayal of human life, the general tenor of his criticism seems to me indicative of a mental twist which inhibits him from depicting the great men of letters of the Victorian age with disinterested objectivity. It is the fate of every generation to have its idols shattered by the hammer blows of the succeeding generation. Since the publication of Lytton Strachey's life of Queen Victoria, there have been many acute and witty *exposés* of the foibles, conventions, and conservatisms of the Victorian era. Yet what so many twentieth-century critics lack is a perception of the dignity, poise, and stability of that era, an ethos contributing to the endowment of its principal personages with nobility of character. To ignore these basic elements in Victorianism in delineating its great men is to view the age through a subtly distorted mirror in which every figure is out of focus.

Every man, it has been said, has the defect of his quality, and it might be added, every poet in his art has the defect of his quality. Browning's energy and vitality at times din the ear and become strident and overpowering. Though "barbarism" is not supposed to be a mid-Victorian vice, there is something unbridled in his rush of passion and the militant romanticism of his verse. He can write metallic poems and rhyming exercises. When he is lost in the Cretan labyrinth of his longer poems, his style is as crabbed and involved as his subject-matter.

But the error and insufficiency of the criticism I have been reviewing seems to be that it fastens exclusively on the negative rather than on the positive aspect of the poet's elemental attribute. For it is precisely the dash or verve of his poetry which constitutes its perennial originality and attractiveness. It is a strain running like an *elixir vitae* through his verse in its golden era, giving it headiness and flavour. We are reminded of the violent rush of a mountain torrent frothing and seething amongst rocks and fretting its channel, but compensating for its lack of smooth rhythmical flow by the spin and dance, the spray and sparkle of its waters. "Passion's too fierce to be in fetters bound." From the critical censure of Browning's energy and impulsiveness we turn away, as our eye falls, perchance, with renewed delight on the opening lines of *Pippa Passes*:

> Day!
> Faster and more fast,
> O'er night's brim, day boils at last:
> Boils, pure gold, o'er the cloud-cup's brim
> Where spurting and suppressed it lay. . . .

The relation between the form and the content of the poetry of Browning is often a tension rather than a harmony. All poetry, he once wrote to Ruskin, is the problem of "putting the infinite within the finite."[8] It would carry us too far afield to show how the antithesis of infinite and finite is perpetually in his thought. But it is clear that the crux of the struggle in his life as an artist was the difficulty of bodying forth the content of his imagination and intellect in adequate poetic forms. In *Sordello*, which in many ways is a confessional document, there is a vivid account of the hero's attempt to forge a new language, in an Italian dialect, capable of expressing the novelty of his thoughts and perceptions. The analogy between this and Browning's wrestling with language is unmistakable. Like Sordello, he was striving to make his diction a suitable vehicle for the new type of analytic poetry he was writing. The arduousness of the process is realistically described:

> He left imagining, to try the stuff
> That held the imaged thing, and, let it writhe
> Never so fiercely, scarce allowed a tithe
> To reach the light—his Language.   (II. 570-73)

Sordello, from the point of view of style, is a gigantic experiment in artistic technique. It is apprentice work of a faulty kind, yet through its convolutions the poet was feeling his way towards his true manner.

The Infinite Moment

And when, after the murkiness of *Sordello,* the art of Browning begins to clear nobly in *Pippa Passes,* discovers its true bent in *Dramatic Lyrics* and *Dramatic Romances,* and reaches its meridian in *Men and Women,* the triumph of his style is all the more impressive because it has been hardly won. In the dramatic monologue of medium length, he found the poetic instrument he had vainly sought in *Sordello.* His metres and diction instinctively adapt themselves to impressionistic vignettes of picturesque situations and crucial moments in the lives of men and women, often enriched by pregnant historical or artistic backgrounds. Tension of style remains, but it is a close-packed, sensitive tension that is responsive to the subtle and varied play of highly charged thought and emotion. The tempo of Browning's diction in his great dramatic monologues is rapid to the point of abruptness. The metres have the beat of a driving energy. The music of his verse is uneven rather than smooth flowing, involving frequent suspensions and resolutions.

Le style c'est l'homme; and the racy, colloquial style of Browning in the best of his dramatic monologues is a revelation of his intrinsic quality. He has used a greater variety of metres than any other modern poet, but his verse is never rigidly set in a conventional mould. In reading Tennyson's lines,

> All in the blue unclouded weather
> Thick-jewell'd shone the saddle-leather,

we realize that the imagery is enclosed in a sedate metrical framework. But when Browning writes,

> To mine, it serves for the old June weather
> Blue above lane and wall,

there is a natural felicity in the utterance which shakes itself free from formal trappings.

Within its own province, there is a finality in the organic structure, the Sophia and Technê of Greek art; where communication is so wedded to inspiration, form to content, that, as Browning has pointed out in *Old Pictures in Florence,* it achieves perfection in the sphere of the finite. But romantic art, as an emanation of the spirit of man in one of the two basic moments of his experience, has a genius of its own. It may lack the radiance of classic art, that clarity and harmony representative of "the depth and not the tumult of the soul." Yet there is a place on the altars of literature for the Dionysiac fire of romantic art: Dionysiac fire at times, but, when it burns as a purer flame, the light of the Holy Grail. Poetry must in certain moods reveal the tension of the spirit straining at the leash of form, and infinite passion shattering the web of finite expression:

> Thoughts hardly to be packed
> Into a narrow act,
> Fancies that broke through language and escaped.

Therefore, despite the frown of the classicist, a lover of Browning's poetry may take pleasure in its romantic beauty and in the free rein given to passion and sensation. He may enjoy its impressionistic glooms and glances, its live and nervous diction responsive to the "moment one and infinite" of electrically charged emotion. He may feel the justification of a content that overweights the form, and a tension that is like the pent-up energy of a storm-cloud:

> There are flashes struck from midnights,
> There are fire-flames noondays kindle. . . .

A few examples of the flair and verve of Browning's verse may be cited at random from the poems composed between 1840 and 1870.

The sensuousness of Browning's imagery is vivid and often opulent, but never cloying or languorous. He has too much energy ever to indulge in the sleepy sensuousness of Spenser. Frequently his imagery is associated with a wealth and exotic splendour of colour. In *Popularity,* his eye revels in the Tyrian blue or purple dye extracted from a secretion in the shell of the murex, and he combines this colour with the lustre of gold in two dazzling pictures. The dye, he tells us, is

> Enough to furnish Solomon
> Such hangings for his cedar-house,
> That, when gold-robed he took the throne

> In that abyss of blue, the Spouse
> Might swear his presence shone
>
> Most like the centre-spike of gold
> Which burns deep in the blue-bell's womb,
> What time, with ardours manifold,
> The bee goes singing to her groom,
> Drunken and overbold.

Images of light, sound, and motion are conjoined in the triumphant close of *Rabbi Ben Ezra,* where the philosophic argument of the Jewish sage takes imaginative wings:

> Look not thou down but up!
> To uses of a cup,
> The festal board, lamp's flash and trumpet's peal,
> The new wine's foaming flow,
> The Master's lips a-glow!
> Thou, heaven's consummate cup, what need'st thou
>   with earth's wheel?   (ll. 175-80)

Abt Vogler is a fine example of a sustained piece of imagery, representing a crescendo of feeling evoked by music. In other poems, imagery flares forth at the peak of an emotional mood like a beacon of passion. How the lines kindle in *The Statue and the Bust* when the cowardly and procrastinating lovers are contrasted with the militant saints of God!

> Only they see not God, I know,
> Nor all that chivalry of his,
> The soldier-saints who, row on row,
> Burn upward each to his point of bliss. . . .   (ll. 220-23)

Browning's descriptions of nature are as impressionistic as his vistas of human life, and reveal to an equal degree his elemental property. There is occasional tranquillity in his landscapes, but as a rule this is the brief hush that follows or precedes a moment of highly wrought emotional tension. As the lovers in *By the Fire-side* wait for the flash of revelation that is to fuse their lives in one, the brooding quietness of evening o'erhangs woodland and mountain.

> Oh moment, one and infinite!
> The water slips o'er stock and stone;
> The West is tender, hardly bright:
> How grey at once is the evening grown—
> One star, its chrysolite!   (ll. 181-85)

But Browning's typical delineation of nature is in keeping with the high tide of dramatic passion that surges through his poetry. In *Pippa Passes,* the lightning seems to search for the guilty lovers, Sebald and Ottima, like the bared sword of divine justice.

> Buried in woods we lay, you recollect;
> Swift ran the searching tempest overhead;
> And ever and anon some bright white shaft
> Burned thro' the pine-tree roof, here burned and there,
> As if God's messenger thro' the close wood screen
> Plunged and replunged his weapon at a venture,
> Feeling for guilty thee and me: then broke
> The thunder like a whole sea overhead....   (I. 190-97)

In *The Ring and the Book,* the Pope's one hope for the salvation of Guido is visualized through a similar piece of fiery landscape painting.

> I stood at Naples once, a night so dark
> I could have scarce conjectured there was earth
> Anywhere, sky or sea or world at all:
> But the night's black was burst through by a blaze—
> Thunder struck blow on blow, earth groaned and bore,
> Through her whole length of mountain visible:
> There lay the city thick and plain with spires,
> And, like a ghost disshrouded, white the sea.
> So may the truth be flashed out by one blow,
> And Guido see, one instant, and be saved.   (X. 219-28)

Browning's delight in brilliant and intense colour blends with his love of Italian scenery. In *De Gustibus,* he prefers a Mediterranean vista, "the great opaque blue breadth of sea without a break," to the pastoral lanes and coppices of England. He takes particular pleasure in the semi-tropical bounty of nature in June in these lines of *Pippa Passes*:

> Well for those who live through June!
> Great noontides, thunder-storms, all glaring pomps
> That triumph at the heels of June the god
> Leading his revel through our leafy world.   (III. 153-56)

The freshness and animation of the poet's landscapes are as typical as their emotional thrust. He pictures Florence as seen in spring "through the live translucent bath of air," when "river and bridge and street and square" are as clear "as the sights in a magic crystal ball." The common phenomenon of the breaking of ice in a pond gives birth, in *The Flight of the Duchess,* to the following exquisite description:

> Well, early in autumn, at first winter-warning,
> When the stag had to break with his foot, of a
> morning,
> A drinking-hole out of the fresh tender ice
> That covered the pond till the sun, in a trice,
> Loosening it, let out a ripple of gold,
> And another and another, and faster and faster,
> Till, dimpling to blindness, the wide water
> rolled. . . .   (ll. 216-22)

Il fait vivre ses phrases. It is, as I have striven to show, the incomparable gusto of Browning's poetry that is its essential quality. And this gusto is not the outpouring in art of the hearty exuberance of a Philistine, or the pietistic enthusiasm of an irresponsible optimist. It is rather—if one may apply to it words used by Arthur Symons in connection with the humour of *The Pied Piper of Hamelin* and *Confessions* — "the jolly laughter of an unaffected nature, the effervescence of a sparkling and overflowing brain."[9] It has its roots in a sound physical constitution, a fine fibre of intellect, and a glow of life which, to cite Elizabeth Barrett's tribute, "shows a heart within blood-tinctured, of a veined humanity."[10]

Undoubtedly, Browning's superb physical health is an element of this gusto. In *Saul,* David sings of "our manhood's prime vigour," the play of muscle and sinew, "the leaping from rock up to rock," and "the plunge in a pool's living water." Idealist though the poet is, there is a genial and aromatic flavour of mother earth in his writings, and he draws sustenance from her which races through his veins like the sap of trees in spring. "Oh, good gigantic smile o' the brown old earth!" he exclaims in *James Lee's Wife*. This touch with earth is reflected in his unique chronicling of insect life, that form of animal existence which is in most intimate conjunction with the soil. The prodigal and spawning energy of nature, riotous with life, is whimsically portrayed in *Sibrandus Schafnaburgensis*. The worm, slug, eft, water-beetle, and newt, invading the covers of a ponderous volume, are symbolic of sheer animal frolic, mocking dry-as-dust pedantry and the dead bones of a musty scholasticism:

> All that life and fun and romping,
> All that frisking and twisting and coupling,
> While slowly our poor friend's leaves were
>   swamping
> And clasps were cracking and covers suppling!

Allied with this love of energy in the physical world is Browning's keen perception of the grotesque. For the grotesque is a bold and peremptory shattering of conventional moulds. As Chesterton has said: "The element of the grotesque in art, like the element of the grotesque in nature, means, in the main, energy, the energy which takes its own forms and goes its own way."[11]

But the *élan* of the poet's art has more subtle and spiritual springs in his intellectual and emotional gifts. These gifts have their extravagances. The suppleness of Browning's mind and his temperamental impetuosity often lead him to strain at the curb of form. Yet the turns and twists of his verse, his metrical liberties, his unexpected and at times somersaulting rhymes, are usually the bubbling-up of irrepressible high spirits, chafing at the yoke of aught that is tame or conventional. It should be noted that he only gives rein to an "outrageous gallop of rhymes" in poems having a certain raciness or bohemianism of content, such as *The Flight of the Duchess, Old Pictures in Florence,* or *Pacchiarotto*. When set in their proper perspective and viewed in relation to the whole body of his poetry, these outward

The Infinite Moment

flourishes of style, even when pushed to the verge of idiosyncrasy, are not to be condemned sweepingly as barbaric wilfulness. They are often the frothings of a superabundant vitality, a tang of life like that of Fra Lippo Lippi, shattering the moulds of artistic decorum in a spirit of Puckish impishness.

> A laugh, a cry, the business of the world . . .
> And my whole soul revolves, the cup runs over,
> The world and life's too big to pass for a dream,
> And I do these wild things in sheer despite,
> And play the fooleries you catch me at,
> In pure rage!   (ll. 247-54)

Though we must look to the future for an impartial evaluation of Victorian literature, it is evident that Browning, with the possible exception of Carlyle, had a more robust and sinewy mind than any of his contemporaries. He is a great humanist; and however deeply and broadly he quarries in the mine of the thoughts and emotions of men and women, the vein never runs thin, though it may lead at times through tortuous tunnels. The horizons of an intellect of such power and fertility are vast; and linked with this amplitude is the gift of communicating the joy and tingle of his contact with life. In this respect he allies himself with Chaucer, Fielding, and Scott. Like theirs his interest in humanity is unflagging, and while he does not maintain their objectivity of representation, he probes deeper than any of his forerunners into the inner springs of character.

As we travel imaginatively with Browning in many climes and ages, a panorama full of light and colour is unrolled. On a spacious canvas, through an astonishing variety of circumstance, he mirrors the subtle and ceaseless play of impulse and motive flaming up in moments of highly wrought passion into the crux of action,

> When a soul declares itself—to wit,
> By its fruit, the thing it does![12]

In speaking of the poems of Browning that culminate with *The Ring and the Book,* Mr. Osbert Burdett has said: "If it be still urged that the poetry of Browning loses for want of repose, the reply is that, in these poems, we do not miss it but are carried by the poet while we read into his own world of vigorous healthy imagination, a world so rich, vivid, and finely fashioned that it is one of the most original and dramatic possessions of our literature."[13]

While individual judgments are always relative, it is a test of quality when we can return in later years with unabated pleasure to the work of a poet loved in youth, and "obey the voice at eve, obeyed at prime." Browning measures up to this test, because the volume of his poetry is "the precious life-blood of a master spirit." Into its pages, through the alchemy of genius, the elixir of a generous personality has been distilled. In a large human sense, the best of Browning's work does not date—always a touchstone of worth.

In the most famous passage of *The Advancement of Learning,* Bacon says of poetry: "And, therefore it was ever thought to have some participation of divineness, because it doth raise and erect the mind, by submitting the shows of things to the desires of the mind." The classicist may complain that Browning bullies "the shows of things" into submission. Despite his recognition of "the value and significance of flesh," he does at times wrest the body of art, its sensuous elements, in order to

> Make new hopes shine through the flesh they fray,
> New fears aggrandize the rags and tatters:
> To bring the invisible full into play!
> Let the visible go to the dogs—what matters?[14]

Yet it is the informing presence of a discursive, fully charged mind that is an unfailing source of enjoyment to the sympathetic reader of his poetry. Like Donne, whom in many ways Browning strikingly resembles, he might have spoken of "the sinewy thread my brain lets fall." In this fibre of thought, interwoven with ardour of temperament, lies the genesis of his verve and originality—that flash of life which I have singled out as the essential quality of his poetry.

2

Browning and Higher Criticism

AMID THE SHIFTING cross currents of religious controversy in England during the middle years of the nineteenth century, there are few points of view equal in freshness and interest to that of Browning. Nor among his brother poets of the Victorian age is there one whose work throws more light on the typical attitude of the English mind in relation to philosophy and religion. Individualism, subjectivity, lack of systematic development, absence of radicalism—attributes which have been singled out as eminently characteristic of English speculative thought in the nineteenth century[1]—are strikingly illustrated in Browning's representation of the religious problems of the mid-Victorian era.

Though Browning's religious views were not, in the traditional sense, orthodox, his attitude towards Higher Criticism, with what he conceived to be its rationalistic interpretation of Christianity, was one of clearly marked antagonism. That this hostility, first expressed in *Christmas-Eve and Easter-Day*, 1850, continued to the close of his life, is shown by the following anecdote concerning the poet, in which Mrs. Humphry Ward refers to his disapproval of the liberal theology of *Robert Elsmere*:

He did not like 'Robert Elsmere' which appeared the year before his death; and I was told a striking story by a common friend of his and mine, who was present at a discussion of the book at a literary house. Browning, said my friend, was of the party. The discussion turned on the divinity of Christ. After listening a while, Browning expressed his entire disagreement with the main argument of the book, repeating with dramatic force the anecdote of Charles Lamb, in conversation with Leigh Hunt on the subject of "Persons one would wish to have seen"; when, after ranging through literature and philosophy, Lamb added, "There is one other Person — If Shakespeare was to come into the room, we should all rise up to meet him; but if that Person was to come into it, we should fall down and try to kiss the hem of his garment!"[2]

Although Mrs. Ward was apparently unaware of them, there are other instances recorded of Browning's quotation of these words of Lamb. One, in particular, occurs twelve years before the occasion to which she alludes. In a letter written in 1876, as a message of comfort to a woman who believed herself to be dying, the poet, while dwelling on the evidences for the power and love of God, speaks of his soul having been thrilled to its depth by the convictions of certain men of genius regarding the person of Christ. Illustrating this statement he writes:

. . . as when Napoleon, shutting up the New Testament, said of Christ: "Do you know that I am an understander of men? Well, He was no man!" ("Savez-vous que je me connais en hommes? Eh bien, celui-là ne fut pas un homme.") Or as when Charles Lamb, in a gay fancy with some friends as to how he and they would feel if the greatest of the dead were to appear suddenly in flesh and blood once more, on the final suggestion, "And if Christ entered this room?" changed his manner at once, and stuttered out, as his manner was when moved, "You see, if Shakespeare entered, we should all rise; if *He* appeared we must kneel."[3]

While the reasons for Browning's dislike of Higher Criticism are more complex than at first appear, his antagonism may in part be attributed to the influence of historical environment. As contrasted with the liberal tendencies of Continental thought, insularity and conservatism dominated English theology from 1800 to 1860. The vast majority of Browning's fellow-countrymen were totally ignorant of the aims and methods of Biblical Criticism. The rank and file of the clergy stoutly adhered to the traditional view of the verbal and mechanical inspiration of the Scriptures. Writing to Julius Hare in 1835 — the year of the publication of Strauss's *Das Leben Jesu*—Thomas Arnold notes as one of the objects of a proposed theological review: "To make some beginnings of Biblical Criticism, which, as far as relates to the Old Testament, is in England almost nonexistent."[4] In 1841, Connop Thirlwall—who had previously declared that at Oxford a knowledge of German exposed a divine to the suspicion of heterodoxy—wrote to a correspondent: ". . . there is no English theological journal connected with the Church which does not *studiously* keep its readers in the dark as to everything that is said and done in German theology."[5]

Nor, despite the broadening influence of *Essays and Reviews,* was the situation changed essentially, so far as the popular mind was concerned, by the time of the publication of Colenso's *The Pentateuch and Book of Joshua Critically Examined* and Renan's *La Vie de Jésus* in the eighteen-sixties. In 1861, the Vicar of St. Mary the Virgin preached a series of sermons at Oxford against *Essays and Reviews,* in which, as has been wittily said, he smote the "seven champions" of these heretical treatises with "the jawbone of an ass." During the course of his fiery philippics he asserts:

The Bible is none other than "the voice of Him that sitteth upon the Throne"! Every book of it—every chapter of it—every verse of it—every syllable of it—(where are we to stop?) every *letter* of it—is the direct utterance of the most High! The Bible is none other than the Word of God—not some part of it more, some part of it less, but all alike, the utterance of Him who sitteth upon the Throne—absolute—faultless—unerring—supreme.[6]

In 1864, eleven thousand clergymen signed the *Oxford Declaration* on inspiration and eternal punishment, in which they pledge themselves to accept "without reserve or qualification the inspiration and Divine authority of the whole canonical Scriptures as, not only containing, but being the Word of God." In the same year, a British reviewer sounds the following note of warning to the public:

Heresy is creeping in through very narrow meshes. We have the poison of the *Essays and Reviews* creeping in through the veins of the talented, the philosophical, and the learned; we have the false arithmetic of Colenso making the books of Moses a cunningly devised fable; we have Renan's "History of Christ," in which our Savior is painted in terms so beautiful as to make him a moon-eyed enthusiast and an unworthy imposter. Are these the times in which we are to remove the landmarks of our fathers?[7]

In 1875, Robertson Smith's article on the Bible in the ninth edition of the *Encyclopaedia Britannica,* was received, as Edmund Gosse has put it, "with a howl of horror," and led to its author's expulsion from his chair of Biblical Exegesis at Aberdeen in 1881. Even as late as 1890, the great English statesman Gladstone, in *The Impregnable Rock of Holy Scripture,* strove to show that, despite the discoveries of modern science and the results of historical criticism, the early chapters of Genesis were infallible.

Nor was the distrust of such writers as Strauss and Renan confined to the orthodox and conservative. Many of the intellectual pioneers of liberal theology in England were repelled by the rationalistic temper of German criticism. Neither the critico-historical group of English liberals represented by Thomas Arnold and the Oriel Noetics, nor the philosophical group represented by Frederick Denison Maurice and the followers of Coleridge, was prepared to subscribe to the findings of *Das Leben Jesu* and *La Vie de Jésus.* Though denounced by Newman as a free thinker, on account of his acceptance of degrees of inspiration in the Old Testament, Arnold, in 1839, expressed his abhorrence of the teachings of the Tübingen school. Amongst various symptoms of the distressed state of the Church, he notes: "And the Zurich Government putting Strauss forward as an instructor of Christians! It is altogether so sad, that if I were to allow myself to dwell much upon it, I think it would utterly paralyse me. I could sit still and pine and die."[8] In like manner, Maurice, who was dismissed from King's College, in 1853, on account of the "dangerous tendency" of his opinions on the doctrine of eternal punishment, was violently repelled by Bishop

Colenso's rationalistic examination of the Hexateuch. In a letter to Llewellyn Davies he says: "The pain which Colenso's book has caused me is more than I can tell you. I used nearly your words, 'It is the most purely negative criticism I ever read,' in writing to him."[9] Even Matthew Arnold, a champion of disinterested criticism and a free lance in theology, ranged himself with the opponents of Colenso, and regarded his work as an unwarranted introduction of the minutiae of science into the sphere of religious truth.[10]

Through their more intimate knowledge of German philosophy and biblical scholarship, the younger group of Broad Churchmen were more sympathetic with the outlook of the Tübingen school than Thomas Arnold or Maurice. The publication of *Essays and Reviews* in 1860 constitutes a landmark in the history of English theology. As Pfleiderer says: "The storm which this collection of theological essays by various authors called up in England had great similarity with the commotion produced in Germany by Strauss's *Leben Jesu*."[11] Yet even these polemical papers indicate the difference between English thought of the most advanced type on the central dogmas of religion and the more radical views of Strauss and Renan. The spirit of free inquiry is tempered by an instinctive absence of revolutionary sentiment, and progress is conjoined with that innate reverence for the past so embedded in the English character.

Were the religious attachments of Browning between 1850 and 1870 such as would incline him to take a more liberal and sympathetic view of the writings of Strauss and Renan than that of the average educated English layman? Fräulein Käthe Göritz declares: "Aus dem Geiste der Broad Church Movement ist Browning's 'Christmas-Eve and Easter-Day' geboren."[12] But the poet opposed the representative Broad Church *Essays and Reviews* and Colenso's *The Pentateuch and Book of Joshua Critically Examined* as vigorously as he did the more drastic works of Strauss and Renan. Witness the following lines from *Gold Hair* published in *Dramatis Personae,* 1864:

> The candid incline to surmise of late
>   That the Christian faith proves false, I find;
> For our Essays-and-Reviews' debate
>   Begins to tell on the public mind,
> And Colenso's words have weight:
>
> I still, to suppose it true, for my part,
>   See reasons and reasons; this, to begin:
> 'T is the faith that launched point-blank her dart
>   At the head of a lie—taught Original Sin,
> The Corruption of Man's Heart.   (ll. 141-50)

Nor, as we have seen, was he any more friendly to *Robert Elsmere,* a book which might truly be said to have been born out of the spirit of the Broad Church movement.

So far as Browning can be claimed by a religious party, his affiliations lie with the Evangelicals rather than with the Broad Churchmen. The poet's family traditions were Nonconformist. His mother had been brought up in the Scottish kirk, but for the last forty-three years of her life she was a devout member of the Independent congregation meeting for worship at York Street, Walworth. His father, originally an Anglican, joined the same congregation in 1820. Browning's marriage in 1846 with Elizabeth Barrett, whose Nonconformist traditions and sympathies were at least as strong as his own, strengthened these early associations. If Mrs. Browning could speak of her husband as having "the blood of all the Puritans in him," she could refer to herself as one of "those schismatiques of Amsterdam"—holders of the Independent church principle—whom Dr. Donne "would have put into the dykes." The correspondence between the two is ample evidence that, however far their religious views outreach the literal and crude puritanism of a "Mount Zion" chapel meeting, they are of the spiritual lineage of the Evangelical movement.[13] It is significant that the narrator in *Christmas-Eve* finds more of the love of Christ in the baldest form of Protestant worship than in the splendour of the midnight mass at St. Peter's, or in the intellectual analysis of Christianity by the professor of Göttingen. Nor can it be doubted that

Browning and Higher Criticism

Browning declares his own preference for a simple and unritualistic type of service in the lines:

> My heart does best to receive in meekness
> That mode of worship, as most to his mind,
> Where earthly aids being cast behind,
> His All in All appears serene
> With the thinnest human veil between,
> Letting the mystic lamps, the seven,
> The many motions of his spirit,
> Pass, as they list, to earth from heaven.   (XXII. 1303-10)[14]

Such influence as Evangelical pietism had upon Browning's attitude towards Biblical Criticism was negative in two respects. Notwithstanding the important contribution of Protestant Evangelicalism to the spiritual life of England, it lacked breadth and freedom of thought. Regarding the Scriptures as a sacred talisman and devoted to a clear-cut but narrow system of doctrinal ideas, the Evangelicals produced no work of the first order in theology, and they were more unwilling than any other party to abandon the theory of verbal inspiration. In their eyes, Higher Criticism was an attack on the very citadel of Protestant faith and a synonym for rationalism and infidelity. While Browning, as is shown by his views on the Atonement and eternal punishment, was far from being a rigid Calvinist, he could scarcely fail to be influenced by that deep-seated distrust of Biblical Criticism felt by the religious party with which he was most closely allied. But the most vital way in which the poet's nonconforming traditions affected his attitude towards the historical criticism of the New Testament and the origins of Christianity, was through their limitation of his education. Up to the year 1854 no Dissenter could take a degree at Cambridge, and no Dissenter could even matriculate at Oxford. As a consequence, Browning's university education was limited to a single term in 1828-29, at the newly founded University of London. During the formative years of his life, he missed that intimate contact with leaders and tendencies of religious thought which a university residence would have given him. Had Browning gone to Oxford in 1828, he would have been in touch with the germinating forces that afterwards bore fruit in the Broad and High Church movements. Oriel, in particular, under the brilliant leadership of Copleston, who was Provost from 1814 to 1828, was the nursery of seedlings destined to produce such different flowerings as *Tracts for the Times* and *Essays and Reviews*. Here, while Newman was beginning his memorable ministry at St. Mary's and Keble was writing *The Christian Year*, Whately, Thomas Arnold, and Hampden were bringing a new breath of intellectual freedom into the Church of England. The Oriel Noetics were pioneers in the field of liberal theology. Yet, through their emphasis on the progressive character of divine revelation, they were laying the foundations for a study of the Bible based upon critical and historical principles. Had Browning become an Oxford student in the eighteen-twenties, Oriel and Whately might have meant to him what Balliol and Jowett meant to Matthew Arnold in the eighteen-forties. It is significant to note, in this connection, that it was not until 1850, seventeen years after the publication of the first *Tract* and the initiation of the Oxford Movement, that the doctrinal controversies of the era find an echo in his poetry.

Apart from the important, though somewhat vague and indeterminate influence of Protestant Nonconformity on Browning's religious views, he cannot be classified as a follower of any particular movement or tendency in English theology. He stands, necessarily, in general relationships to the religious background of the mid-Victorian epoch. But to regard Browning's representation of Christianity as the mere by-product of his historical environment is to miss its flavour and distinction. So far from reflecting the influence of a school or body of theological opinion, he is typically English in the rugged individuality of his thought. His approach to the problems of religion is inseparably bound up with the characteristic attitudes of mind, or dispositions of spirit, traceable throughout his poetry. As has been said: "It is not as a creed, still less as a body of religious opinion, that Christianity attracts Browning. It is as a living experience that its spell is potent."[15] The "incidents in the development of a soul" with which he is primarily concerned centre about the paradox that man is a being in whom the claims and purposes of the finite and infinite, body and soul, flesh and spirit, time and eternity, meet and must each receive due recognition. While, from one point of view, life must be an unceasing aspiration in pursuit of an infinite ideal, from another it must be a continuous stooping to a world of weakness and finitude. Justice must be done to the natural and human as well as to the mystic and divine aspect of personality. Likewise, it must be borne in mind that Browning frequently attains to the cardinal truths of Christian faith in undogmatic fashion, by regarding these as a corollary to what has been called "the richest vein of pure ore" in his poetry, his view of the nature and function of love. In the poet's philosophy of life—for it may reasonably be called that—with its profound sense of human experience as poised between the absolute and the relative lay a natural channel of approach to the Christian doctrine of the Incarnation.

The direct references of Browning to Biblical Criticism lie in a group of poems published between 1850 and 1870. These are, *Christmas-Eve and Easter-Day*, 1850; *Bishop Blougram's Apology*, 1855; *Gold Hair*, 1864; *A Death in the Desert*, 1864; *Epilogue* to *Dramatis Personae*, 1864. With this group should be linked certain writings which deal with evidences for the Incarnation and thus practically involve the issues of Biblical Criticism. The most important of these are, "The Pope," in *The Ring and the Book*, 1869; "The Sun," in *Ferishtah's Fancies*, 1884; "Bernard de Mandeville," in *Parleyings with Certain People of Importance in Their Day*, 1887. The following poems allude to the theme of the Incarnation in a more general way: *Saul*, x-xix, 1855; *An Epistle containing the Strange Medical Experience of Karshish, the Arab Physician*, 1855; *Cleon*, 1855; "A Pillar at Sebzevar," in *Ferishtah's Fancies*, 1884.

Browning was married in 1846 and the influence of the devout religious spirit of his wife may be discerned in the composition of *Christmas-Eve and Easter-Day*. But the primary reason for his vivid sketches of Evangelical Nonconformity, Roman Catholic ritualism, and German criticism, in this poem, lies in the pressure of the religious controversies which were rife in England around the year 1850. In particular, the description of the teaching of the German professor at the University of Göttingen is, under a thin dramatic disguise, the expression of Browning's own reaction to the writings of Strauss and his followers.

The publication of *Das Leben Jesu* in 1835 was an epoch-making event in the history of Biblical Criticism, and the theological upheaval that followed in its wake may be traced in a variety of ways. Beginning, in England, with Charles Hennell's *Inquiry concerning the Origin of Christianity*, 1838, it gave rise to a continuous series of books and articles. Amongst the more important writings that reflect the influence of Strauss's work, in the decade of Browning's *Christmas-Eve and Easter-Day*, are Theodore Parker's "The Transient and Permanent in Christianity," 1841; J. A. Froude's *Shadows of the Clouds*, 1847, and *The Nemesis of Faith*, 1849; Arthur Hugh Clough's *Epi-Strauss-ium* and *Easter Day*, 1849; Francis Newman's *The Soul*, 1849, and *Phases of Faith*, 1850; William Rathbone Greg's *The Creed of Christendom*, 1851. While the classic English version of *Das Leben Jesu* was that of George Eliot in 1846, it was not the first translation of the book. As early as 1841, John Sterling writes: "But the oddest sign of the Times I know, is a cheap Translation of Strauss's *Leben Jesu,* now publishing in numbers, and said to be circulating far and wide."[16] Two years before this, Sterling had read much of this critical life of Jesus and foresaw the effect of it on the thought of his generation. In a letter of 1839 he tells Carlyle: "In this way I have gone through a good deal of Strauss's Book; which is exceedingly clever and clear-headed; with more of insight, and less of destructive rage than I expected. It will work deep and far, in such a time as ours."[17] The wide circulation of *Das Leben Jesu* in the eighteen-forties is attested to by one of the leaders of the Oxford

Movement. In 1843, W. G. Ward[18] noted that Strauss's work was selling more than any other book.

In considering Browning's references to Higher Criticism in *Christmas-Eve* and elsewhere, it must be remembered that he writes as an artist, not as a theologian, and that he deals with the facts of religion in an individualistic and untechnical way. By comparison with the equipment of such English men of letters as Coleridge and Carlyle, his knowledge of the historical and philosophical backgrounds of Biblical Criticism was slight. According to Mrs. Orr, Browning professed his ignorance of German philosophy, being "emphatic in his assurance that he knew neither the German philosophers nor their reflection in Coleridge, who would have seemed a likely medium between them and him."[19] Yet in 1843 he writes to Domett that he reads German tolerably and is using Schlegel and Tieck's translation of Shakespeare to aid him in the study of the language.[20] Again, he informs Domett that certain quarterlies contain articles on Leibnitz, Spinoza, and Descartes.[21] The evidence seems to show that Browning was not completely ignorant of German thought, as Mrs. Orr has represented. On the other hand, his acquaintance with it was, indisputably, superficial and sporadic. It could not have enabled him to meet a writer like Strauss on his own ground, nor does he attempt to do so. The arguments used to refute the conclusions of the Göttingen professor, in *Christmas-Eve,* are those of the ordinary "Christian" man, rather than those of the theological expert. At the same time, the native power and insight of the poet's mind, conjoined with the emotional intuitions of genius, enable him to throw illuminating flashes on the problems of the religious consciousness.

In his *apologia* for Christianity in sections xv-xvii of *Christmas-Eve,* Browning takes a general survey of the rationalistic tendencies of the day. The professor of Göttingen is an imaginative creation and therefore not to be identified arbitrarily with any particular critic of the German school. Yet the fact that *Das Leben Jesu* was a storm centre of controversy in the eighteen-fifties, and the references to the "Myth of Christ" in the text of the poem, make it unmistakably evident that the poet has Strauss in mind. In the lines,

> It matters little for the name,
> So the idea be left the same   (xv. 866-67)

the distinction which Strauss draws between the transient and the permanent elements in Christianity is clearly indicated. But in the general outline of the Christmas-Eve discourse, lines of demarcation between various critics of a rationalistic temper are blurred. Starting with the premises of Strauss, the Göttingen professor draws conclusions which resemble those of Comte and Matthew Arnold rather than those set forth in the *Leben Jesu* and the *Vergängliches und Bleibendes im Christentum*.

With Hegel's conception of the relationship between idea and reality in mind, Strauss regarded the doctrine of Christ's divinity as unaffected by the results of Biblical Criticism. His position is plainly stated in the preface to the first German edition of his life of Jesus, where he writes: "The author is aware that the essence of the Christian faith is perfectly independent of his criticism. The supernatural birth of Christ, his miracles, his resurrection and ascension, remain eternal truths, whatever doubts may be cast on their reality as historical facts."[22] It is this distinction—made more explicit in the *Vergängliches und Bleibendes im Christentum*—between the symbolic and temporally conditioned representation of the Incarnation in the historical life of Jesus and its absolute realization in the Christ of religious consciousness, that is pivotal in Strauss's thought.

Apart from the initial reference to the contrast between "name" and "idea," no allusion is made in *Christmas-Eve* to the philosophical implications that lie back of Strauss's "mythical theory." The conclusions of the professor in his lecture room at Göttingen are frankly rationalistic. He does not attempt, in the spirit of Strauss, to substitute a metaphysical for a historical concept of "the God in Christ." On the contrary he dispels the myth of Christ's divinity to disclose

Browning and Higher Criticism

> A Man!—a right true man, however,
> Whose work was worthy a man's endeavour. . . .
> (xv. 878-79)

Thus Christ becomes a purely human figure whose virtue lies in his teaching rather than in the uniqueness of his person, and religion is reduced to "morality touched with emotion."

Without attempting to weigh historical evidences, or to consider specifically the problems of miracle and revelation, Browning attacks this position on several grounds. In the first place, he regards it as inconsistent with the claim of Christ to be divine and "one with the Creator." In the second place, he feels that it is wholly inadequate to satisfy the craving of the religious consciousness. It is not a mere knowledge of God's truth, but power to act upon such knowledge that is the supreme need of humanity. A moral code or a body of teaching lacks the spiritual dynamic

> to furnish a motive and injunction
> For practising what we know already. (xv. 1041-42)

This can only be supplied through the enkindling and transfiguring power of a divine personality operative in the lives of men. As Browning phrases it:

> Morality to the uttermost,
> Supreme in Christ as we all confess,
> Why need we prove would avail no jot
> To make him God, if God he were not?
> What is the point where himself lays stress?
> Does the precept run "Believe in good,
> In justice, truth, now understood
> For the first time?" — or, "Believe in me,
> Who lived and died, yet essentially
> Am Lord of Life?" (ll. 1047-56)[23]

While *Cleon, Saul,* x-xix, and *An Epistle of Karshish* deal with the Christian concept of the Incarnation in a general way, the only direct allusion in the poetry of Browning between 1850 and 1864 to contemporary Biblical Criticism occurs in *Bishop*

Blougram's Apology. Here Cardinal Wiseman, under a thin disguise, is placed in limbo between St. Paul and Luther as types of ardent faith and Strauss as a type of "bold unbelief."[24] Here, too, curiously enough, that argument for faith in the Christian revelation based upon the relativity and fallible character of human knowledge, on which Browning was afterwards to lay so much stress, first makes its appearance in the ingenious web of casuistry woven by his subtle prelate.

The publication of *Dramatis Personae* in 1864 coincides in point of time with the signing of the *Oxford Declaration* by eleven thousand clergymen of the establishment. It was a restless and troubled epoch in the religious thought of England, when the theological controversies stirred up by Biblical Criticism were reaching an acute stage. The printing of *Essays and Reviews* in 1860, followed by Colenso's rationalistic work on the Hexateuch in 1862, provoked a storm of hostility in orthodox circles. This was widened and intensified by the publication of Renan's *La Vie de Jésus* in 1863. The popular and dramatic qualities of Renan's book ensured its rapid circulation. With the possible exception of Strauss's *Das Leben Jesu,* no work in the whole range of Higher Criticism caused such an immediate sensation, or became the focus of such heated controversy. The book was published on June 23, 1863, and in November of the same year sixty-five thousand copies had been sold.

Browning's interest in the problems of Biblical Criticism that were agitating the religious thought of England in the eighteen-sixties is strikingly revealed in *Dramatis Personae*. Reference has already been made to his outspoken criticism of *Essays and Reviews* and the writings of Bishop Colenso, as voiced in *Gold Hair,* one of the minor pieces in this collection.[25] In the *Epilogue* to *Dramatis Personae,* Renan is one of the three speakers, and the subject of the poem is Browning's assertion of the essential divinity of Christ, in answer to what he regards as the thoroughly negative conclusions of the French theologian.

With the single exception of the Pope's monologue in *The Ring and the Book, A Death in the Desert* is the most elaborate and closely reasoned *apologia* for Christianity throughout Browning's poetry. In common with *Christmas-Eve* the poem deals with the general idea of Christ's divinity, but it also treats of the origins of Christianity, the question of miracles, and the historical development of the Christian faith. *A Death in the Desert* is Browning's most direct rejoinder to the attack made upon the historical basis of Christianity by the critics of the Tübingen school. Here, as in *Christmas-Eve and Easter-Day,* the influence of Strauss's *Das Leben Jesu* is unmistakable.

Does the poem also echo the turmoil of the second great inbreak of religious controversy reaching England from Continental shores during the lifetime of Browning? In view of the allusion to Renan in the *Epilogue* to *Dramatis Personae* and the extraordinary furore stirred up by *La Vie de Jésus* in 1863, it is tempting to hazard the inference that the polemical elements in *A Death in the Desert* were aimed in part at Renan's famous book.

Such a conjecture, however, runs contrary to a statement made by the Reverend J. Llewellyn Davies at a meeting of the Browning Society on February 25, 1887. In the minutes of the discussion that succeeded the reading of Mrs. M. G. Glazebrook's paper on *A Death in the Desert,* a digest is made of Mr. Davies' remarks as follows: "The poem was published in the 'Dramatis Personae,' which came out soon after Renan's 'Life of Jesus'—and consequently many people imagined it referred to that. But Browning wrote the poem long prior to the publication of Renan's work; and he thought Mrs. Glazebrook was right in assuming it to be an answer to Strauss; for in reading it we can see that Browning recognizes all the force of that destructive writer's reasoning."[26]

Though many of the poems included in *Dramatis Personae* may have been written anywhere between 1855 and 1864, this is the only statement to my knowledge that definitely places the composition of *A Death in the Desert* prior to the year 1863. All other testimony leads to the conclusion of Sir Frederic Kenyon regarding this poem that "no direct evidence of its date remains."[27]

There is, however, in the letters of Browning to Isabella Blagden, an important passage which throws light on his attitude towards Renan's *La Vie de Jésus* and fixes the date of his first reading of the work. In a letter to Miss Blagden of November 19, 1863, he writes as follows:

> I have just read Renan's book, and find it weaker and less honest than I was led to expect. I am glad it is written; if he thinks he can prove what he says, he has fewer doubts on the subject than I, but mine are none of his. As to the Strauss school, I don't understand their complacency about the book, he admits many points they have thought it essential to dispute, and substitutes his explanation, which I think impossible. The want of candour is remarkable: you could no more deduce the character of his text from the substance of his notes, than rewrite a novel from simply reading the mottoes at the head of each chapter: they often mean quite another thing, unless he cuts away the awkward part, as in the parable of the Rich Man & Lazarus. His admissions & criticisms on St. John are curious. I make no doubt he imagines *himself* stating a fact, with the inevitable license, so must John have done. His argument against the genuineness of Matthew, from the reference to what Papias says of the λογία is altogether too gross a blunder to be believed in a Scholar, and is yet repeated half a dozen times throughout the book: if Pen, in three . . . . means, an oracle or revelation . . . . he'll stand badly off for . . . . honest, old Tom Paine stands . . . . miracles were cheats, and their author a cheat! What do think of the figure *he* cuts who makes his hero participate in the wretched affair with Lazarus, and then calls him all the pretty names that follow? Take away every claim to man's respect from Christ and then give him a wreath of gum-roses and calico-lilies, or, as Constance says to Arthur in King John "Give Grannam King John and it grannam will give it a plum, an apple and a fig."[28]

The feeling aroused in Browning by the reading of *La Vie de Jésus,* and, in particular, his hostility to Renan's views on St. John and miracles, would suggest the likelihood of *A Death in the Desert* being either composed or revised between November, 1863, and the publication of the poem in 1864.

In view of this, one could wish that Mr. Davies had stated the source of his information that it was written "long prior to the publication of Renan's work." There is, however, no positive circumstantial evidence that *La Vie de Jésus* was in the poet's mind when he wrote *A Death in the Desert*. The attacks upon the historicity of the fourth gospel made by Strauss and his immediate followers are in themselves sufficient to account for the form and the subject-matter of the poem. Then, too, it must be recalled that in *An Epistle of Karshish,* printed as early as 1855, eight years before the appearance of Renan's life of Jesus, Browning's interest in the Johannine gospel is already evident. A further point, in support of Mrs. Glazebrook's and Llewellyn Davies' contention that *A Death in the Desert* is aimed primarily at the Tübingen school, is that the views of Strauss and Baur on the Johannine gospel were much more radical than those of Renan. Strauss maintained that the fourth gospel was a controversial book written late in the second century after Christ by a theologian of the Greek Gnostic and anti-Jewish school. Renan, on the other hand, considered it to be in substance the work of the Apostle John, though possibly revised and retouched by his disciples. It is plainly the position of Strauss rather than Renan that the poet has in mind in *A Death in the Desert* when he pictures St. John, with prophetic insight, hearing "unborn people in strange lands" inquire:

> Was John at all, and did he say he saw?
> Assure us, ere we ask what he might see!   (ll. 196-97)

Nevertheless, were it not for Mr. Davies' explicit statement to the contrary, I should have conjectured that Browning's keen interest in Renan's life of Jesus, as shown by his letter to Miss Blagden of November 19, 1863, and his reference to Renan in the *Epilogue* to *Dramatis Personae,* was in part responsible for the composition of *A Death in the Desert*. The vigorous hostile comment in the Isa Blagden letter is evidence, at least, that in the year preceding the publication of the poem, Browning was stirred up by the reading of *La Vie de Jésus* and associated Renan with Strauss as a rationalistic and destructive critic of Christianity.[29]

There are a number of reasons why *A Death in the Desert* is a pivotal poem, in a study which seeks to define the attitude of

Browning towards Biblical Criticism. While less profound than the soliloquy of the Pope in *The Ring and the Book*—one of the greatest examples of constructive religious thought in nineteenth-century poetry—it is in more intimate touch with the contemporary situation created by the assaults of Higher critics on orthodox views of the inspiration of the New Testament. It also illustrates clearly Browning's way of approach to the basic truths of Christianity, and his central and unwavering position on the question of the divinity of Christ. As Professor Herford has pointed out, the poet makes no attempt in *A Death in the Desert* to meet Strauss on his own ground, with the weapons of history and comparative religion. Even had he wished to do this, his lack of expert knowledge would have precluded it. Only amongst the more advanced leaders of the Broad Church party in England, outside of the camp of Positivism, was there any genuine understanding of the historical groundwork and philosophical inheritance of such a work as *Das Leben Jesu*. With neither of these movements was Browning allied by tradition or education. To approach the writings of Strauss from the standpoint of the authors of *Essays and Reviews* and Matthew Arnold, would have been as alien to him as to sit with George Eliot at the feet of the father of the Tübingen school. His attitude towards Higher Criticism was very much that of the average English layman in the eighteen-sixties, distrustful of it as a product "made in Germany," fearful of its iconoclastic tendencies, and with little sympathy for its sifting of documentary evidence and patient work of scientific investigation.

Nor should it be forgotten that Browning, with all his intellectual bent, exercises the artist's prerogative to roam experience rather than to systematize it. The problems involved in the method and technique of Biblical Criticism, the evaluation of historical data, the scrutiny of origins and sources, the reconstruction of a complex religious environment, lay beyond the poet's ken. Moreover, in seeking to cut the Gordian knot of these difficulties, Browning, to an even greater degree than Tennyson, made a distinction between love and reason, feeling and intelligence, which led him eventually to adopt a sceptical view of human knowledge.

As a consequence, particularly in his later writings, he came to regard the Incarnation and the Crucifixion as historical facts, incapable of proof or disproof. On the other hand, his faith in the intuitive testimony of the heart to the existence of a loving, self-sacrificing God, working with redemptive and transfiguring power in human experience, never wavers. The clue to Browning's religious position lies in the recognition of the fact that with him, as with many of his contemporaries, it is the function of the heart to "melt the freezing reason's colder part." His gnosticism is primarily emotional.

In accordance with this basic distinction between faith and reason, the natural stress of Browning's *apologia* for Christianity is on the evaluation of it as a living experience rather than as an historical creed. In this way he seeks to turn the flank of the attack made by rationalistic criticism on the historic foundations of Christianity. Untechnical as Browning's approach to the critical problems of the New Testament, in such a work as *A Death in the Desert,* undeniably is, the depth and discernment of his religious intuition give it genuine significance. The purport of the argument of the poem as put into the mouth of St. John, the beloved disciple, is to represent Christianity as a religion of the spirit, with love as its inspiring motive. While the authority of the New Testament sources is not questioned, the poet tends to minimize the importance of the appeal to history, and refuses to base the truth of Christianity on an intellectual proof of the factual character of a series of past events. It is the realization and appropriation of the divine love of God in the lives of men and women, the abiding presence of the ever living Christ in the hearts of his disciples, that he regards as an irrefutable proof of the validity of the Christian faith. Approaching Christianity from the human rather than the dogmatic side, Browning finds its sovereign credential in the fact that it harmonizes with the central truths of man's experience. Though the historical character of the Christian revelation cannot be proven by reason, it satisfies the reason. It does this because it discloses that conception of the nature of God and his relationship to man which has already been attested by the independent witness of the heart and revealed as the supreme factor in the creative moulding of personality.

> ... the acknowledgment of God in Christ
> Accepted by thy reason, solves for thee
> All questions in the earth and out of it,
> And has so far advanced thee to be wise. (ll. 474-77)

It is therefore plain that Browning considers the historical evidences of Christianity only as a corollary to what may be called the gospel of the eternal Christ, or, less theologically, the unceasing revelation of the infinite love and self-sacrifice of a divine being in lives transfigured by his presence.

> To me, that story—ay, that Life and Death
> Of which I wrote "it was"—to me, it is;
> —Is, here and now: I apprehend nought else.
> Is not God now i' the world His power first made?
> Is not His love at issue still with sin
> Visibly when a wrong is done on earth?
> Love, wrong, and pain, what see I else around?
> Yea, and the Resurrection and Uprise
> To the right hand of the throne. . . . (ll. 208-16)

In a classic of literary criticism, *Browning as a Philosophical and Religious Teacher,* Professor Henry Jones has given a brilliant analysis of that cleavage between Reason and Love which he characterizes as "the fundamental error of the poet's philosophy." The same line of demarcation may be traced throughout Browning's reflection on the cardinal doctrines of Christianity. Whenever he is on the ground of historical evidences, there is a note of uncertainty and ambiguity in his utterance, for which his sceptical theory of knowledge is directly responsible. On the other hand, whenever he dwells on the inner witness of the heart to the universal truth of Christianity, he is absolutely unfaltering in his convictions. He then speaks with as infallible accents as the Pope in *The Ring and the Book*:

I
> Put no such dreadful question to myself,
> Within whose circle of experience burns
> The central truth, Power, Wisdom, Goodness,—
>   God: ....
> No,—I have light nor fear the dark at all.
>   (X. 1631-34, 1660)

One of the most striking illustrations of the purely relative and subordinate value which Browning attached to the historical evidences of Christianity is a conversation with Mrs. Orr in 1869, which the latter records in an article in the *Contemporary Review,* on "The Religious Opinions of Robert Browning." Nothing could more forcibly exemplify the pervasive ambiguity which the poet's intellectual agnosticism involved him in, when dealing with Christianity as a historical revelation, than the following words cited by Mrs. Orr:

"I know the difficulty of believing," he once said to me, when some question had arisen concerning the Christian scheme of salvation. "I know all that may be said against it, on the ground of history, of reason, of even moral sense. I grant even that it may be a fiction. But I am none the less convinced that the life and death of Christ, as Christians apprehend them, supply something which their humanity requires, and that it is true for them." He then proceeded to say why, in his judgment, humanity required Christ. "The evidence of Divine power is everywhere about us; not so the evidence of Divine love. That love could only reveal itself to the human heart by some supreme act of *human* tenderness and devotion; the fact, or fancy, of Christ's cross and passion could alone supply such a revelation."[30]

Without a comprehension of the theoretical difficulty in which the poet through his distrust of reason was enmeshed, these words might seem to justify Mrs. Orr's conclusion that "the one consistent fact of Mr. Browning's heterodoxy was its exclusion of any belief in revelation." In reality they mean nothing of the kind, and the whole tenor of Browning's poetry as well as the evidence of his life refute Mrs. Orr's statement. What he does deny is that the historical character of the events of the life of Christ recorded in the New Testament can be demonstrated by reason, in the sense that the events in the life of Napoleon are matters of factual knowledge. But this is accompanied by an unswerving faith in the revelation of the Incarnation and "Christ's cross and passion" within the spiritual experience of humanity.

Yet it is evident that Browning's abnegation of reason continually sprains his argument whenever he is dealing with the historical bases of Christianity. For, if the incidents of the gospel narrative are placed beyond the pale of reason, it is difficult to show how they possess objective validity. The vacillation of the poet's own point of view on this ground is a testimony to the unsoundness of his premise.[31] At times, while disavowing the possibility of an intellectual proof of the historical truth of the New Testament story, he puts into the lips of such characters as St. John and Pope Innocent XII, words which ascribe to it a high degree of rational probability. Thus the Pope soliloquizes in *The Ring and the Book*:

> There is, beside the works, a tale of Thee
> In the world's mouth, which I find credible:
> I love it with my heart: unsatisfied,
> I try it with my reason, nor discept
> From any point I probe and pronounce sound.
> (X. 1348-52)

In addition, the Pope supports the reasonableness of the gospel narrative by an argument drawn from the disparity between man's inner and outward experience. Within the heart of man, the trinity of God's love, power, and wisdom is subjectively revealed. But in the world without, while there is ample evidence of divine strength and intelligence, the goodness of God is not equally apparent. The life and death of Christ, therefore, provide an objective manifestation of God's love and self-sacrifice and bring the testimony of the visible universe regarding his nature into harmony with the ideal conception of the heart:

> What lacks, then, of perfection fit for God
> But just the instance which this tale supplies

Browning and Higher Criticism

>   Of love without a limit? So is strength,
>   So is intelligence; let love be so,
>   Unlimited in its self-sacrifice,
>   Then is the tale true and God shows complete.
>   (X. 1367-72)[32]

But in the poet's later writings, where his intellectual agnosticism is most pronounced, he becomes extremely sceptical of any approach to religious truth through the exercise of reason,

>   Were knowledge all thy faculty, then God
>   Must be ignored: love gains him by first leap.[33]

In laying exclusive stress on love, he is inclined to regard the historical evidences of Christianity, not merely as unproven, but as embodying a narrative of events which are absolutely inconceivable from the point of view of reason. In the parable of "The Sun," the intellect of Ferishtah's disciple is staggered by the notion that "God once assumed on earth a human shape."

>   Wherefrom
>   What is to follow—if I take thy sense—
>   But that the sun—the inconceivable
>   Confessed by man—comprises, all the same,
>   Man's every-day conception of himself—
>   No less remaining unconceived![34]

Nor does Ferishtah's answer offer any solution of the paradox. As a matter of fact he admits the intellectual contradiction of the doctrine of the Incarnation, but bids his pupil fall back on the intuitive response of the heart to such a faith.

>   "How?
>   An union inconceivable was fact?"

>   "Son, if the stranger have convinced himself
>   Fancy is fact—the sun, besides a fire,
>   Holds earthly substance somehow fire pervades
>   And yet consumes not,—earth, he understands,
>   With essence he remains a stranger to,—
>   Fitlier thou saidst 'I stand appalled before

>   Conception unattainable by me
>   Who need it most'. . . ."   (ll. 164-73)

Though the cry of Tennyson "I stretch weak hands of faith and grope" seems inadequate to express the invincible optimism of Browning's creed, "God! Thou art love! I build my faith on that," the pressure of the problems of the day drove Browning to a more sceptical theory of knowledge than even Tennyson ever contemplated. Yet the theoretical difficulties which the poet has conjured up by his denial of knowledge do not prevent his practical acceptance of the essential truths of Christianity. For, in Browning's eyes, the validity of the New Testament narrative is quite independent of a proof of its historical authenticity. Its warrant lies first in the fruitage of the life and teachings of Christ as a creative spiritual power operative in the lives of his disciples throughout the ages. From a study of the origins and documentary sources of Christianity, which his fear of the sophistries of reason and his dislike of the coldly rationalistic temper of Higher Criticism made him profoundly distrust, he appeals to Christian experience.

> It is the idea, the feeling and the love,
> God means mankind should strive for and show
>   forth
> Whatever be the process to that end,—
> And not historic knowledge, logic sound,
> And metaphysical acumen, sure!
> "What think ye of Christ," friend? when all's
>   done and said,
> Like you this Christianity or not?[35]

Sensitive, as an artist, to all that rich play of imagination and poetic sentiment which forms the mystic penumbra of Christian faith, his heart revolts at the devitalizing of it in the critical laboratory. In addition he sees, and in this is in accord with the ripest thought of today, that history can never say the last, or indeed the most important, word regarding such doctrines as the Incarnation and Crucifixion. That these truths, in their highest reaches, set aside temporal limitations and express the universal significance of God's love and self-sacrifice, as manifest in human experience, is a cardinal article of Browning's belief.

As a matter of fact, the doubts and uncertainties which the scrutiny of Biblical Criticism casts upon the New Testament story are frequently regarded by the poet as providentially arranged to give scope for the exercise of faith. They are like the apparent breaks in a mountain road, due to the imperfect vision of the traveller, which prove at last

> The most consummate of contrivances
> To train a man's eye, teach him what is faith.[36]

Regarding man's life on earth as a period of probation, and acutely conscious of the relativity and finiteness of his intelligence, Browning never ascribes to the historical evidences of Christianity an absolute value. Their authority is not inherent, but derived from the fact that they are a pendant to a larger revelation of the divine nature within the spirit of man. Paradoxical as it may seem, in view of his attitude towards Strauss, the words of the Tübingen critic in the preface to the first edition of *Das Leben Jesu,* already quoted, precisely state Browning's position: "The supernatural birth of Christ, his miracles, his resurrection and ascension, remain eternal truths, whatever doubts may be cast on their reality as historical facts." Nor does the analogy cease here. In Browning's constant wavering regarding the character of the evidences for Christianity enshrined in the gospel story, his doubt whether these are fact or fancy, history or fiction, reality or symbol, there is much that recalls the famous "mythical theory" of Strauss. The poet, however, by placing the whole subject beyond the pale of reason, avoids forcing the issue. That is to say, the vital thing, to him, is that the New Testament narrative supports the intuitive faith of his heart and harmonizes with that conception of God and his dealings grasped through personal experience.

In *A Death in the Desert, The Ring and the Book, Ferishtah's Fancies,* and *Parleyings with Certain People of Importance,* Browning constantly reiterates his conviction that the validity of the gospel story is independent of a proof of its historical character. In his greatest religious monologue, he makes the Pope refuse to pronounce on the historicity of the Christian tale handed down through the centuries, and even speak as if this were a matter of indifference.

> ... whether a fact,
> Absolute, abstract, independent truth,
> Historic, not reduced to suit man's mind,—
> Or only truth reverberate, changed, made pass
> A spectrum into mind, the narrow eye,—
> The same and not the same, else unconceived—
> Though quite conceivable to the next grade
> Above it in intelligence,—as truth
> Easy to man were blindness to the beast
> By parity of procedure,—the same truth
> In a new form, but changed in either case:
> What matter so intelligence be filled? ...
>   so my heart be struck,
> What care I,—by God's gloved hand or the bare?
>   (X. 1388-99, 1406-7)

In view of the relative and subordinate character assigned to it, the question arises, does the poet regard this temporally conditioned Christian story, hovering indeterminately between fact and fable, as having a permanent significance for humanity in its own right? Or is it merely a stepping stone to be dispensed with, when men have apprehended the absolute spiritual truth which the tale expresses in historical or symbolic guise? In connection with this query it should be noted that in *Christmas-Eve, Saul, The Ring and the Book,* and other religious poems, Browning has depicted characters who apprehend the essential nature of God's infinite love and self-sacrifice without the aid of an historical revelation. In *A Death in the Desert* St. John draws a distinction between his own spiritual vision of an eternal and ever present manifestation of God's being, and the feebler sight of those who, as he says,

> needs must apprehend what truth
> I see, reduced to plain historic fact,

Browning and Higher Criticism

>   Diminished into clearness, proved a point
>   And far away: ye would withdraw your sense
>   From out eternity, strain it upon time.... (ll. 235-39)

Here the poet makes the apostle of love the spokesman of the truth that the embodiment of spiritual realities in the gospel story brings these within the comprehension of the average man and woman. This conception of the adaptation of the historical life and death of Christ to the need and understanding of common humanity, has been exquisitely voiced by Tennyson in *In Memoriam*.

>   For Wisdom dealt with mortal powers,
>   Where truth in closest words shall fail,
>   When truth embodied in a tale
>   Shall enter in at lowly doors. (XXXVI. 5-8)

In summing up Browning's attitude towards the historical evidences of Christianity it must be borne in mind that, in conjunction with a spirit of romantic idealism which aspires towards the infinite, he has a very deep sense of the necessity of stooping to the limited and finite channels of human experience. To disdain or reject the revelations of truth, goodness, and beauty vouchsafed to man on earth, because they are relative or imperfect, is to attempt like Sordello to overleap the conditions of life. Therefore the poet considers the deflection of the absolute truth concerning God's nature, in passing through the prism of the gospel narrative, a means whereby it is fitted to the relative scale of man's faculties. By robing itself in the prismatic colours of imagery and symbol the Christian story captivates the heart, where the white radiance of absolute truth, like Lazarus's vision of heaven, would sear and blind through excess of light.

>   Clouds obscure—
>   But for which obscuration all were bright?
>   Too hastily concluded! Sun-suffused,
>   A cloud may soothe the eye made blind by blaze,—
>   Better the very clarity of heaven:
>   The soft streaks are the beautiful and dear.

> What but the weakness in a faith supplies
> The incentive to humanity, no strength
> Absolute, irresistible comports?
> How can man love but what he yearns to help?
> And that which men think weakness within strength,
> But angels know for strength and stronger yet—
> What were it else but the first things made new,
> But repetition of the miracle,
> The divine instance of self-sacrifice
> That never ends and aye begins for man?[37]

Though the Incarnation is a stumbling block for the abstract reason, such a stooping of God to human ken is recognized by the heart as in exquisite harmony with the nature and function of love. This paradox is dramatically illustrated in *An Epistle of Karshish*, where the Arab physician, repelled by the intellectual difficulty of a belief in Christ's divinity, is, nevertheless, thrilled to the depths of his being by this representation of an infinite love submitting itself in the spirit of lowliness and self-sacrifice to the limitations of man's lot.

> The very God! think, Abib; dost thou think?
> So, the All-Great, were the All-Loving too—
> So, through the thunder comes a human voice
> Saying, "O heart I made, a heart beats here!
> Face, my hands fashioned, see it in myself!
> Thou hast no power nor mayst conceive of mine,
> But love I gave thee, with myself to love,
> And thou must love me who have died for thee!"
>   (ll. 304-11)

In like manner, David attains to a prophetic vision of the Incarnation, through his realization of the tender humanity that lies at the heart of God, disclosing itself in a love stooping to conquer and triumphing in the midst of conflict and suffering.

> He who did most, shall bear most; the strongest
>   shall stand the most weak.
> 'T is the weakness in strength, that I cry for! my
>   flesh, that I seek
> In the Godhead! I seek and I find it. O Saul, it

Browning and Higher Criticism

>shall be
>A Face like my face that receives thee; a Man like to me,
>Thou shalt love and be loved by, for ever: A Hand like this hand
>Shall throw open the gates of new life to thee! See the Christ stand![38]

If proof were needed that Browning's sceptical theory of knowledge never shook his faith in the validity of the Christian revelation, it would be furnished by the fact that it is in his later works, where his intellectual agnosticism is so marked, that he feels most keenly the human worth of the gospel story of "Christ's cross and passion." The parables of Ferishtah revolve about the thought of God's condescension to human weakness, and the unfolding of his divine nature through relative, symbolic, means of representation adapted to the lowliness and finiteness of man. A still more striking illustration occurs in the "Bernard de Mandeville" section of *Parleyings with Certain People of Importance*. Here, through the analogy of Prometheus confining the Sun's fire in a tube for the service of man, Browning lays stress upon the truth that a God whose perfection excludes all human attributes is for man a mere negation and abstraction. His experience of God, as distinguished from a definition of his absolute nature, must be that of a personal being, or, at least, one who includes within himself the attributes which in humanity are bound up with personality. Before Prometheus brought fire from heaven to earth, man strove in vain to understand the nature of the Sun. But once a spark was obtained which men could use, then the Sun's self was made palpable. It is true that the fire thus won is "glass-conglobed," and narrowed to "a pin-point circle." Nevertheless it is "the very Sun in little," sharing its elemental nature,

>Comprising the Sun's self, but Sun disrobed
>Of that else-unconceived essential flame
>Borne by no naked sight. (ll. 307-9)[39]

The myth of Prometheus is a symbol of Christ's revelation of God to man. As man is able to repeat the miracle of the Titan by using the flame once won, so the concentration of the fire of divine love in the person of Christ enables man to repeat the miracle of the Incarnation. He too achieves a creative type of personality informed by and radiating the sovereign energies of God's love. In this way he satisfies the deepest instinct of his being.

> I solely crave that one of all the beams
> Which do Sun's work in darkness, at my will
> Should operate—myself for once have skill
> To realize the energy which streams
> Flooding the universe.   (ll. 275-81)

Yet, along with this perception of the human worth and significance of the life and death of Christ as set forth in the New Testament, the poet believes that the partial gleams of God's infinite love, discerned through the prism of history and symbol, are meant to "sting with hunger for full light." The task of man, while not disdaining the props of earth, is to unceasingly correct and enlarge his relative vision of truth, so that it may approximate, ever more closely, to an absolute and spiritual conception of God's being. In this connection, Browning suggests that criticism of the traditional record and report of Christ's life may be necessary to prevent men from looking upon the historical revelation of Christianity as final and absolute.

Pope Innocent XII is represented as hearing "whispers of time to come" when, as he declares, an age of doubt will "shake this torpor of assurance from our creed." As Christianity shattered the beliefs of paganism, so it may be needful to shatter faith in an infallible Christian record to avert the danger of substituting the historically conditioned, and therefore relative, conception of God's love enshrined there, for its absolute content.

> As we broke up that old faith of the world,
> Have we, next age, to break up this the new—
> Faith, in the thing, grown faith in the report—
> Whence need to bravely disbelieve report
> Through increased faith i' the thing reports
>   belie? . . .

> Correct the portrait by the living face,
> Man's God, by God's God in the mind of man?
> (X. 1864-68, 1873-74)

Yet, while the trying and testing of Christianity in the crucible of rationalistic criticism may ultimately lead to an enlargement of faith, Browning takes pains to point out that Pope Innocent would have been repelled had he foreseen the ruthless iconoclasm that the age of reason was to let loose upon the world.

> If he thought doubt would do the next age good,
> 'T is pity he died unapprised what birth
> His reign may boast of, be remembered by—
> Terrible Pope, too, of a kind,—Voltaire.[40]

I have reserved the *Epilogue* to *Dramatis Personae* for final consideration, because in it Browning has practically dropped his dramatic disguise to state the essence of his faith in the divinity of Christ. Moreover, he contrasts his own belief with the points of view of two great movements, Tractarianism and Higher Criticism, which were agitating the religious life and thought of mid-Victorian England. Surveying the tendencies of his day in matters of faith, the poet sees men driven by various winds of doctrine towards the Scylla of formalism on the one hand, and the Charybdis of scepticism on the other.

The first speaker of the *Epilogue*, represented as David, dwells upon the manifestation of God's presence in a sensuous and material form within the precincts of the temple at Jerusalem. That Browning, under the symbolic guise of the Old Testament dispensation, is here alluding to the sacerdotalism and legalism of the Oxford Movement and the Church of Rome, has been convincingly shown by Professor Kirkconnell in his article on the *Epilogue* to *Dramatis Personae*.[41] In a more general way, the poet criticizes the dogmatic materialism which would regard as final a revelation of God localized in place and time, or confuse a symbolic and sensuous representation, adapted to man's childhood, with a spiritual perception of the absolute qualities of the divine nature.

Renan, the second speaker, typifies the negative, rationalistic temper of Continental Biblical Criticism in the eighteen-sixties. This division of the *Epilogue* centres about the thought that Higher Criticism, as exemplified by Renan, leads to a denial of an historical revelation of God's being in the person of Christ. The rays of that star which once shone out upon the world, so that men discerned God through the semblance of a human face, now contract and vanish. In addition, the loss of faith in this illusion is accompanied by a sceptical attitude towards all revelation. As a consequence, God is "lost in the night at last." He becomes a vague unknowable, whose abstract and infinite being is beyond human ken.

In the opening lines of the third part of the *Epilogue*, Browning, abandoning dramatic disguise, criticizes the traditional and sceptical points of view set forth in the preceding sections of the poem.

> Witless alike of will and way divine,
> How heaven's high with earth's low should intertwine!
> Friends, I have seen through your eyes: now use mine!   (ll. 65-67)

The lines that follow present a spiritual conception of the relation between God and man which is akin to St. John's exposition of Christianity in *A Death in the Desert*. The revelation of God is not limited to temple courts, nor to a chosen people. Neither is it dependent upon a single historical event. Rather, God is eternally manifesting himself throughout the whole scheme of the visible creation and the heart of man. In particular, his divine providence is revealed in the way in which the multitudinous play of outward circumstances is all directed to the supreme end of fashioning character and the development of individual personality. Thus, as the third speaker reflects on the manner of God's self-manifestation, temporal symbols expand and give place to eternal verities:

> Why, where's the need of Temple, when the walls
> O' the world are that?   (ll. 95-96)

Browning and Higher Criticism

In *A Death in the Desert,* St. John had pointed out that the contemplation of divine love "reduced to plain historic fact" in the story of Christ's life and death, should lead men on to the realization of the universal revelation of God's love in human experience:

> Then stand before that fact, that Life and Death,
> Stay there at gaze, till it dispart, dispread,
> As though a star should open out, all sides,
> Grow the world on you, as it is my world.   (ll. 240-43)

So, as the third speaker in the *Epilogue* to *Dramatis Personae* gazes on the face of Christ, instead of beholding it withdraw from man's ken and disappear in the dark, it becomes an object of infinite personal significance:

> That one Face, far from vanish, rather grows,
> Or decomposes but to recompose,
> Become my universe that feels and knows.   (ll. 99-101)

How intimately these lines record Browning's own religious belief concerning the person of Christ, is shown by his comment to Mrs. Orr after reading them to her: "That Face, is the face of Christ. That is how I feel him."[42]

3

"Our Lady of Bellosguardo": A Pastel Portrait

IN AN ARTICLE printed in the *Atlantic Monthly,* December, 1864, Kate Field writes: "Florence without the Trollopes and our Lady of Bellosguardo would be like bread without salt. A blessing, then, upon houses which have been spiritual asylums to many forlorn Americans!—a blessing upon their inmates, whose hearts are as large and whose hands are as open as their minds are broad and catholic!" Miss Field's reference to "our Lady of Bellosguardo" conjures up the memory of a charming and vivacious little woman, whose kindly nature so radiated friendship that she became the centre of the social life of the English and American colony in Florence during mid-Victorian times. It was probably in 1849 that Jane Isabella Blagden, familiarly called Isa by her numerous friends, came to Florence and established her home at Villa Bricchieri on the height of Bellosguardo. From that time until her death in 1873, without possessing such assets as rank, fortune, or genius, but through the magnetism of her personal qualities, she was the focus of a distinguished Anglo-Florentine group amongst whom are men and women of renown in the annals of nineteenth-century literature.

Isabella Blagden is a remarkable example of a woman whose shadowy yet secure immortality in the remembrance of posterity has been attained indirectly. During her life she strove to win recognition as an authoress. She wrote five novels, copies of which may now be found in the British Museum. They are conventional and mediocre, Victorian in essence. Henry James dismisses her contribution to the old Tauchnitz volumes as "the inevitable nice novel or two of the wandering English spinster."[1] Miss Blagden's essays, published in English magazines such as the *Cornhill* and the *Athenaeum,* deserve more attention. They reveal her intimate knowledge of Italy; and are kindled by a romantic response to the variegated panorama of Florence and Venice, so full of colour and movement, flowing beneath her eyes. But Isabella Blagden's best work in literature lies in the sphere of poetry. Her poems, collected and edited by Alfred Austin, are thirty-three in number, filling sixty-four pages of a slim volume. The poems vary in merit, but some of them, especially the sonnet series entitled "The Seven Chords of the Lyre," achieve distinction. Austin has noted as a characteristic of Isa Blagden that "she appeared incapable of thought apart from feeling."[2] Charm of sentiment springing from a generous, impulsive nature, conjoined with an ardent but genuine romantic idealism, give flavour and poignancy to these lyrics. They are not works of genius, but have human and imaginative value.

Yet Miss Blagden's literary reputation, fragile enough in her own day, was too evanescent to withstand the touch of time. We recapture her, not as an authoress but as a personality, in her proper setting as the focus of a gifted social *milieu*. In order therefore to appreciate her significance a brief survey of this *milieu* is necessary.

Van Wyck Brooks has spoken of "the Romantic exiles" who left America to live at Rome or Florence in the middle years of the nineteenth century. The designation is equally applicable to the English sojourners in these cities during this period. Lured by the historical and artistic traditions and by the semi-tropical clime of Italy, the land of the orange and myrtle, these Romantic exiles became the nucleus of a fascinating cross-section of mid-Victorian society transplanted overseas. The Anglo-American colony of permanent residents of Rome and Florence was not numerous, but it was of unusual quality. With it may be linked a constant flow of notable English and American travellers who visited Rome and Florence in the period extending from 1850 to 1870.

The coterie settled in Italy had its literary and artistic core. Poetry was represented by Landor, the Brownings, Frederick Tennyson, Robert Lytton, and, later, Alfred Austin. The sculptors were in the main Americans—Hiram Powers, Thomas Crawford, William Wetmore Story, and Harriet Hosmer. Another American living in Florence, James Jackson Jarves, was the author of various books dealing with painting and sculpture. Thomas Adolphus Trollope, a familiar figure in Florence for many years, was a historian of merit, while his mother, Frances Trollope, and Isabella Blagden were minor Victorian novelists. In touch with the artists, through their literary sympathies and as writers of journalistic essays, were two American women of vivid personality. Margaret Fuller, the meteoric and eccentric New England transcendentalist, had her home in Italy as the Marchesa d'Ossoli between 1846 and 1850. She was succeeded by Kate Field, a reincarnation of Margaret in vitality and idealism, though not in abnormality. Among the outstanding characters of the Florentine circle was George Seymour Kirkup, an English artist, whose dabblings in spiritualism foreshadowed the advent of the prince of mediums, Daniel Home. Home's impostures, despite the stout scepticism of Robert Browning, were responsible for a veritable cult of spiritualism in the midst of the Anglo-American community.

When we turn to the travellers, who as they came and went gravitated about the nucleus of their compatriots in Florence and Rome, the ramifications are wide. Thackeray, Anthony Trollope, Dickens, George Eliot, Mrs. Jameson, Emerson, Hawthorne, Lowell, Longfellow, Henry James, Mrs. Stowe—names of import in the literary history of England and America—pass across the canvas. Well-known painters such as Sir Frederic Leighton, the talented American actress Charlotte Cushman, the Irish authoress and philanthropist Frances Cobbe, Charles Eliot Norton, on his road of transition from the counting office to a professorship at Harvard, and other men and women in various walks of life, became for the time being members of the Florentine group or the kindred company at Rome.

It seems at first a paradox that Isabella Blagden should have been the centre of a circle including within it so many people of eminence. Isa was in no sense a *grande dame*. Her literary talents, as has been stated, were mediocre. Her talk was animated and merry, but she never exhibited those intellectual qualities of sparkling wit and incisive reflection which enabled the brilliant Countess of Blessington to dominate her Italian salon. Engirt by the clever and gifted coterie of which she was the connecting link, she invariably occupies the background rather than the foreground of the picture. She was unfailingly modest in the estimation of her own abilities, and Henry James was struck by the self-abnegation of her nature.

The distinction of Miss Blagden lies in her attributes of heart rather than of head, in her temperament rather than in her intellect. Isa was genuinely unspoiled and unselfish. It has been well said of her that "she must have had the rare gift of drawing out the best from other persons, of forgetting herself, of turning all thoughts away from her back to her friend."[3] Browning called her "perfect in friendship,"[4] and Adolphus Trollope wrote that she "was . . . more universally beloved than any other individual among us."[5] The unobtrusive radiation of the character of Isa Blagden, combining as she did a love of human nature with a sweet-tempered disposition and a generous, loyal spirit, was the magnet which drew together men and women whose intellect and genius were more scintillating than her own.

It is symbolic of the shadowy, elusive, yet pervasive individuality of Isabella Blagden that she should appear upon the Florentine scene with her origins shrouded in mystery. She was evidently a Eurasian. Rumour has toyed with the fancy that she was the daughter of an Indian rajah, but in all probability her father was an Englishman and her mother an East Indian. Miss Lilian Whiting thought that she was the daughter of an English gentleman and a Hindu princess.[6] However, this statement regarding the rank of her parents seems a mere conjecture. Beyond the fact that she was a Eurasian nothing definite is known of her ancestry.

Miss Blagden must have met the Brownings shortly after her arrival at Florence in 1849. During the winter of 1849-50 she saw them frequently and acquaintance speedily ripened into friendship. Browning describes Isa as "a bright, delicate, electric woman."[7] Mrs. Browning's first recorded letter to her was written in Siena, September, 1850. Soon she became Elizabeth's most intimate friend. In addition to their constant companionship at Florence, they were frequently together in the summer excursions of the Brownings to Bagni di Lucca and Siena.

During the autumn of 1852, Robert Lytton came to Florence. When he arrived he presented himself at Casa Guidi with a letter of introduction from John Forster. He was cordially received by the Brownings and through them met Isabella Blagden. She quickly became one of his closest friends. Four years later, in a letter written to Browning from The Hague in June, 1856, Lytton reveals the warmth of his affection for Isa. "A dozen or more good and dear women must have gone to the making of that one little body. I know of none so essentially lovable and absolutely to be loved, through and through."[8]

This attachment was deepened by an episode which took place in 1857. During the summer of that year, while the Brownings, Robert Lytton, and Isabella Blagden were at Bagni di Lucca, the young Englishman was seriously ill for sixteen days with an attack of gastric fever. Throughout this period Miss Blagden was his constant nurse. "Nothing," Mrs. Browning writes, "can exceed her devotion to him by night or day."[9]

Indirect but unmistakable statements in the letters of the Brownings reveal their hopes that Lytton might marry Isa. The frustration of these hopes was undoubtedly one factor in the subsequent cooling of the friendship between Robert Browning and Lytton. It is clear, however, that the poet and his wife read more into the attachment than the circumstances justified. The barriers to any prospect of a marriage were great. Lytton at that time had doubtless no prevision of his future career as Viceroy of India; had he married a Eurasian, the position would have been forever beyond his reach. Moreover he was fifteen years younger than Isabella Blagden. His attachment, such as it was, must be regarded as the impulsive sentiment of a young man —and he was chock-full of romance—for a charming and lovable woman whose social setting and environment blended inextricably in his thoughts with the spell of enchantment that Italy had laid upon him. Though the Brownings were disappointed and inclined to censure Robert Lytton because he did not marry Isa, it is difficult to see how any blame can be attached to him. He appreciated to the full her warmth of heart and unselfishness of spirit, but his feeling for her was that of friendship rather than of passion, although a certain amount of romantic sentiment did enter into it. As for Isa, whatever her secret hopes may have been, it is clear that she never wore her heart on her sleeve or for one moment o'er-stepped the bounds of modesty and decorum. Her feelings were probably more deeply engaged than those of Lytton, but she gave no outward sign of it. Her devotion to him as a nurse was not exceptional. In the last illnesses of Elizabeth Browning and Theodosia Trollope she was equally self-sacrificing in her loving care, as their husbands have gratefully testified.

It is with some hesitation that one trespasses upon the ground of an intimate personal relationship, yet it seems to me to have definite importance for the literary historian. Lytton's poetry has a vein in it which is semi-autobiographical in character. As Mrs. A. B. Harlan has shown in her book on "Owen Meredith," his portrayal of Irene in *The Wanderer,* 1858, is a reminiscence of his romantic infatuation for Mrs. Fleetwood Wilson at the time of his residence in Florence. Browning and his wife, however, regarded the "Cordelia poems" of *The Wanderer* as having a connection with Isabella Blagden. Mr. E. C. McAleer of the University of Tennessee has recently informed me of an unpublished letter of Mrs. Browning to Isa, February 15, 1859, and has kindly allowed me to cite from it:

But Lytton's book is out—"The Wanderer"—& you observe how the Athenaeum praises it, *don't you Cordelia?* . . . The book is to come to us from the publisher, Mr. Chapman writes to us—and he tells us also that the poet is to marry his Dutch love . . . (the same I suppose,) . . . a "Baroness or something of the kind," says the bookseller with a touch of satisfied awe. Is it good for him indeed Isa?—and is it not bad for HER, indeed?—Pray be humane, you who are magnanimous—or do the great virtues exclude the small?[10]

Mrs. Browning's identification of Cordelia in *The Wanderer* with Isabella Blagden may be open to question, but I am convinced that Lytton's later and best-known poem, *Lucile,* 1860, which he published under his pen name, Owen Meredith, is definitely coloured by his attachment to Isa.

A portion of the narrative material of *Lucile* was taken from George Sand's *nouvelle, Lavinia.* The borrowed material, however, is confined to the opening cantos of the poem, and its author asserts: "Every character in *Lucile* is fundamentally different from any character in *Lavinia.*" One striking alteration in the borrowed material has a bearing on my argument. George Sand's Lavinia is represented as the daughter of a Portuguese banker. Lytton's Lucile is depicted as a Eurasian, her mother being a wealthy East Indian of Mysore. In view of the fact that Isabella Blagden was a Eurasian, the significance of the change is unmistakable. Lytton follows George Sand in describing his heroine as a mature woman no longer youthful. When Lord Alfred sees Lucile we are told:

> The woman that now met, unshrinking, his gaze,
> Seem'd to bask in the silent but sumptuous haze
> Of that soft second summer, more ripe than the first,
> Which returns when the bud to the blossom hath burst
> In despite of the stormiest April. . . . (I. III. ix. 1-5)

Although the maturity of Lucile is in accord with that of Lavinia, Lytton might also have in mind the correspondence of her age with Isa's. The physical characteristics of Lucile, who is portrayed as slight in stature, a brunette, with dusky hair, dark eyes, and cheeks of "pure olive hue," are in harmony with those of Isa. The minute analysis of Lucile's character, a completely original part of Lytton's poem, has touches applicable to Isa, and the account of the heroine's villa at Serchon recalls Villa

Bricchieri. In the latter part of Owen Meredith's romantic tale, to which there is no analogy in *Lavinia,* Lucile, as the Sœur Seraphine, nurses the wounded son of Lord Alfred, and is untiring in her watch by his couch. The first edition of *Lucile* was printed in 1860. Who can doubt that in this episode Lytton has in mind the gentle, faithful woman who had nursed him during his serious illness of 1857 at Bagni di Lucca? It would be pressing the correspondence too far to imply that Lucile is meant to be a literal portraiture of her. The comparisons that I have drawn attention to are glancing and incidental. But that Lytton's delineation of his heroine is coloured by his relationship with Isa seems self-evident.

I am again indebted to Mr. McAleer for knowledge of a reference of Mrs. Browning which reveals that she had no doubt of the influence of Isabella Blagden on *Lucile.* In a letter to Isa of May 10, 1860, she comments on a review of *Lucile* in the *Athenaeum,* April 21, 1860. Alluding to a long quotation from the poem (I. VI. ix) cited in the review, she writes of Lytton: "His prayer to you is very amusing."[11]

Of the two women whose indirect portraiture enters into *The Wanderer* and *Lucile,* I am inclined to think that Isa made the more lasting impression upon Lytton. His affection for her was not the romantic passion he felt for Mrs. Wilson, but his cherished friendship burnt with a steadier flame. Lytton was decidedly susceptible, and his infatuation for Mrs. Wilson, prompted by his volatile and impulsive temperament, is paralleled by later episodes. Referring to him in a letter of November 19, 1863, Browning writes to Isa: " . . . 'Je connais Mon. L.' and, *given* the piquant brunette, with a husband, the rest follows as the cat & fiddle follows hi-diddle-diddle."[12]

Reference has been made to Miss Blagden's home in Florence, the Villa Bricchieri on the height of Bellosguardo. This beautiful and picturesque villa has been imaginatively described by Elizabeth Browning in the seventh book of *Aurora Lee.* It enshrines, above all other spots, the social memories of the Anglo-American colony in Florence during the middle years of the nineteenth century. One can only pick and choose a few reminiscences of the company who were wont to assemble there. Since I have dwelt on the intimacy of Robert Lytton's connection with Isa, it is appropriate to begin with an extract from a letter of Mrs. Anna Jameson written at Florence, on July 25, 1857:

> Last night after sunset I went up to the villa on Bellosquardo [sic] belonging to an English lady (Miss Blagden). The Brownings, Mr. Bulwer Lytton (a son of Sir Edward) and myself formed the party. We sat on a Balcony, with the starry night above our heads and Florence spread in the valley at our feet. Mr. Lytton read us with a charming voice and expression some of his own poems of great beauty and originality. The scene was very striking on the whole and in itself poetical.[13]

In the spring of 1859, a clever and attractive young American woman, twenty years of age, arrived at Florence, who was at once taken to the hearts of the Anglo-American circle there. Kate Field, coming to Italy to study music and the languages, was placed in the care of Isabella Blagden. Her personality has been well summed up by Miss Whiting: "Kate Field was a woman who impressed the imagination. She abounded in spiritual vitality. Delicate in physique, artistic in temperament, exquisite in taste, lofty in all poetic and heroic feeling, she had that intense and finely strung nature that leaves in some form or other its haunting impress."[14] Landor, the Brownings, and Isa were captivated by this brilliant American girl, and for five or six years she is a central figure in the Florentine group. Her series of articles, published in the *Atlantic Monthly* between 1861 and 1868, on "English Authors in Florence," and on individual poets such as Walter Savage Landor and Mrs. Browning, contain intimate glimpses of her gifted friends and their environment. I have already cited her glowing tribute to Isabella Blagden. She writes frequently of Villa Bricchieri, its hostess and guests, as in the following passage: "The inmate of this villa was a little lady with blue-black hair and sparkling jet eyes, a writer whose dawn is one of promise, a chosen friend of the noblest and best, and on her terrace the Brownings, Walter Savage Landor, and many choice spirits have sipped tea while their eyes drank in such a

"Our Lady of Bellosguardo"

vision of beauty as Nature and Art have never equalled elsewhere."[15] It was on a summer evening of July, 1860, at Bellosguardo, when Kate Field, her mother, Landor, and the Brownings were being entertained by Miss Blagden, that the pretty young American girl "earned her poem" from the venerable Nestor of Victorian literature by greeting him with a kiss. As Landor wrote in mock-heroic vein:

> She came across nor greatly feared
> The horrid brake of wintry beard.

The lines recall, by way of contrast, Mrs. Browning's more appreciative tribute to Landor's facial adornment: "He has the most beautiful sea-foam of a beard you ever saw, all in a curl and white bubblement of beauty."

Around 1860, Villa Bricchieri was the scene of many gay and happy social gatherings. The dark pillar of Mrs. Browning's death in 1861 had not yet cast its shadow over the brilliant circle who foregathered there. Nathaniel Hawthorne spent the summer of 1859 in Florence, and occupied Villa Mont' Auto on Bellosguardo in the immediate vicinity of Villa Bricchieri. As Kate Field has noted, it is Bellosguardo "which he transformed by the magic of his pen into the Monte Bene of the 'Marble Faun.' "[16] He was frequently a guest of Miss Blagden, and it was at one of her afternoon receptions that he met Browning and Adolphus Trollope.

In the spring of 1860, Miss Frances Power Cobbe, the Irish author and philanthropist, came to Florence and shared for a time Isabella Blagden's home. To Miss Cobbe's pen we are indebted for a graphic and intimate picture of Villa Bricchieri and her companionship with Isa. These were providential times when a comfortable life in Italy was compatible with a slender purse. Miss Cobbe writes:

We were both of us poor, but in those days poverty in Florence permitted us to rent fourteen well-furnished rooms in a charming villa, and to keep a maid and a man-servant. The latter bought our meals every morning in Florence, cooked and served them; being always clean and respectably dressed. He swept our floors and he opened our doors and announced our company and served our ices and tea with uniform quietness and success. A treasure, indeed, was good old Ansano! Also we were able to engage an open carriage with a pair of horses to do our shopping and pay our visits in Florence as often as we needed. And what does the reader think it cost us to live like this, fire and candles and food for four included? In those halycon days under the old *régime*, it was precisely £20 a month! We divided everything exactly and it never exceeded £10 apiece.[17]

Miss Cobbe's reminiscences include frequent references to Browning as a visitor at Bellosguardo. She speaks of his light and playful conversation; of the ripple of laughter round the sofa where he used to seat himself; of his eagerness and intensity; of his affectionate wrangling with Isa. On one occasion she recalls that when she was at the Villa Niccolini, half a mile away from the Villa Bricchieri, "some singular condition of sonority" in the night air carried the voices of Browning and Isabella Blagden between the walls of the two villas. They were engaged in an animated controversy regarding spirit-rapping—Robert Browning denouncing spiritualism, while Isa, who shared his wife's views on this subject, defended it.

With the possible exception of a brilliant Roman season in the winter of 1853-54, the year 1860 may be singled out as representing the apogee of Anglo-American life in Italy during mid-Victorian times. In addition to Miss Cobbe, Harriet Hosmer, the talented American sculptress, was a guest of Miss Blagden at Bellosguardo in the spring of this year. William Wetmore Story, another distinguished American sculptor, and his family, saw much of the Brownings and Isabella Blagden at Siena during the summer. George Eliot was with G. H. Lewes in Florence, the English novelist being engaged in making studies for *Romola*. They were the guests of Thomas Adolphus Trollope. Theodore Parker, the noted Unitarian divine, was also at Florence. In October, 1860, Anthony Trollope came to Florence, where he was captivated by the beauty and intelligence of Kate Field. The failing health of Mrs. Browning was the only cloud on the horizon of this memorable year.

"Our Lady of Bellosguardo"

The death of Elizabeth Browning, in June, 1861, was the first and the greatest tragic break in Isabella Blagden's circle of friends. Mrs. Browning's letters between 1849 and 1861 reveal the warmth of attachment between the two women: "Dearest Isa, I miss you and love you. How perfect you are to me always. . . . You are an angel, dearest Isa, with the tact of a woman of the world."[18] Immediately after Elizabeth's death, Isabella took Browning's young son to Bellosguardo, and induced the poet to spend the nights at her home. Browning never forgot her unflagging and loving friendship in these days of grief and suffering. "Isa Blagden, perfect in all kindness to me," he wrote to Miss Haworth in a letter dated July 20, 1861.[19] When in the month of August the poet and Penini left Florence, she went with them as far as Paris. Writing to a friend at this time, Browning says: "I did leave Florence at last, accompanied by Miss Blagden, who has devoted herself to me, and Pen, disregarding health, inconvenience, and all other considerations."[20] Nine years later, in a letter to Isa, the poet recalled the comfort she had given him the night after his wife's death: "It was this day that I went to your house in the evening: how utterly good and kind you were, and always have been, before and since. . . ."[21]

As Browning left Florence forever in 1861, his personal intercourse with Isa in Italy came to an end; but 1861 marks the beginning of an extensive correspondence between them. Their letters were monthly, Miss Blagden writing on the twelfth and the poet replying on the nineteenth. They cover a period of twelve years from 1861 to 1872. Isabella's claim to immortality lies in the recollections of her friends, and it seems in keeping with this fact that none of her numerous letters to Browning have survived. They were destroyed by the poet in accordance with a mutual agreement, but Isa kept the poet's letters, though she may have intended to burn them before her death.

With the single exception of the love letters written to Elizabeth Barrett, the letters of Browning to Isabella Blagden are his most important correspondence. Mrs. Orr, the poet's first biographer, cites extracts from these letters. The bulk of them were published by Professor Armstrong in 1923, and the remainder in the Thomas Wise collection of Browning letters edited by Professor Hood in 1933. They have proved a valuable mine of information for students of the poet. They are quite unlike the letters written to Miss Barrett. The reader will not find in them any intimate self-revelation. Nor, though they contain data regarding the composition of certain of Browning's works, do they deal with the intrinsic content of his poems. There are no analytic discussions of *The Ring and the Book* such as mark the poet's correspondence with that literary blue stocking, Julia Wedgwood. Browning's letters to Isa are chatty and familiar in tone. They dwell on his manifold interests and activities in the world of affairs as well as his periods of relaxation. The poet's London life, his holidays in Brittany or the south of France, his friends in England and Italy, family news—these are the customary themes of the Isabella Blagden letters. Old memories blend with fresh associations. Interspersed are shrewd and penetrating comments on men and women of historical and literary importance. Amongst these are references to Napoleon III, Cardinal Manning, Benjamin Jowett, Byron, Carlyle, Matthew Arnold, Renan, and other people of note. The correspondence is pervaded by an endearing vein of affection. It is a tribute to one of the oldest and deepest of Browning's friendships, hallowed by his consciousness of Isa Blagden's intimate relationship with his wife.

Though the death of Mrs. Browning and her husband's departure from Italy were irreparable breaks in the Florentine circle, Miss Blagden's life was still enriched by manifold social contacts. Her friendship with Thomas Adolphus Trollope and his wife was particularly close. In his book of memoirs, *What I Remember,* Trollope describes Isa as "a very bright, very warm-hearted, very clever little woman, who knew everybody and was, I think, more universally beloved than any other individual among us."[22] At the time of his wife's last illness and death in 1865, Isabella was as great a comfort to him as she had previously been to Browning. In a letter of October 27, 1865, addressed to Kate Field, Miss Blagden writes:

Your last came when I was getting very anxious about poor Mrs. Trollope, which anxiety was justified by the event. Not many weeks afterwards I went to stay with her and never left her until her death. She died in my arms, I might say, though not actually, but mine was the last voice she heard and the last hand she pressed in this world. When I saw that she was passing away I gave up my place to Mr. Trollope. I stood a little behind him. I sat up with him that night and took Beatrice home with me the next morning and she remained with me till Anthony Trollope fetched her himself.[23]

One of the most interesting of Isabella Blagden's later associations is her connection with Alfred Austin. It is surely a mark of the catholicity as well as the perfection of her friendship, that she should have an affectionate regard for the poet whom Browning savagely assailed in *Pacchiarotto*. The two men were at daggers drawn, and yet both were embraced in the mantle of Miss Blagden's generous and loving spirit. Her qualities of heart endowed her with that rare magnetism of sympathetic friendliness which attracted men and women of the most diverse tastes and temperaments. After Isabella's death, Alfred Austin edited her poems; and in his introductory memoir recalls with gratitude the aid she gave him in establishing himself in Florence.

I well remember how busy she was in the spring of 1865, yet with what alacrity she assisted me, weary after seven months even of the streets of Florence, to bivouac in an unfurnished villa outside the Porta Romana, and not far from the Villa Giglione she herself then tenanted; lending me or finding me linen, plate and crockery, and pressing into service the handsome barefooted daughters of the Podere that adjoined it, one of whom used to compute the length of time one's eggs for breakfast should be left in boiling water, by counting two hundred beats of her pulse.[24]

In the *Life, Letters, and Memories* of Charlotte Cushman, various references are made to Miss Blagden. The American actress always stayed with her for a while when she visited Florence, and the two women became fast friends. Miss Cushman, herself a dog lover, alludes to Isa's fondness for animals. Her dogs and cats were generally waifs and strays. An ugly poodle, "without form, and void of grace and comeliness," had been rescued from some boys who were drowning it in Venice. It was appropriately christened Venezia. Another dog whom she had saved received the name of a low comedian, "from his unaristocratic and comic appearance." The list of these four-footed adoptions would be a long one. In common with the Brownings, Miss Blagden was vehemently opposed to vivisection; and she once took an active part in drawing up a resolution of protest against this surgical practice. Her affection for animals deserves passing notice as in accord with the tenderness of her nature.

Towards the close of December, 1872, Browning wrote, in what was destined to be his last letter to Isabella Blagden: "Well, dearest, here is another year's end, the eleventh: the years that come & go, the Races drop in the grave, but never the love does so!"[25] Miss Blagden died in the following month, on January 20, 1873. There is an element of pathos in her death, as movingly described by Adolphus Trollope. She was living alone at the time preceding her death except for the attendance of a couple of old servants. Trollope, probably her closest friend next to Browning, was in Siena. He thought had he been present he could have persuaded her to call a doctor, but in his absence she obstinately refused to take medical advice. Trollope believed that her life might have been saved had she received proper attention. A few of her friends were with her in the last days of her brief illness, and Madame Pasquale Villari was by her bed-side when she died.

Isabella Blagden was buried in the lovely cypress-shaded English cemetery just outside the old walls of Florence. There are two burial grounds in Italy hallowed by the associations of English poetry. One is the Protestant cemetery at Rome where the body of Keats and the ashes of Shelley were placed. The other is the English cemetery at Florence where Landor and Mrs. Browning were buried. It is fitting that Isa's grave should be in this beautiful spot in the Florence she loved so well, close to the graves of her friends, Mrs. Browning and the Trollopes.

The personality of Isa Blagden is revealed to us in oblique fashion through the numerous vignettes of her friends. With her

"Our Lady of Bellosguardo"

origins veiled in mystery, her literary reputation transitory, her nature modest and unpretentious, she seems but a humble member of the gifted coterie by whom she was surrounded. She lacked, as has been said, any distinction of rank or advantages of fortune. And yet when we seek a focus for the talented Anglo-Florentine group, it is not to be found in Browning, a poet of genius, in Adolphus Trollope, a scholarly historian, in Kate Field, a beautiful woman endowed with literary and musical sensitivity; but rather in Isa, whose primary qualities were a warm heart and a limitless capacity for friendship. Villa Bricchieri, not Casa Guidi or Villino Trollope, was the English and American social centre of Florence between 1850 and 1870. Relatively unimportant in herself, Isabella Blagden is the pivotal figure of a galaxy of men and women whose names are still bright in the remembrance of posterity. A minor personage, a pastel portrait, this little woman, a Eurasian yet so typically Victorian, has an illumined niche in the reflected light of that brilliant social *milieu* from which she can never be severed.

It was reserved for Henry James, the great psychological novelist, to capture the spiritual distillation of Isa's personality. He had only talked with her during one brief morning at Bellosguardo, but the interview left an indelible impression. He recorded this after her death with the intuitive vision of the artist. In his "salutation to the hovering shade" of Miss Blagden, he writes of her devotion to the Brownings, and recalls how she had "befriended the lonely, cheered the exile and nursed the sick." "These friendships and generosities," he continues, "in a setting of Florentine villas and views, of overhanging terraces and arched *pianterreni*, of Italian loyalties and English longings, of shy literary yearning and confessed literary starvation—these things formed her kindly little legend. . . ." The American novelist then describes the morning he spent with Isa amid the springtime air of a garden at Bellosguardo.

I feel again the sun of Florence in the morning walk out of Porta Romana and up the long winding hill; I catch again, in the great softness, the "accent" of the straight, black cypresses; I lose myself again in the sense of the large, cool villa, already then a centre of histories, memories, echoes, all generations deep; I face the Val d'Arno, vast and delicate, as if it were a painted picture; in special I talk with an eager little lady who has gentle, gay black eyes and whose type gives, visibly enough, the hint of East-Indian blood. The villa had, as I say, a past then, and has much more of one now; which romantic actualities and possibilities, a crowd of international relations, hung about us as we lingered and talked, making, for the victim of this first impression of the place, a mere fond fable of lives led and work done and troubles suffered there. She had seen the procession, the human panorama, more or less polyglot; there were odd people—oh, "precursors" enough, in *her* list!—whom she had known, and of whom I knew; and then we had friends in common, figures of the Florentine legend, to my knowledge of whom she added; with which, moreover, there were wistful questions that were at the same time, for the passer-by, provocations of envy: the books she would have liked to read, the news she would have liked to get, the people she would have liked to see, amounting all, in their absence, as I remember ingenuously thinking, to nothing more than a sign of how deep one might be in Italy.[26]

Possibly this sketch of personal reminiscence, from the pen of Henry James, is a little over-romanticized. Isa as an echo of the past, a repository of historic memories, literary associations, and Italian settings, is withdrawn into the shadows and becomes "a hovering ghost." In life she had her own sparkle. Her friends speak of her animation and enthusiasm, her freedom from ennui and boredom, her habitual cheerfulness. As Alfred Austin testifies: "The news, 'Isa is coming,' invariably filled with an almost childlike delight a certain Florentine circle." Dulness, outward or inward, was foreign to Isabella Blagden. Her biographer notes: "She gloried in the gorgeous apparel of the external world, just as—many will remember—she delighted in bright textures and vivid colours for feminine adornment."[27]

In words which recall the reference of Henry James to Isa Blagden as one who had "befriended the lonely, cheered the exile and nursed the sick," Alfred Austin pays glowing tribute to the unselfishness of her character. "Practical benevolence" he tells us "was her religion."[28] Instance after instance might be cited illustrating her kindness of heart.

"Our Lady of Bellosguardo"

In a letter to her sister Henrietta, December 30, 1853, Mrs. Browning writes of Isa: "She devotes herself to a poor little invalid friend whom she brought from England, last Monday."[29] This "invalid" friend was Louisa Alexander. She was taken care of by Miss Blagden for two years, until in 1855 she departed for India with a servant. Three years later she died in India, and Mrs. Browning refers to this in a letter of sympathy written to Isa, October 2, 1858:

I am saddened, saddened by your letter. We both are. Indeed, this last news from India must have struck—I know it did. Still, to your generous nature, long regret for your dear Louisa will be impossible; and you, so given to forget yourself, will come to forget a grief which is only your own. For she was in the world, as not of it, in a painful sense; she was cut off from the cheerful, natural development of ordinary human beings. . . . Rather praise God for her therefore, dearest Isa, that she is gone above the cloud, gone where she can exercise active virtues and charities, instead of being the mild patient object of the charities and virtues of her friends. Perhaps she ministers to *you* now instead of being ministered to by you. . . .[30]

Was this Louisa, cared for and beloved by Isabella Blagden, who died in India, possibly a Eurasian like Isa, and conceivably a blood relation?

We can only conjecture, but the supposition is strengthened by the fact that when Browning met Louisa's mother in England he wrote to Isa: " . . . I liked her much, fancied her like you somewhat in face. . . ."[31] When Miss Blagden was in England she gave the Alexander home in London to various correspondents in Italy as her forwarding address; and when Mrs. Alexander died, Browning wrote to Isa: "I was sorry to hear of Mrs. Alexander's death, in the certainty it would bring greater sorrow to you. . . ."[32]

The essays of Isa, which are superior to her novels, reveal her eye for the picturesque and her love of brilliant hues. Illustrations may be cited from a charming article called "A Holiday in Venice," printed in the *Cornhill Magazine* for October, 1865. After nursing Mrs. Trollope in her last illness, Miss Blagden went to Venice for a month to recuperate. Of her visit she wrote to Kate Field: "I enjoyed it thoroughly and entirely—No place has so completely enchanted me."[33] Her sketch in the *Cornhill* was a record of her impressions. Isa was "deep in Italy," and passages in this essay reflect the magic and richness of Venetian scenery, and the ever shifting colours of those gay water fêtes in which the natives of Venice delight.

The gondola shot from the steps of the garden, and for a few minutes we seemed to be alone on the canal. Above, was the soft darkness of the sky; around, a shimmering haze of transparent air, pregnant of stars soon to be born; below, the liquid shining blackness, through which we cut our way. But suddenly, far off, we heard sounds of music, and then, as if evoked by the sound, there floated slowly towards us a train of luminous apparitions; gondolas, with rows of coloured lamps of every tint and shape, slung to the square rods of the awnings, and rowed by gondoliers in their holiday costume of white, with particoloured sashes looped up at the sides. . . .

The effect was beautiful. The two illuminated barges containing the two orchestras were moored, one at the Rialto and one at the Piazzetta, and it seemed as if beds of gay flowers were gliding down the canal, from end to end, between two lofty variegated banks; or as if a flight of those fairy birds, with silver beaks and peacock tails, of which Eastern stories tell us, were fluttering to and fro their jewelled nests over a magic lake.

Limitations of space preclude the citation of the fine description of St. Mark's Cathedral in "A Holiday in Venice," or the graphic account of a visit to Vallombrosa in another article contributed by Isa to the *Cornhill Magazine,* October, 1864, entitled "A Tuscan Village—A Tuscan Sanctuary."

Isabella Blagden had a sunny but not a shallow nature. Her sweetness was never cloying, nor did her genial temperament lack edge, as her whimsical sparring with Browning evinces. In a letter of 1870, the poet affectionately reminds her: "Yet so are we made that I suppose we should teaze each other again if the seas and lands did not separate us, whom *does* one care to teaze that one does not also care to kiss? 'Love both ways, kiss and teaze.' "[34] Despite Miss Blagden's gaiety of disposition, her life was not one of unalloyed happiness. She was such an unfailing source of comfort and good cheer to her friends that it is difficult to realize her lack of family ties and relationships. She might well have been a lonely woman but for her hospitality and benevolence. Her genius for friendship had its root in the qualities of her heart, and so inspired her that it became a philosophy of life. "Women must love or their blood turns to vinegar," one of her novels ends; and in expressing the conviction of Mrs. Spencer, a character in her fiction, Isa voices her own: "It is better, believe me, to love, than to be loved: the loving love longer than the beloved."

Isabella Blagden was a brave yet a sensitive spirit; and in her poetry we glimpse a gentle melancholy which she concealed from the men and women whose worldly paths she brightened. Occasionally the melancholy became passionate rather than gentle, but even in a storm-tossed mood Isa exhibits strength and fortitude, as her sonnet to Endurance testifies:

> Wild heart be still! From yon lone mount, a star
> Looks singly forth on the dark world. Art thou
> Less brave? To thee thy fears and sorrow are
> As night to yon bright orb; yet is its brow
> Radiant and calm, as when amid the joy
> Of the young earth its light flashed forth from God!
> Can summer suns, or gentle moons alloy
> The immemorial woe to which art vowed,
> O cypress-tree? Yet dost thou sternly bear
> Thy mournful doom, and with a brave despair
> Droop'st not, albeit no smiles of vernal spring
> To thy funereal crown new light can bring.
> Lo! these bear up 'gainst Fate a steadfast war;
> Am I less noble than the tree or star?

Seventy years have passed since the death of Isabella Blagden. She left no diary or journal to perpetuate her name; her few surviving letters are scraps and jottings; her contributions to literature, while far from contemptible, are of transient worth. It is only in her setting as the social centre of the Anglo-Florentine colony of her day that she has a claim to remembrance. Ultimately we return to Henry James's vision of Isa as a reflection of the associations, traditions, and memories clustering about the notable English and American men and women who lived in or visited Florence between 1850 and 1870. She is, in this sense, a pastel portrait, or a prism dyed with colours when touched by the ambient light of the sun. Though she left scant record of herself, it is doubtful whether any other woman has received so many affectionate tributes from people of high distinction in the middle years of the nineteenth century. Hers was the Florence of Landor and the Brownings, and towards it flowed streams of pilgrimage from England and America. A runnel of Victorian society, devoted to arts and letters, intermingled there with a rivulet of the painters, sculptors, and *literati* of New England in its golden age. Florence, even more than Rome, is representative of this conflux, symbolically significant of the cousinship between English and American artists and men of letters. And in Florence, the Villa Bricchieri was like an *imperium in imperio,* with Isa Blagden the unassuming yet acknowledged mistress of her little salon.

Villa Bricchieri still endures. It stands about a mile outside the walls of Florence on the height of Bellosguardo commanding a lovely view of the city and the valley of the Arno. Beyond these rise the cypress-covered slopes of Fiesole interspersed with white villas and topped by the gray tower of a medieval cathedral silhouetted against the sky. The large cool villa, with its terrace, balcony, and adjoining garden, has romantic charm and beauty. The Italian history of Villa Bricchieri both antedates and follows the residence there of Isabella Blagden.

> It has had its scenes, its joys and crimes,
> But that is its own affair.

The English or American visitor to Florence will, however, always link Villa Bricchieri with the years it was tenanted by Isa. Historic shades seem to haunt it—the hovering ghosts of Landor, the Brownings, Robert Lytton, the Trollopes, Kate Field, Frances Cobbe, Charlotte Cushman, the Storys, Harriet Hosmer, Hawthorne and others—who in life walked in the garden, drank tea on the terrace, looked at the stars from the balcony, discussed music, painting, sculpture, and literature in the reception room, or wrangled over spiritualism and chit-chatted there. Above all, the villa enshrines the memory of the kindly, merry Isa, unendowed with genius, fortune, or title, but rich in the possession of a loving heart; whose "greatest poem," as it has been aptly put, "was her life—her generous gift of human sympathy and love."

It is a vanished society now, this cross-section of Victorianism with its shibboleths, conventions, artistic interests, and ideals—interblended with a dash of New England transcendentalism. The cobwebs and creepers of time have dimmed some of its lustre; the searchlight of modern criticism has exposed some of its weakness. The Anglo-Florentine colony was in certain respects an exotic bloom. A choice company, but few in numbers, its members did not escape the foibles, the pruderies, the innate conservatisms of the Victorian age, but they also exhibit the dignity and poise of that era. Now that the dykes of this settled and long-established order have broken down, and the world like a labouring ship tosses in the stress of the tempest, we may look back at times with longing to the idyllic havens where our Victorian fathers dwelt. A contemplation of this little cameo of English and American life, centring about Isa Blagden and the Villa Bricchieri, may bring momentary respite and spiritual refreshment. Like Kipling's "Three-Decker," the Victorians, with their love of form and ceremony, carried more *impedimenta* than we do. Yet their voyage was more leisurely and better charted. Under a stately sail, with "tiering canvas in sheeted silver spread," they have passed to a far horizon, having completed the measure of their days. Whatever vicissitudes of weather they encountered, they enjoyed to the full life's halcyon harbours, and often attained outward happiness and a serenity of mind that we may envy. So, recalling in connection with a literary study that Art is a way of escape, we may pause for a brief interval in the midst of a cataclysmic world to wish the Victorian "Three-Decker" a *bon voyage* to "the Islands of the Blest."

Hull down—hull down and under—she dwindles to
 a speck,
With noise of pleasant music and dancing on her
 deck.
All's well—all's well aboard her—she's left you far
 behind,
With a scent of old-world roses through the fog
 that ties you blind.

4

New Light on the Genesis of "The Ring and the Book"

FOREWORD: The essays on the genesis and the documentary sources of *The Ring and the Book* were first printed in the June and November, 1928 issues of *MLN*. My findings in these were afterwards accepted by Browning scholars, and they appear in such works as W. C. DeVane's *A Browning Handbook,* 1935, and the revised edition of Griffin and Minchin's *The Life of Robert Browning,* 1938. Since 1928, the publication of additional letters of Browning has confirmed my conclusions regarding the dates of his visits to Cambo and Biarritz in 1864. As the process of reasoning by which my results were established was based upon the information available in 1928, it seems best to reprint the articles as originally written, and to refer to the later confirmatory evidence in an addendum.

The date of Browning's first reference in writing to the story of *The Ring and the Book*, has generally been regarded as determined by a letter of his to Miss Isabella Blagden, cited by Mrs. Orr, in part as follows:

Biarritz, Maison Gastonbide: Sept. 19, '62.

. . . I stayed a month at green pleasant little Cambo, and then came here from pure inability to go elsewhere—St.-Jean de Luz, on which I had reckoned, being still fuller of Spaniards who profit by the new railway. . . . I stay till the end of the month, then go to Paris, and then get my neck back into the old collar again. Pen has managed to get more enjoyment out of his holiday than seemed at first likely. . . . For me, I have got on by having a great read at Euripides—the one book I brought with me, besides attending to my own matters, my new poem that is about to be; and of which the whole is pretty well in my head,—the Roman murder story you know. . . .[1]

This letter, as printed by Mrs. Orr, appears to fix the date of Browning's first literary allusion to the story of *The Ring and the Book* as September 19, 1862. It also seems to confirm the accuracy of her account of the poet's holiday trips to France—his stay at Cambo and Biarritz in 1862 and his initial visit to Pornic, Brittany, in 1863.

So far as I have knowledge, the validity of the date prefixed to the Isabella Blagden letter, and the correctness of Mrs. Orr's chronology with respect to Browning's residences in France in 1862 and 1863, have never been questioned.[2] On the contrary, all of his biographers cite the Biarritz letter to Miss Blagden as indisputable proof that the poet was occupied with the theme of *The Ring and the Book* in 1862, and that he was in the neighbourhood of the Pyrenees in the summer and early autumn of this year.

Yet, notwithstanding this unanimity of statement, there exists definite circumstantial evidence that Browning was not at Cambo and Biarritz in 1862, and that the letter which Mrs. Orr quotes is misdated by two years.

In the *Letters of Robert Browning to Miss Isa Blagden,* edited by Professor A. J. Armstrong, and published in 1923 by Baylor University Press, there are two letters of the poet written at Ste Marie près Pornic, on August 18 and September 19 of the year 1862.[3] It is of particular note that the date of the second Pornic letter, September 19, 1862, and the date of the Biarritz letter as printed by Mrs. Orr, are identical, and that both letters are addressed to Miss Blagden. Obviously, Browning cannot have written to Isabella Blagden from Brittany and the Pyrenees on the same day, and, consequently, one of these letters must be misdated. But, while the date of the Biarritz letter, as cited by Mrs. Orr, is unconfirmed by other testimony, the evidence that the poet was at Pornic in 1862 comes from a variety of sources and is of positive character.

The Ring and the Book

The confusion in which Mrs. Orr is involved through her acceptance of the date of the Biarritz letter as September 19, 1862, is shown by the fact that it compels her to regard 1863 as the year of Browning's initial stay at Pornic. She apparently substantiates this by an extract from another letter of the poet's to Isabella Blagden, in which he describes his first summer spent in the vicinity of Pornic as follows:

. . . This is a wild little place in Brittany, something like that village where we stayed last year. Close to the sea—a hamlet of a dozen houses, perfectly lonely—one may walk on the edge of the low rocks by the sea for miles.[4]

Though Mrs. Orr does not print the heading of this letter, she tells us that it was written on August 18, 1863. This fits in with her belief that Browning was at Cambo and Biarritz, and not in Brittany, during the summer of 1862. But a reference to the superscription and full text of this particular letter, as published in the *Letters of Robert Browning to Miss Isa Blagden,* shows that the correct date is 1862 not 1863.[5] The heading there reads: "Chez M. La Raison, Maire de St. Marie, Pornic, Loire Inférieure. Aug. 18, '62." If Mrs. Orr's dates were accurate, the "village where we stayed last year" would be "green pleasant little Cambo," an inland hamlet; which would scarcely justify the comparison to Ste Marie, "a wild little place in Brittany." The allusion is plainly to St. Enogat, near Dinard, another Breton village, where Browning spent a vacation of two months in 1861.

The two long Ste Marie letters of August 18 and September 19 would, of themselves, be sufficient to establish the fact of the poet's residence at Pornic in 1862. They supplement each other and give a circumstantial and somewhat detailed account of his interests and diversions in Brittany.[6] From these and a preceding letter from Warwick Crescent, we can definitely trace Browning's itinerary, in France, throughout the months of August and September, 1862. He left London for Paris on August 2, arrived at Pornic before the 18th, remained there till the end of September, and then, after a week in Paris, returned to London. Further evidence of Browning's stay at Pornic in this year is provided by subsequent letters to Miss Blagden. Writing to her from

Warwick Crescent, London, on "Oct. 18, '62," he speaks of the physical benefit derived from his summer in Brittany: "You suppose I was dull at Ste Marie. On the contrary I stayed a week longer than the allotted time, and could have done well there for ever: it was in my scheme to read, walk & do nothing but think there;. . . . My health is much improved I should tell you, for I was regularly ill when I left town."[7] Again, in a Ste Marie letter of August 19, 1863, telling Miss Blagden of his second arrival at Pornic, he writes of having "left on the 9th. for Tours, thence, next day to Nantes and this old place, where I find nothing altered."[8]

The testimony of these various "Blagden" letters is conclusive, but a final proof of the poet's residence in Brittany in 1862 may be cited from an independent source. In a letter to the American sculptor, W. W. Story, and his family, dated from "Ste.-Marie, près Pornic, Brittany, Sept. 5th, 1863," Browning writes: "Here are we in the old place, just as we left it last year, and I rather like it better on acquaintance."[9]

The evidence that Browning was at Pornic on September 19, 1862,[10] proves that the Biarritz letter with its allusion to the Roman murder story, as quoted by Mrs. Orr, is wrongly dated. This, however, is a purely negative result. Is it possible to establish with certainty the true date of the letter in question? I feel convinced that this can be done beyond any reasonable doubt.

There is, in the first place, indisputable evidence to show that Browning paid a visit to Cambo and Biarritz in the year 1864. As a matter of fact this has been recognized by Edward Dowden and by W. Hall Griffin in their admirable biographies of the poet. Deriving his information from letters written in 1864 by Browning to Mrs. Story and Francis Palgrave, which contain references to this particular trip, Professor Dowden notes: "In 1864 Browning again 'braved the awful Biarritz' and stayed at Cambo. On this occasion he visited Fontarabia."[11] Professor Griffin also alludes to an 1864 letter from Browning to Tennyson, and records his itinerary in southern France with a little more

The Ring and the Book

detail. "When the second sojourn at Sainte Marie ended, he had a fancy to see what Arcachon was like. Finding it noisy and modern, he and his party pushed on to St. Jean-de-Luz, and thence, there being no accommodation, to Cambo once more. From this village he visited the *pas de Roland,* which, as letters to Story and to Tennyson testify, impressed him greatly."[12]

Yet, while fully aware that Browning went to the Basses-Pyrénées in 1864, Dowden and Griffin fall into the error of accepting the date given by Mrs. Orr for the Biarritz letter of 1862. Consequently they regard the poet's visit to the Basque region of France in 1864 as his second stay at Cambo and Biarritz, the first being in 1862. They also, in common with other biographers and literary critics, follow Mrs. Orr in her erroneous statement that the first summer spent by Browning at Pornic was in 1863.

As has been shown, the Ste Marie letters to Isabella Blagden in 1862-63 furnish decisive proof that the poet was in Brittany during the months of August and September, 1862, and that the date printed by Mrs. Orr for the Biarritz letter, "Sept. 19, '62," is untenable. But, apart from the Pornic letters, a careful reading of the accounts given by Browning of his vacation in the south of France in 1864 reveals the fact that he is visiting the Pyrenees for the first time. Here, too, valuable supplementary information is available through the publication of the *Letters of Robert Browning to Miss Isa Blagden.* Fortunately the comparison of the letters we now possess does more than disprove the date of the Biarritz letter. It shows that the latter was written shortly after letters of Browning from Cambo to Mrs. Story in August, 1864 and deals with the same trip to the Pyrenees. It enables us to fix the date of the Biarritz letter, with assurance, as September 19, 1864, instead of September 19, 1862.

At this point I cite, in chronological order, extracts from Browning's correspondence, descriptive of his visit to the Pyrenees in 1864, which have a bearing on the date of the Biarritz letter. The first citation is from a letter to Isabella Blagden.

Aug. 19, '64.
Cambo près Bayonne,
Basses Pyrénées.

DEAREST ISA,

You will wonder to find me so far South: we had a fancy to go to Arcachon, a newish place by Bourdeaux, but found it crammed with strangers: we tried St. Jean de Luz and Biaritz to no better purpose, and having to make the best of a mistake, settled ourselves in this pleasant little place for a month, meaning to get two or three weeks of sea-bathing at St. Jean (as charming as Biaritz is ugly.) . . . Pen amuses himself very well, having a knack that way. . . . I shall be able to spin the month out. . . .[13]

The second extract is from a letter, written at Cambo, addressed to Mrs. Story, the wife of the American sculptor. This is undated. A comparison, however, with the letter just quoted shows that it also was written in August, 1864.

CAMBO, près BAYONNE, BASSES PYRÉNÉES.

. . . We had a fancy to try a new place, Arcachon by Bordeaux, and reached it in two days' easy journeying only to find what was a few years ago a beautiful pine-forest turned into a toy-town, . . . and the whole full to the edge of strangers . . . we determined to go on to Bayonne, and did so, hoping for rest to the foot-sole at St-Jean-de-Luz. This is really an exquisite little place, with a delicious sea, and great mountains in the background; (but with) every house taken, every *one* of not a few. Last we braved the awful Biarritz, but liked the noise and crowd of it still less than Arcachon. . . . There seemed no course open to us—pushed up at the very end of France as we were—but to lie by in some quiet place till the bathers should begin to leave St-Jean; they never stay long, in France, but come and go in a crowd. So here we are at Cambo, a village in the Pyrénées fifteen or sixteen miles from Bayonne. . . .

I went two days ago to see a famous mountain-pass, *le pas de Roland,* so called because that paladin kicked a hole in a rock, which blocked the way, to allow Charlemagne's army to pass. . . . Well, our plan is to stay here three weeks longer, till the 13th, and then spend the rest of our holiday at St-Jean—say three weeks, bathing assiduously to make up for lost time. . . . I hold for my original scheme till forced to strike my flag. Be where we may we return to Paris in the first week of October. . . .[14]

The third citation is from a letter of Browning's to Tennyson acknowledging the receipt of a copy of the *Enoch Arden* volume.

19 WARWICK CRESCENT,
Oct. 13th, 1864.

DEAR TENNYSON,
    I have been two months away, and only just find your book now. . . . "Boadicea," the new metre, is admirable, a paladin's achievement in its way. I am thinking of Roland's Pass in the Pyrenees, where he hollowed a rock that had hitherto blocked the road, by one kick of his boot:. . . . Give my congratulations to Mrs. Tennyson. I looked a long look three days ago at the Hôtel de Douvres, where I met her first; and of you I was thinking particularly at Amiens station next afternoon. . . .[15]

A note to Francis Palgrave, written a few days after the letter to Tennyson, contains a brief mention of Browning's visit to the Basque country.

19 Warwick Crescent: Oct. 19, 1864.

My dear Palgrave,—Thank you indeed for your letter and the pleasant news of your return. We were not near each other in France—I went southward to the Pyrenees and Biarritz—indeed, I saw Fontarabia and St. Sebastian. . . .[16]

Through a comparison of these various sources of information, we may trace Browning's route in the south of France during August and September, 1864, with precision. In the opening lines of his letter to Mrs. Story, Browning writes of reaching Arcachon by Bordeaux "in two days' easy journeying." After a couple of days there, he and his party go on to Bayonne with the intention of staying at St.-Jean-de-Luz, a seaside resort twelve miles to the south-west of that town. Finding every house taken at St.-Jean, they try Biarritz, five miles west-south-west of Bayonne, but are repelled by the noise, crowd, and high prices. From Biarritz they proceed to Cambo, "a village in the Pyrenees fifteen

82   *The Infinite Moment*

or sixteen miles from Bayonne." While the date of Browning's sojourn at Cambo is not indicated in his letter to Mrs. Story, this is supplied by his letter to Miss Blagden of "Aug. 19, '64," from the same place. The likeness between these two letters is so close, extending even to parallel phrasing, that they were evidently composed at the same time, or within one or two days of each other. The letter to Miss Blagden, like that to Mrs. Story, begins with an account of Browning's journey from Arcachon to Cambo via St.-Jean-de-Luz and Biarritz. While it is impossible to tell the exact date of his arrival at Cambo, these letters, one of which is headed "Aug. 19," were undoubtedly written in the early part of his residence there.

In both the Blagden and the Story letters there are descriptions which make it plain that the poet was visiting this region for the first time in 1864. With Florence in mind, he writes to Miss Blagden:

It is very saddening to me to feel the Southern influence again: the mountains under which we are, are just like the Tuscan ranges: the verdure and vegetation more flourishing and abundant, and the villages less picturesquely distributed by far: but there are *cicale* on the trees, and much the same blue sky as of old: few vines, but great fields of maize, and plenty of fern and heather. No, it is not anything near Italy after all, but dearer for what is like.[17]

This is a definite statement that the trip to the Pyrenees was Browning's first visit to the south since he had left Italy in 1861. In similar vein, describing a region that is new to him, he tells Mrs. Story:

The country is exceedingly beautiful, the mountains just like the Tuscan ranges, with plenty of oak and chestnut woods, and everywhere the greenest of meadows—the great characteristic of the place. The little fresh river that winds in and out of the hills and vales, the Nive, comes from Spain, which is three hours' walk off. This is the Basque country, moreover, the people talk French with difficulty, and charming girl-faces abound.[18]

Again, in writing to Mrs. Story, he contrasts his first impression of Cambo in 1864 with his memories of Ste Marie in the two preceding years, as follows:

... for the last two years in the dear rough old Ste. Marie, stark-naked as she was of all comfort to the British mind, put this smug little village in unpleasant relief. I don't see the sea all day long.[19]

In the Biarritz letter, cited by Mrs. Orr, Browning declared, "I stayed a month at green pleasant little Cambo." This corresponds exactly with the period indicated by the Cambo letters to Miss Blagden and Mrs. Story of August, 1864. For instance, when writing to Isabella Blagden on the 19th, he tells her that he and his party have "settled" themselves "in this pleasant little place for a month," and adds "I shall be able to spin the month out."

To establish the precise date of the Biarritz letter, it is of particular importance to note Browning's mention of his future movements in the Cambo letters. In coming to Cambo the poet had made a virtue of necessity, not being able to find accommodation at either of the popular French watering places, St.-Jean-de-Luz or Biarritz. As he writes to Mrs. Story: "There seemed no course open to us—pushed up at the very end of France as we were—but to lie by in some quiet place till the bathers should begin to leave St.-Jean." Browning's intention was, therefore, to return to St.-Jean-de-Luz later on in the season. He gives Mrs. Story the following definite information on this point: "Well, our plan is to stay here three weeks longer, till the 13th, and then spend the rest of our holiday at St-Jean—say three weeks, bathing assiduously to make up for lost time."[20] The parallel reference, in the Blagden letter of August 19, 1864, tells of his purpose "to get two or three weeks of sea-bathing at St. Jean" after the month's stay at Cambo. Browning's plan was, then, to leave Cambo for St.-Jean-de-Luz on September 13; spend about three weeks of bathing there; and, as we learn from a later allusion in the Story letter, "return to Paris in the first week of October."

One alteration in this plan must be accounted for. If the letter of September 19, cited by Mrs. Orr, should be dated 1864, how is it that we find the poet, not at St.-Jean, but at the neighbouring town of Biarritz? The reason is explained by Browning himself, in the opening lines of the letter: " . . . I stayed a month at green pleasant little Cambo, and then came here from pure inability to go elsewhere—St.-Jean de Luz, on which I had reckoned, being still fuller of Spaniards who profit by the new railway."[21]

This Biarritz letter to Miss Blagden, when given its proper date of September 19, 1864, fits in precisely with our knowledge of Browning's intended schedule derived from the Cambo letters of the previous month. It fills in the gap between his departure from Cambo on September 13 and his arrival at Paris about the beginning of October.[22] His statement in this letter, "I stay till the end of the month, then go to Paris, and then get my neck back into the old collar again," corresponds with his purpose, as he wrote to Mrs. Story, to return to Paris in the first week of October. Browning was back in London by October 13. His letters from Warwick Crescent of the 13th and the 19th to Tennyson and Palgrave, respectively, contain interesting reminiscences of his vacation in the Pyrenees. They also give a little additional information concerning the closing incidents of his holiday in 1864. In his letter of October 13, he tells Tennyson that he "looked a long look three days ago at the Hôtel de Douvres" and was "at Amiens station next afternoon." He was, therefore, still in France on the 10th and 11th of the month, having in all probability spent several days in Paris.

The correct dating of the Biarritz letter as 1864, not 1862, harmonizes the allusion to the Roman murder story with facts already ascertained regarding the genesis of *The Ring and the Book*. Browning speaks in this letter as if his "new poem that is about to be" were very much in the forefront of his thoughts. The whole of it, he informs Miss Blagden, is pretty well in his head. This points to a time when he seriously addressed himself to the composition of *The Ring and the Book*. Though the Old Yellow Book was discovered at Florence in June, 1860, there is evidence to prove that it was not until 1864 that Browning threw his energies into the writing of the poem. In his apostrophe to the Yellow Book at the close of *The Ring and the Book* he exclaims:

> How will it be, my four-years'-intimate,
> When thou and I part company anon?   (XII. 227-28)

As these lines were, in all likelihood, written shortly before the publication of the poem in the winter of 1868-69, they carry us back to the latter part of the year 1864 as the time when Browning definitely began the composition of *The Ring and the Book*.

Other sources of information reveal that it was in the late summer and autumn of 1864 that the plan of *The Ring and the Book* took shape in the poet's mind. From the point of view of the date of the Biarritz letter with its allusion to the Roman murder story, the most noteworthy of these references is an entry in W. M. Rossetti's diary of March 15, 1868, which he made immediately after a visit from Browning. Here, on the authority of his talk with the poet, Rossetti directly connects the genesis of *The Ring and the Book* with the Basses-Pyrénées trip of 1864. He notes:

Browning's forthcoming poem exceeds 20,000 lines: it may probably be out in July, but he would defer it if he finds that more conducive to the satisfactory completion of the work. He began it in October '64. Was staying at Bayonne, and walked out to a mountain-gorge traditionally said to have been cut or kicked out by Roland, and there laid out the full plan of his twelve cantos, accurately carried out in the execution.[23]

The fidelity of this report is attested by comparing it with similar accounts of Browning's visit in letters to Tennyson and Mrs. Story in 1864. He tells Tennyson: "I am thinking of Roland's Pass in the Pyrenees, where he hollowed a rock that had hitherto blocked the road, by one kick of his boot."[24] In like manner he writes to Mrs. Story: "I went two days ago to see a famous mountain-pass, *le pas de Roland,* so called because that paladin kicked a hole in a rock, which blocked the way, to allow Charlemagne's army to pass."[25] The passage in the letter to Mrs. Story shows, however, that the visit to *le pas de Roland* was not made from Bayonne in October, as Rossetti recalls it, but from the neighbouring village of Cambo, about August 20.[26]

Browning's recollection that he laid out the full plan of his twelve cantos of *The Ring and the Book* at this gorge is, therefore, in perfect accord with his statement to Miss Blagden regarding the Roman murder story in his Biarritz letter of September 19. Here, writing about a month after his expedition to the mountain gorge immortalized by Roland, he tells her that the whole of his prospective poem is pretty well in his head.[27]

When the poet returned to London, at the close of his trip to the Pyrenees, he was still absorbed in the subject-matter of *The Ring and the Book*. In the postscript of a letter to Frederic Leighton, written on October 17, 1864, he asks the painter to furnish him with certain details regarding the Church of San Lorenzo in Lucina.[28] These, he says, will be of great use to him. This church was the scene of Pompilia's marriage and also of the exposure of the bodies of the Comparini. The information supplied by Lord Leighton was subsequently made use of in Book II of *The Ring and the Book*.

The restoration of the correct date of the Biarritz letter, September 19, 1864, sets the allusion to the Roman murder story, with exactitude, in its proper context. After Browning's hands were freed by the publication of *Dramatis Personae* in June, 1864, he turned with zest to his new poetic venture. Standing beside the historic pass of Roland, in the latter part of August, his imagination received a fillip and "the full plan" of the twelve cantos of *The Ring and the Book* was actually conceived. With his mind still full of the subject he writes to Miss Blagden from Biarritz on September 19:

For me, I have got on by having a great read at Euripides—the one book I brought with me, besides attending to my own matters, my new poem that is about to be; and of which the whole is pretty well in my head,—the Roman murder story you know.[29]

The letter to Frederic Leighton, written on October 17, shows his anxiety to secure information on particular details and his unabated interest in the theme of *The Ring and the Book*.

Were no fresh information available, the correction in the date of the Biarritz letter would widen the gap between the discovery

The Ring and the Book

of the Yellow Book and the first known reference of Browning, in writing, to the story of *The Ring and the Book,* by a space of two years. It would extend from 1860 to 1864 instead of from 1860 to 1862. The alteration in the date of the letter does, of course, transfer this particular mention of the Roman murder story from 1862 to 1864 and, up to the present, it has been regarded as the first literary allusion of its kind. There is, however, an earlier, though hitherto unnoticed, reference to the genesis of *The Ring and the Book* of an interesting and important character. With this I shall deal in the following essay.

ADDENDUM

Additional evidence in confirmation of this article of 1928 appeared in 1933 with the publication of the *Letters of Robert Browning,* collected by Thomas L. Wise and edited by Thurman L. Hood. In the poet's correspondence with Isabella Blagden, printed there, may be found passages bearing out the facts that Browning was at Pornic in the autumn of 1862 and at Biarritz in the autumn of 1864. In particular, my conclusion that, after leaving Cambo on September 13, 1864, Browning spent three weeks at Biarritz, writing there on the 19th the letter to Miss Blagden containing the familiar reference to *The Ring and the Book,* is substantiated by passages in another letter to her from London dated "Oct. 19. '64": "I returned on the 11th—We stayed three weeks at Biarritz;. . . . I hope to have a long poem ready by the summer, my Italian murder thing."[30]

In this collection of letters there also appears a very definite statement of Browning's, in a letter to Isabella Blagden of May 19, 1866, which it seems to me is indisputable evidence that the literary composition of *The Ring and the Book* began in the autumn of 1864. The poet writes:

My poem is nearly done—won't be out for a year or perhaps more. . . . 16,000 lines, or over,—done in less than two years, Isa! —I having done other work besides,—and giving the precious *earlier* hours of the morning to it, moreover, which take the strength out of one.[31]

In the summer of 1928 I read at Baylor University the then unpublished letters of Browning and Robert Lytton, amongst which was a letter of Browning to Lytton written at "Ste. Marie —near Pornic, Loire-Inférieure," and dated "Sept. 27, '62." This letter has since been included in the book, *Letters from Owen Meredith to Robert and Elizabeth Barrett Browning*, 1936.[32] It would in itself be sufficient proof of Browning's residence in Pornic in 1862.

The publication in 1937 of the correspondence between Robert Browning and Julia Wedgwood, further confirmed my findings of 1928 regarding the dates of the poet's visits to various places in southern France in 1864.

In a letter to Julia Wedgwood written from Cambo, begun August 19, 1864, and continued on the two following days, Browning refers specifically to his excursion to "Le pas de Roland," which took place on August 20, as I had conjectured.

20th. I went this morning to see the mountain-pass called "Le pas de Roland"—the tradition being that he opened a way through a rock that effectually blocks it up, by one kick of his boot, and so let Charlemagne's army pass:....[33]

On September 19, 1864, Browning wrote a letter to Julia Wedgwood from Maison Gastonbide, Biarritz.[34] This, without other confirmation, is indisputable proof of the correct date of the Biarritz letter written by the poet to Isabella Blagden, which Mrs. Orr misdated by two years. A reading of these letters, penned on the same day to Julia Wedgwood and Isabella Blagden, reveals sentences almost identical in phrasing as well as content.

5

Browning's First Mention of the Documentary Sources of "The Ring and the Book"

IN THE PRECEDING essay on the genesis of *The Ring and the Book,* originally printed in *MLN,* June, 1928, I have shown that Browning's letter written from Biarritz to Miss Isabella Blagden, containing his allusion to "the Roman murder story," should be dated September 19, 1864, not September 19, 1862. Were no new information at hand, this would place the first known reference in the poet's correspondence to the origins of *The Ring and the Book* two years later than has hitherto been supposed. But, at this point, the letter of September 19, 1862, written by Browning to Isabella Blagden from Ste Marie près Pornic, noted in my previous article, makes an *amende honorable*. It proves, convincingly, that the Biarritz letter to Miss Blagden, with its allusion to the theme of *The Ring and the Book,* cannot have been written on September 19, 1862. Then, having shifted the accepted date of the first known mention, in writing, of the Roman murder story, it obligingly provides us with a new and, up to the present, unnoticed reference to the documents used in the composition of *The Ring and the Book.* "The wheel is come full circle" and, curiously enough in view of what has transpired, the first literary allusion of Browning to the sources of the poem is contained, as has always been supposed, in a letter addressed to Isabella Blagden on September 19, 1862.[1] Only, this initial mention of the narrative on which the poem was based, occurs in the 1862 letter written at Ste Marie, Brittany, not in the 1864 letter written at Biarritz in the Basses-Pyrénées.

Browning's reference to the source of *The Ring and the Book,* in his Ste Marie letter to Miss Blagden of "Sept. 19. '62," is as follows:

> If you see Mrs. Baker, tell her that I was quite unable to call on her during the day or two she was at Bayswater, & that I am sorry for it. Another thing, she promised to lend me a MS. account of the trial of Count Francesco Guidi for the murder of his wife, which I am anxious to collate with my own collection of papers on the subject: she told me she had lent it to Trollope, along with other documents which she thought might interest him, and that he had found nothing in this subject to his purpose. Can you ask him if there was no mistake in her statement, if the account really related to *my* Count Francesco Guidi of Arezzo? Because, in that case, with her leave (which I shall beg your kindness to ask) I should greatly like to see it, would find some friend to bring me the papers and would return them safely and expeditiously.[2]

On his return to London, Browning found the desired manuscript awaiting him. On "Oct. 18, '62," he writes to Miss Blagden from Warwick Crescent:

> Thank you most truly for attending to my request so promptly, in the matter of the Account of the Murder &c. which I found on my return. Pray thank Mrs. Baker for her kindness, & say it will be particularly useful to me: it would be of little use to anybody without my documents, nor is it correct in several respects, but it contains a few notices of the execution &c. subsequent to my account that I can turn to good: I am going to make a regular poem of it.[3]

The query naturally arises: what was this manuscript account of the trial and execution of Count Francesco Guido which Mrs. Baker sent to the poet in 1862? In addition to the Yellow Book, Browning is known to have used what Professor C. W. Hodell has called the Secondary Source in the composition of *The Ring and the Book.* This was an Italian pamphlet, in manuscript, giving

The Ring and the Book

a contemporary version of the murder story, and supplementing the narrative of the Yellow Book with many important details.

A third document dealing with this famous trial was found in a library at Rome and has been printed by Professor Griffin in an English translation. But, as this manuscript was not discovered till after the poet's death, it is not one of his sources. The question, therefore, is, whether the document sent by Mrs. Baker to Browning is the Secondary Source, or a third source used by him, though unknown to us today.

The date of the discovery of the Secondary Source has been a matter of debate and uncertainty. As information derived solely from it is used freely in the first two cantos of *The Ring and the Book,* internal evidence shows that it was in Browning's hands before he began the composition of the poem. Mrs. Orr, who has translated certain passages from the manuscript in her *Handbook* to the poet's works, writes concerning it: "This pamphlet has supplied Mr. Browning with some of his most curious facts. It fell into his hands in London."[4] Professor Hodell refers more definitely to the discovery of the document: "It was found in London by one of Browning's acquaintances, who, knowing the poet's interest in the subject, sent it to him."[5] Professor W. Hall Griffin cites the following reminiscence, which may have a bearing on the date of the Secondary Source: "Mr. Cartwright, who spent a night or two at Warwick Crescent, about 1864 or '5, remembers that Browning then told him that he was engaged upon a poem based on the Franceschini affair, as to which, he added, he had procured further information: this would be that contained in a reprint of a contemporary manuscript pamphlet, sent him by a friend, containing an account of the murder and of Guido's trial and execution."[6]

Mr. Arthur K. Cook, in *A Commentary upon Browning's The Ring and the Book,* has suggested a possible connection between the poet's letter to Frederic Leighton asking him for particulars about the Church of San Lorenzo in Lucina, and the discovery of the Secondary Source.[7] As has been noted, the Secondary

Source contains the account of the marriage of Pompilia and of the exposure of the bodies of the Comparini within the walls of this church. Mr. Cook, therefore, conjectures that Browning's request to Leighton on October 17, 1864, was inspired by the finding of this important document. He also thinks that the discovery may account, in part, for the heightening of his interest in the subject-matter of *The Ring and the Book* at this particular time. There is, however, no positive evidence to prove that the Secondary Source was sent to Browning in the year 1864. Mr. Cartwright's reminiscence of 1864 or 1865 does not state how long before that the poet "procured further information" concerning "the Franceschini affair." Mr. Cook's connection of the finding of the Secondary Source with the letter to Lord Leighton is in the nature of a surmise. On the other hand, Professor Hodell's statement that the manuscript was sent to Browning by an acquaintance of his who had found it in London, does not quite fit in with the theory that the document obtained by him from Mrs. Baker in 1862 was the Secondary Source.

The manuscript owned by Mrs. Baker was sent to Browning from Florence, and reached him on his return to London in October, 1862. Previous to this, the poet states, "she had lent it to Trollope, along with other documents which she thought might interest him." This was, presumably, not Anthony Trollope, the novelist, but his brother Thomas Adolphus Trollope, the author of a *History of Florence* and other works on Italian life of a biographical and historical character. He was a close friend both of Browning and of Isabella Blagden and made his home in Florence, having built a villa in the Piazza Independenza. It is, of course, possible that Mrs. Baker may have found the manuscript in London. But since she sent it to Browning from Florence, after it had been examined by Trollope, there is a strong presumption that it was discovered in Italy, as the nature of the document would lead us to expect. Such an assumption does not, however, disprove the identity of Mrs. Baker's manuscript with the Secondary Source. Professor Griffin and Sir

The Ring and the Book

Frederic Kenyon merely say that the Secondary Source was sent to the poet by a friend. Mrs. Orr's expression, "it fell into his hands in London," might readily have had its source in the dispatch of Mrs. Baker's document from Florence to Browning at Warwick Crescent, London. The detail added by Professor Hodell that "it was found in London," may easily be a slip.

The most important evidence, in this connection, lies in Browning's reference to the title and contents of Mrs. Baker's manuscript. When begging the loan of the document he calls it "a MS. account of the trial of Count Francesco Guidi for the murder of his wife." In acknowledging its receipt he refers to it as "the Account of the Murder &c." and tells Miss Blagden:

> . . . it will be particularly useful to me: it would be of little use to anybody without my documents, nor is it correct in several respects, but it contains a few notices of the execution &c. subsequent to my account that I can turn to good: I am going to make a regular poem of it.[8]

Browning's words, "it will be particularly useful to me," and his statement that, in conjunction with his other documents, he intends "to make a regular poem of it" are worthy of note. This establishes the fact that the account of the murder which he received from Mrs. Baker was used in the composition of *The Ring and the Book*. Since the Secondary Source is the only report of the trial and execution of Guido, in addition to the Yellow Book, that the poet is known to have used, it would seem a reasonable conjecture to identify this with Mrs. Baker's manuscript.

The most direct and telling evidence, however, is comprised in the comment of Browning: ". . . it contains a few notices of the execution &c. subsequent to my account that I can turn to good." This is in exact accord with the supplementary matter that the poet obtained from the Secondary Source, in writing *The Ring and the Book*. In his English translation of the Secondary Source, Professor Hodell has printed in italics the new material that Browning derived from it.[9] The entire account of the execution at the end of the Secondary Source, containing about 350 words, is italicized. A comparison between this passage and the description of the execution of Guido and his compatriots in *The Ring and the Book* (XII. 118-207), shows that the poet is following the Secondary Source almost verbatim. Browning's singling out of the notices of the execution in Mrs. Baker's manuscript as material that he "can turn to good" is, consequently, a strong argument in favour of the identification of this document with the Secondary Source.

6

Browning's Roman Murder Story as Recorded in a Hitherto Unknown Italian Contemporary Manuscript

THE DISCOVERY of additional accounts of the Roman murder story on which *The Ring and the Book* is based cannot fail to be of interest to readers and students of Browning's poetry. Previous to 1939 only three accounts were known. These are: the Old Yellow Book, found by Browning at Florence in 1860; the so-called Secondary Source, sent to the poet from Florence in 1862 by Mrs. Baker; and a pamphlet discovered in the Royal Casanatense Library at Rome in 1900. The Old Yellow Book, Browning's main source, is an extensive collection of documents, the bulk of which are in print, constituting a lawyer's file of the Franceschini case. They centre about the trial of Guido, the arguments of the opposing lawyers, and the evidence of witnesses. The Secondary Source and the Casanatense manuscripts are short, popular recitals of the criminal career, trial, and execution of Guido. From the Secondary Source Browning derived important material, but whether he used or even saw the Casanatense pamphlet is a debatable question.

The first addition to the previously known versions of the Roman murder story is the manuscript which is the subject of this essay. An English translation of it, made by my colleague Professor E. H. Yarrill, was printed in the *Baylor Bulletin*, December, 1939. In the course of editing and translating the volume in which it was contained, the existence of other hitherto unknown accounts was ascertained by Dr. Beatrice Corrigan of the Italian Department of the University of Toronto. Microfilms of some five of these, together with additional collateral documents bearing on this notorious criminal case, have been obtained from the Italian libraries that house the originals. Miss Corrigan has almost completed the translation of this fresh material. When the results of her findings have been edited and published, the number of known documents dealing with the tale on which *The Ring and the Book* is based will be more than doubled, and a considerable amount of historical information, unknown to Browning, of the course of events leading up to the murder of the Comparini will be revealed.

The Baylor University manuscript with which I shall now deal, since it is the first of these finds to be translated, is the last of three Italian pamphlets bound in a vellum-covered book containing 191 pages of $7\frac{1}{2}$ by $5\frac{1}{4}$ inches. The volume as a whole is a representative specimen of collections of narratives based on the villainies and wretched deaths of notorious rogues. These "penny dreadfuls" of a bygone age seem to have been common in Italy around the year 1700. Each pamphlet has as its theme the history of an individual criminal. The reader who scans in order of sequence the picaresque documents of this book has a thrill in store. The first and second narratives are of general interest to a student of the bypaths of Italian history, but the third has particular and intimate association with a *magnum opus* of Victorian literature. It is a hitherto unknown contemporary account, in 63 pages of Italian script, of the Roman murder tale that is the theme of Browning's *The Ring and the Book*.

The wanderings and vicissitudes of manuscripts have an element of romance; and it may not be irrelevant to speak briefly of the discovery of this volume before reviewing its contents. A note in the fly-leaf states that the book was found in Rome in 1913 by W. H. Woodward. Shortly after being entrusted with the editing of the volume, I was able to identify Mr. Woodward as a Professor Emeritus of the University of Liverpool and an

The Ring and the Book

Italian scholar of repute. Correspondence followed, and Professor Woodward informed me that he found the Roman murder story manuscript "in a bookseller's shop in the Piazza San Claudio at Rome many years ago." He added: "I was not certain of its value when I found it on the shelf, but its connection with Browning's poem was obvious. I meant to translate it and define its relation to the other Sources, but my work lay in quite other directions and I came to Canada (Quebec City) for three or four years. . . . I spent the winter months in Rome (and Italy) for fifteen years, and Rome is in truth my second home."

Some time after Mr. Woodward purchased this collection of Italian manuscripts in 1913, he parted with the book, and nothing is known of its whereabouts for twenty-three years. Fortunately, in 1936, Professor A. J. Armstrong of Baylor University, Texas—to whose indefatigable zeal as a collector of Browning material, students of the poet are deeply indebted—bought this volume from Barnet J. Beyer, Incorporated, of New York, dealers in rare and antiquarian books. Dr. Armstrong was, however, under the misapprehension that the version of the Roman murder tale in the volume was the Secondary Source of *The Ring and the Book*. The text of this is known to scholars, though the original manuscript has been lost. The book was therefore simply housed amongst the other Browning rarities at Baylor University. A chance inquiry of mine in 1939 regarding the Secondary Source led to Dr. Armstrong's lending me this collection of pamphlets for examination. When the nature of the Guido manuscript was ascertained as an independent and unknown account of the Franceschini murder case, Dr. Armstrong kindly entrusted me with its editorship. In this way, seventy-nine years after the discovery of the Old Yellow Book and half a century after the death of Browning, the fourth of the documents dealing with the narrative revivified in *The Ring and the Book* has been saved from oblivion.

The Baylor manuscript is a general account of the Roman murder story similar in character to the Secondary Source and the Casanatense pamphlet, but longer and fuller in detail than either of these. That it is a contemporary account of the crime and punishment of Guido Franceschini is attested in various ways. It was penned when the events described were of recent and popular interest. It has many touches of what might be called "local colour." Here, for instance, is one which has reference to the gruesome sight of the mutilated bodies of Pietro and Violante exposed in "the cemetery room" of the parish of San Lorenzo in Lucina:

Curiosity urged many to go there to see; there going also a relative of mine who told me that he had not seen a like spectacle in his lifetime, seeing two old people, one over seventy years old, who was Comparini, and the other of about sixty-five years of age, so barbarously murdered; for not only had they butchered them so that their heads scarcely remained attached to their trunks, but both of them were riddled with wounds, and mostly so the woman who had very many of them in her face; yet its effigy was recognizable.

There is no clue to the identity of the author of the Baylor manuscript, but he was either a lawyer or a man well versed in legal procedure. He introduces technical legal terms and, unlike the author of the Secondary Source, frequently alludes to the lawyers' documents now embraced in the Old Yellow Book. Whoever he may have been, he was endowed with dramatic feeling, for his narrative abounds in picturesque touches and stresses the sensational incidents of the murder story. He occasionally pauses in his recital of events to appeal to sentiment or to indulge in a vein of moralistic reflection. He pities Pompilia and invokes the reader's compassion as he dwells on the wretched situation of the hapless girl.

Before dealing with the independent material of this manuscript and its contribution to our knowledge of the Roman murder case, reference should be made to the relationship between it and the other accounts. Comparisons with the two manuscripts of like general scope reveal that it is much more akin to the Secondary Source than to the Casanatense pamphlet. The sequence of events is parallel to that followed in the Secondary Source and the wording is often strikingly similar. In this connection, the Italian text of the manuscript under review has been carefully compared with the Italian transcription of the Secondary Source printed in the *Miscellanies of the Philobiblon Society,* Volume XII, 1868-69. The correspondences suggest two possibilities. Either the writer of the present manuscript was acquainted with the text of the Secondary Source and enlarged upon it, supplying certain details from the documents now collected in the Old Yellow Book and others from his personal knowledge, or the Secondary Source is a condensed version of this manuscript. Yet even in the parallel material there are noteworthy divergences which seem to point to the relative independence of the two narratives. If there is an actual connection, I would hazard the conjecture that the shorter and more concise account of the Secondary Source is the earlier, but the question is a debatable one. Mr. Woodward, the original owner of the recently discovered manuscript, claimed that it was written before the Secondary Source and the Casanatense document. Certainly its freshness of impression, its circumstantial character, its echoing of emotions and excitement stirred up by the bizarre and lurid happenings of the Roman murder case, are evidence that it was composed shortly after the execution of Guido.

The relation between the Baylor University manuscript and the pamphlets of the Old Yellow Book is perfectly clear. Its author makes frequent reference to the legal documents linked with the trial of Guido, to the attestations of various witnesses, and is evidently familiar with the whole corpus of information now gathered in the Old Yellow Book. Where the pamphlets of the Old Yellow Book differ from the Secondary Source it is interesting to note that he follows the former. For example, he represents Violante as being locked out of the Franceschini home along with Pietro; not Pompilia, as in the Secondary Source. A large portion of the material of his manuscript not found in the Secondary Source is in accord with the documents of the Old Yellow Book.

Yet when all elements that may be paralleled in other accounts are set aside, there remains a not inconsiderable residuum of material peculiar to this manuscript, and much of it of arresting and dramatic quality. The bulk of such original matter is in the latter part of the narrative, dealing with incidents that fall outside the compass of the Old Yellow Book. In the earlier part, with the exception of digressions in which the writer of this version of the murder tale gives rein to a vein of sentiment or moralistic comment, the additions are of minor import. But beginning with the account of the massacre of the Comparini family, they become more significant. The outline of events is similar to that of the Secondary Source, but vivid strokes of description are added. Violante runs to the doorway of a neighbour and is there barbarously killed. Pompilia, when attacked, invokes the Blessed Virgin Mary, as in the Secondary Source; but also "promised to carry her vow to her miraculous image located at the Fornaci, supplicating her to give her grace to survive so long that she might receive the most sacred sacraments." A neighbour cries out and raises an alarm. One of the guards at the door, becoming frightened, flees from the Comparini home, but subsequently returns and rejoins his fellows. In the Secondary Source one of the assassins leaves his cloak behind. This manuscript gives fuller particulars. "There remained because of the haste the cloak of Franceschini and also the cap, which was recognized by the half dead Pompilia; also one of the said men had taken from Comparini his spectacle case, and it too, when he was imprisoned, was sent to the same woman to be recognized."

While this author's account of the death of Pompilia is along the lines of the testimony of Fra Celestino Angelo in the Old Yellow Book, his references to the inflammation of Pompilia's wounds and the efforts of surgeons to save her life by blood letting are original. A paragraph of description is devoted to the funeral obsequies of Pompilia in her parish church of San Lorenzo in Lucina. No mention of this is made in any other document. The representation of the carrying of the body of Pompilia into the Church of San Lorenzo, where it was "laid on a rich covering of gilded embroidery on the ground with many candles"; the reference to the celebration of requiem masses "to which

The Ring and the Book

there came so many people both noble and not noble that they could not be contained in the church"; the emphasis on the costliness and pomp of the funeral, arranged by the heirs of Pompilia "without regard for any expense," are examples of the individual and pictorial touches through which the writer of this most recently found record of the Roman murder story enhances his report of the pivotal events of the tragedy.

It is, however, in the climactic scene of the execution of Guido and his fellow criminals that the Baylor manuscript decidedly surpasses any previously known pamphlet in fullness of detail and tragic poignancy. Elaborate accounts are given of the remorse and confessions of the murderers. The Casanatense document refers briefly to the halt of the cart containing the criminals at the Church of the Agonizing, but the picture of Domenico Gambasini receiving there the benediction of the most saintly Solita, where "he performed so many acts of compunction that many of the beholders burst into tears," is one of the frequent arresting incidents peculiar to the Baylor University manuscript. From it too we learn that the scaffold on which Guido was beheaded was near the Consorteria built for greater convenience in a corridor of a garden of the Reverend Fathers of the Madonna of the People. The narrator dilates on the throngs of people who attended the executions; and, with his characteristic eye for detail, tells us that while the criminals were being put to death "a stand fell because of excessive weight, so that if it had not been quickly held up the death of several persons would have resulted. One person also nearly fell from a roof, and was miraculously drawn back." The windows and balconies were so crowded with princes, ladies, and *cavalieri* that "one could not throw there, so to speak, a bag of grain." Guido mounts the scaffold blindfolded, with the manacles placed on him by the executioner. The account of the final act of the tragedy in the Baylor University manuscript is grim and sanguinary, but dramatic. "The signal was given to the executioner; the cord controlling the *mannaia* was cut and the head was severed, which, if the executioner had not been ready to take it, would have fallen from the scaffold; but he took it up and cried several times in a loud voice: 'This is the head of Guido Franceschini!' "

One of the most imaginative episodes of the aftermath of the executions, recorded exclusively in this pamphlet, is the carrying of the bodies of the murderers by the Venerable Confraternity of Mercy to the shrine of "St. John the Beheaded of the Florentine nation." We may surmise how Browning, who wrote in *Fra Lippo Lippi* of "Saint John, because he saves the Florentines," would have seized upon an account of the conveyance of the beheaded Guido to the shrine of a beheaded saint as material for *The Ring and the Book,* had he ever set eyes upon this manuscript.

Attention may now be drawn to a number of interesting details, some of which evidence the first-hand knowledge of the writer of the narrative I am reviewing. He is, as a rule, definite and accurate in his dates and in the names of places. A signal instance of this occurs in connection with Guido. The only mention of the age of Guido at the time of his execution in previously known records of the Roman murder story is in the Secondary Source. He is there represented as a man of fifty. Browning follows the Secondary Source in this respect in *The Ring and the Book*. However, an entry in the baptismal register of the Pieve Church reveals that Guido was baptized on January 14, 1657, and consequently was forty when he died upon the scaffold. The Baylor University manuscript gives his age as forty, which is correct. In the Secondary Source, Pietro and Violante Comparini are referred to at the time of their assassination as "two old septuagenarians." The Baylor University manuscript states that Pietro was over seventy years old and Violante about sixty-five years of age. The register of deaths in the Church of San Lorenzo shows that Pietro was sixty-nine and Violante sixty-six. The Secondary Source describes Alessandro Baldeschi, one of the criminals, as a man of twenty-two. The Baylor University manuscript alludes to him as "one who is believed to have stained his hands in human blood many times: he might have

The Ring and the Book

been sixty." Since the Casanatense pamphlet refers to Alessandro as a daring and wicked cut-throat, and since no attempt was made to save him from the gallows on the ground of his youth, a plea urged on behalf of another criminal, it is probable that the more advanced age is true to fact.

The Secondary Source states that Pompilia was married during December, 1693, in San Lorenzo in Lucina. The Baylor University manuscript declares that the marriage was performed secretly late in the month of November, 1693, in the Church of Sts. Simon and Jude. Neither date is correct, for the marriage register of the Church of San Lorenzo proves that Pompilia was married on September 6, 1693. The author of the Baylor University manuscript is plainly in error in writing of the ceremony as being performed in the Church of Sts. Simon and Jude. His mistake is inexplicable, yet it shows the independence of his narrative.

There has been some confusion regarding the location of the house of the Comparini where the family was murdered. Misled by his misinterpretation of an allusion in the Old Yellow Book, Browning thought that Pietro and Violante had two homes, one in the Via Vittoria, and another in a suburban villa on the outskirts of Rome. He places the scene of the assassinations at the villa, and refers to it as a solitary place, "smothered up in vines." The source of Browning's error has been pointed out by Sir Frederick Treves, but the Baylor manuscript supplies a positive identification of the house in question. In it, Guido is represented as stationing two spies to watch the home of the Comparini, one in the direction of the Popolo and the other in the direction of the Piazza di Spagna. This reference proves that the house in the Via Vittoria, near the heart of Rome, was the scene of the murders.

The time of important happenings is often marked with precision. We are informed that the slaying of the Comparini family took place on Thursday, January 2, at about seven in the evening. This, however, is also noted in the Secondary Source.

But the Baylor University manuscript alone tells us that the executions of Guido and his followers began at half-past three in the afternoon and ended at half-past five.

There are one or two interesting variants in names in this pamphlet. The Secondary Source alludes to Guido stopping at Ponte Milvio on his way to Rome. In the Baylor University manuscript we read of Guido "hiding in the vineyard of the Abate his brother, situated on the mountain before reaching Ponte Mollo" (Molle). The Ponte Milvio bridge is commonly called the Ponte Molle, so that the writer of the Baylor University manuscript uses the more popular form. As a minor detail we learn from this account that the Christian name of Captain Patrizi, the chief constable who arrested Guido, was Andrea. It should be noted that in the Italian text of this document there are various spellings of the names of principal personages. These have been reproduced literally in the English translation without any attempt to reduce them to uniformity.

Such are some of the general and particular features of this lately discovered manuscript. It deserves a place beside the previously known accounts of the Roman murder story. Longer and more circumstantial than either the Secondary Source or the Casanatense pamphlet, it can well bear comparison with them in human and dramatic interest.

7

Browning's Dark Mood: A Study of "Fifine at the Fair"

Vous plaît-il, don Juan, nous éclaircir ces beaux mystères?
IN VIEW OF the contemporary reception of *Fifine at the Fair*, this opening line of the passage from Molière's *Don Juan*, used by Browning as a motto for one of the most subtle and esoteric of his monologues, has an almost ironical ring. The reaction of the majority of the poet's readers to the casuistry of a work approaching *Sordello* in intellectual complexity and containing a moral enigma was not unlike that of the puzzled Donna Elvire as she questions her wayward husband:

> Don Juan, might you please to help one give a
>   guess,
> Hold up a candle, clear this fine mysteriousness?

"That piece of perplexing cynicism," Mrs. Orr wrote of *Fifine*, and her apologetic comment on the poem[1] reflects the embarrassment of many admirers of Browning who were at a loss to explain what seemed to them an inconsistency between his ethics and his handling of the moral delinquencies of Don Juan.

In a measure, Browning anticipated the controversy that followed the printing of *Fifine*. In April, 1872, he told Alfred Domett that he was very doubtful as to its reception by the public.[2] The critical reviews of the later years of the nineteenth century show that these misgivings were not without foundation. A typical example of their tone may be cited from Mr. Mortimer's "Note on Browning" in the *Scottish Art Review* for December, 1889, in which the writer assumes that the casuistry of Don Juan voices the poet's own sentiment. As summarized by Mrs. Orr,[3] Mr. Mortimer's argument runs that *Fifine at the Fair* should be linked with *The Statue and the Bust,* both poems showing that Browning "prescribes action at any price, even that of defying the restrictions of moral law." The poet, consequently, "in the person of his *Don Juan,* defends a husband's claim to relieve the fixity of conjugal affection by varied adventure in the world of temporary loves." Though this critic concludes by placing Browning in the exalted company of Goethe, Shelley, and Byron, above the moral convention under which we habitually view life, such an interpretation might well bemuse those orthodox readers who constituted the rank and file of the Browning Society.

Nor was this bewilderment lessened by the apparition of strange champions that *Fifine* enlisted. Swinburne, who, after the publication of his pagan and hedonistic *Poems and Ballads* of 1866, was regarded by a large section of the British public as a veritable reincarnation of Don Juan, said of *Fifine*: "This is far better than anything Browning has yet written. Here is his true province."[4] It was, apparently, his appreciation of *Fifine* that led Swinburne, in his introduction to the poems of Chapman, printed in 1875, to comment so enthusiastically on Browning's verse—a tribute which we are told perplexed the older poet as much as it gratified him.[5] The praise of such an advocate would undoubtedly embarrass Browning, by adding to the misapprehension of a poem so delicately poised on the tight-rope of moral casuistry. He must have realized that Swinburne's panegyric, hailing the author of *Fifine* as a fellow spirit, would cause many an old friend to murmur, "Que diable allait-il faire dans cette galère?" The flutter of the dove-cotes continued for a number of years and at times ruffled the meetings of the Browning Society. Dr. Furnivall, however, in his pontifical capacity as President, was able to repreen the feathers by stating on the poet's authority that his idea in *Fifine* "was to show merely how a Don Juan might justify himself, partly by truth, somewhat by sophistry."[6]

The background of *Fifine at the Fair* may, I believe, be instructively studied from two standpoints, though the division

Fifine at the Fair　　　　　　　　　　　　　　　　　107

is somewhat arbitrary: first, the historical setting of the poem, so far as this has a basis in Browning's experience and can be regarded as the reflection of a personal mood induced by outward circumstance or event; second, the character of the poem as a casuistical monologue.

Is it, however, necessary, in view of Browning's dramatic bent, to assume that *Fifine* has a discernible connection with the actual happenings of his life or a mood induced by them? There have not been wanting competent reviewers of this poem who deny any such relationship. Thus, Sir F. G. Kenyon writes of *Fifine*: "No one, of course, should (and probably very few ever did) suppose that it contained any autobiographical element, or in any way represented Browning's personal opinions. It is as purely dramatic as anything he ever wrote."[7]

More recently, Mr. Osbert Burdett, in his able book on the Brownings,[8] has challenged Mrs. Orr's conclusion that "some leaven of bitterness" must have been working within the poet when he wrote *Fifine*. He does admit the possibility that, as Mrs. Orr suggests, Browning's active participation in social life—the "friendly greeting" of the present—may have appeared to his imagination as a kind of disloyalty to his old allegiance. Nevertheless, Mr. Burdett refuses to believe that there was any real wavering in the poet's devotion to the memory of his wife which might have evoked a dark mood reflected in the writing of *Fifine*. Hence he characterizes Mrs. Orr's oracular, half-veiled hints regarding "some leaven of bitterness" responsible for "that piece of perplexing cynicism," as "foolish remarks" which have given rise to baseless conjecture and unfortunate misunderstanding. In particular, he criticizes her tentative surmise that we may read into Browning's letters of 1870 "that eerie, haunting sadness of a cherished memory from which, in spite of ourselves, life is bearing us away." On the whole, Mr. Burdett is inclined to dismiss the inquiry into personal circumstances connected with the composition of *Fifine* as irrelevant. The poem, he thinks, can be accounted for, on purely objective grounds, as an illustration of Browning's love of case-making, of his increasing disposition to use the casuistical monologue as a medium for gratifying his imaginative curiosity. In common with *Prince Hohenstiel-Schwangau, Red Cotton Night-Cap Country,* and *Aristophanes' Apology, Fifine at the Fair* represents "an exploration of psychology." Therefore, Mr. Burdett concludes, to probe beneath this for subjective motives which link themselves with the poet's personal experience is to inquire too curiously.

But a right understanding of Browning's poetic method and a knowledge of the facts connected with the composition of his major works, both refute the idea that his poems have no important foothold in the events of his life or the mood induced by these. Professor Santayana has spoken of the arrest of Browning's dramatic art at soliloquy, and has gone to the length of maintaining that his art is all self-expression or satire. "Even in the poems where the effort at impersonality is most successful, the dramatic disguise is usually thrown off in a preface, epilogue or parenthesis."[9] Such criticism, however, overshoots the mark and fails to appreciate the distinctive nature of the poet's dramatic portraiture, with its stress on the psychology of character. Dealing, as he does, with "the incidents in the development of a soul" disclosed in motive and aspiration rather than with personality revealed in outward action, Browning, as he puts it in his essay on Shelley, "digs where he stands," seeking "the primal elements of humanity" in his own soul as a reflex of the absolute mind. In reality, Browning's analysis of Shelley's genius applies in many ways to himself. He, in as true a sense as Shelley, is "the subjective poet of modern classification" who bodies forth his characters not through external event, but through the imaginative realization of the potentialities of their motives sublimated in the alembic of his own spirit.[10] As a matter of fact, the very inwardness of the drama that he presents involves a personal interpretation, and a closer nexus between subjective and objective elements than exists in the more explicitly embodied art of the theatre.

Yet, in his later poems, it is evident that Browning fails to preserve the semi-independence of characterization that he achieves in the golden period of his poetry between 1840 and 1870. More and more after 1870, his tendency is to make his characters mouthpieces of his intellectual and emotional convictions—his philosophy of life—till, at last, in *Parleyings with Certain People of Importance,* the disguise is practically cast aside. In *Fifine,* as in almost all of Browning's later verse, there is a direct and immediate connection between the subjective elements of the poet's individuality and his writings. If, in the Shakespearean sense, the characters of his earlier poetry are but half dramatized, of the personages of *Fifine* it may be said: "The best in this kind are but shadows, and the worst are no worse, if imagination amend them."

Is there, however, a truly subjective factor that must be taken into the reckoning as a primary motive in the composition of *Fifine at the Fair?* Do the troubled waters of the poem reflect a dark mood of Browning's spirit, which has its origin in an intimate personal experience linked with his private life, or is its casuistry and sophistical dallying with hedonism sufficiently accounted for by a fillip given to his dramatic imagination through the agency of an external impulse or interest of an objective and social character?

In support of the latter supposition, it may be urged that a number of Browning's poems have a close relation to contemporary movements and controversial issues, artistic, religious, and political. Moreover, the interest which colours each one of the poems in question is not of an abstract nature, but definitely focused in a person, writing, or sequence of event. *Christmas-Eve* takes its point of departure from Strauss's *Das Leben Jesu; Bishop Blougram's Apology* from the career of Cardinal Wiseman; *Cleon* from Matthew Arnold's *Empedocles; A Death in the Desert* from Renan's *La Vie de Jésus; Mr. Sludge, "the Medium,"* from the trickery of the spiritualistic faker Home; *Prince Hohenstiel-Schwangau* from the opportunism of Napoleon III; "Bernard de Mandeville" from the philosophical views of Carlyle; "George Bubb Dodington" from the political chicanery of Disraeli. The inception of such poems in contemporary incident and Browning's flair for case-making suggest the plausibility of the genesis of *Fifine at the Fair* in an issue of controversial character which was a matter of public concern at the time of its composition, between December, 1871 and April, 1872.

This point of view has been adopted by one of the foremost Browning scholars of America, Professor William Clyde DeVane, who, in an article entitled, "The Harlot and the Thoughtful Young Man,"[11] has made a study of the relation which, he feels, exists between Rossetti's *Jenny* and Browning's *Fifine at the Fair*.

In support of his argument, Mr. DeVane stresses the fact that *Fifine* was written at the height of the famous Pre-Raphaelite controversy which followed the publication of Rossetti's *Poems* of 1870. The storm of hostility that had been brewing since Swinburne in his *Poems and Ballads* of 1866 shocked the Puritan conscience of England, broke in fury over Rossetti's head, when Robert Buchanan launched his savage bolt, "The Fleshly School of Poetry," in the *Contemporary Review* for October, 1871. As Mr. DeVane has shown, there were many reasons why Browning could not fail to be keenly interested in this literary quarrel. From a purely personal point of view, his sympathies must have been divided. Both Buchanan and Rossetti were friends of Browning, and the latter an avowed disciple. In attacking *Jenny,* Buchanan was criticizing a poem containing reminiscences of Browning's own work, in style, character portrayal, and manner of handling a dramatic situation. Yet, from the standpoint of poetic and spiritual conviction, it is clear that Browning regarded with suspicion and growing dislike the artistic cult of Pre-Raphaelitism —burning incense before strange altars—of which Rossetti was the acknowledged leader. Its over-sensuousness, its epicurean outlook on life, its tendency to divorce art from morality, ran counter to the central Victorian tradition. Though Browning might deprecate the virulence of Buchanan's article, his private comments show that he was at heart in sympathy with the cause that the critic espoused.

With this attitude in mind, Professor DeVane undertakes to show that *Fifine at the Fair* was prompted by Rossetti's *Jenny* and is a veiled criticism of the latter poem. Since *Jenny* was the most important of the four poems pilloried by Buchanan's scathing denunciation, Browning's interest would naturally gravitate to it, particularly as it contained echoes of his own manner. In this connection, Mr. DeVane draws attention to the striking similarity in theme of *Jenny* and *Fifine*. Both are dramatic monologues centring on the relation between a man of reflective and philosophical bent and a woman of loose character. Yet there is a significant difference of outlook. Rossetti, despite the noble justification of the spirit of *Jenny* in his dignified reply to Buchanan's vilification, lays himself open to the charge of confusing the standards of right and wrong by depicting a hero who, in Ruskin's phrase, "reasons and feels entirely like a wise and just man" while engaged in immoral practices. Browning, on the contrary, guards his poem against any such misapprehension. Through an ingenious *dénouement,* the viciousness of Don Juan is exposed and his previous self-justification branded as sophistry—the devil quoting Scripture for his purpose. Therefore (to follow the course of Mr. DeVane's argument) Browning, through a clever stroke of irony, is indirectly hitting at *Jenny* by revealing the moral duplicity underlying a vein of reflection which Rossetti had represented as proceeding from an honest rather than a casuistical mind. In the light of this analysis, Rossetti's conviction that certain passages of *Fifine* were an attack upon himself was not entirely the delusion of a morbid and overwrought brain. Browning, of course, had no thought of impugning Rossetti's moral character or of raising a personal issue with his old friend and brother poet. Yet, since he wrote his poem with *Jenny* in mind, criticizing its interpretation of life and human nature, the passionate indignation which led the already half-maddened Rossetti, after the reading of *Fifine,* to break off a friendship of twenty-five years' standing with Browning, can be understood if not justified.

The assumption that Browning in writing *Fifine at the Fair* was influenced to some extent by the stir of Pre-Raphaelite controversy in 1871 seems to me a reasonable hypothesis. As Mr. DeVane has elsewhere pointed out,[12] sixteen years later in

Parleyings with Certain People of Importance, the poet wrote with unmistakable reference to the leaders of the Aesthetic Movement, contrasting their theory of art for art's sake with his own belief in the ultimate moral import of beauty. Can it, however, be shown that the primary source of the inspiration of *Fifine* was Rossetti's *Jenny,* or was this merely an incidental factor in connection with the composition of the poem? Poetry, as Tennyson defined it, "is like shot silk with many glancing colours," and, in dealing with such a catholic mind as Browning's, we may recognize the presence of a weft in his artistic creation without regarding it as the dominating pattern of the web. Before subscribing to Mr. DeVane's view in its entirety, the question must be faced as to whether there is not a more poignant and subjective influence at work in *Fifine* than Rossetti's *Jenny*; whether, from the standpoint of its relation to Browning's life, the genesis of *Fifine* is to be sought in the Pre-Raphaelite controversy—an interest largely social and objective—or in the depths of the poet's own personal experience.

Though the verdict of contemporary criticism on a question of this nature cannot be regarded as final, it has the advantage of being in closer touch with the pulse of the time than the judgment of posterity. It is, therefore, not without significance that the weight of such opinion is in agreement with Mrs. Orr when she ascribes the dark mood of *Fifine* to "some leaven of bitterness" working within Browning's own spirit. Commenting on the poet's state of mind when he composed *Fifine,* Edward Dowden writes:

The internal suggestion, as Mrs Orr hints, lay in a certain mood of resentment against himself arising from the fact that the encroachments of the world seemed to estrange in some degree a part of his complex being from entire fidelity to his own past. The world, in fact, seemed to be playing with Browning the part of a Fifine.[13]

Dowden is here referring to the following paragraph cited from Mrs. Orr's review of *Fifine at the Fair.*

Fifine at the Fair

The sweet and the bitter lay, indeed, very close to each other at the sources of Mr. Browning's inspiration. Both proceeded, in great measure, from his spiritual allegiance to the past—that past by which it was impossible that he should linger, but which he could not yet leave behind. The present came to him with friendly greeting. He was unconsciously, perhaps inevitably, unjust to what it brought. The injustice reacted upon himself, and developed by degrees into the cynical mood of fancy which became manifest in *Fifine at the Fair*.[14]

Are we justified in regarding Mrs. Orr's opinion, re-echoed by Dowden, as more than an ingenious conjecture? *Fifine,* as it stands, deals with a situation which has no correspondence with the real incidents of Browning's life. It is, as Chesterton sums it up, "the soliloquy of an epicurean who seeks half-playfully to justify upon moral grounds an infidelity into which he afterwards actually falls."[15] To identify Don Juan with Browning, in any literal sense, would be a palpable absurdity. The question, however, is not one of a correspondence in situation, but of the reflection in *Fifine* of a mood which has its inception in the poet's personal history.

Amidst a maze of intermingled truth and sophistry, the cardinal motif of *Fifine,* as it revolves about Elvire and the gipsy, is the subtle lure that lawlessness has in linking itself with the desire for change, with the craving to shatter the shackles of form and convention, with the impulse that represents, in a left-handed way, freedom of the spirit as attained through an outburst into a realm of fresh thought and emotion.

> Frenetic to be free! And, do you know, there beats
> Something within my breast, as sensitive?—repeats
> The fever of the flag? My heart makes just the same
> Passionate stretch, fires up for lawlessness, ... (VI. 43-46)

This passionate stretch of the heart for lawlessness is bound up in *Fifine* with a discussion of the problem of sex, centring on the married relationship. Why, with full recognition of the value and uniqueness of the bond between husband and wife, is a man tempted by a Bohemian instinct of the heart to be false to that allegiance in thought or deed? The theme of *Fifine,* as Stopford Brooke remarks,[16] is what the French, pithily, call *La Crise* in married life.

It is, of course, possible to approach such a theme from an objective standpoint, and Browning's keen interest in case-making and the intellectual sword-play of casuistry, as well as the dramatic element in his work, must not be discounted as factors in the composition of *Fifine.* Yet, I believe it can be shown, both from the poem itself and from the circumstances of Browning's life in 1872, that Mrs. Orr and Professor Dowden are right in associating *Fifine* with a mood whose source lies in the poet's own experience.

So far as explicit statement is concerned, these contemporaries of Browning seem to base their opinion on general grounds. They refer to the passage of time that had elapsed between Mrs. Browning's death and the composition of *Fifine.* They stress the inevitable "encroachments of the world" which to the sensitive conscience of the poet seemed to be bearing him away from the past and disturbing his whole-hearted devotion to the memory of his wife. It was in keeping with the strength of fibre of Browning's character and the whole trend of his religious faith that after the death of his wife he should resolutely determine, as he told Story, to begin life afresh, "to break up everything, go to England and live and work and write."[17] In order to avoid morbid brooding over the past, he turned to literary and social activities in London and widened rather than narrowed his circle of friends. The present, as Mrs. Orr puts it, "came to him with friendly greeting," a panacea to keep grief at bay and soften the blow that death had dealt him. Yet the gifts of the present, with their natural attraction for a man of such physical and mental vigour, must frequently have seemed to him subtle snares luring his spirit from the shrine of the love of his life. Despite the optimism of Browning's temperament, there are notes of despondency in his later lyrics which reveal him as acutely conscious of

Fifine at the Fair

the peril that lies in the exposure of human affections to the corroding work of time. In moments of spiritual depression, the world must have presented itself to him in the guise of a beguiling but treacherous gipsy, "an enemy sly and serpentine," dazzling his eyes with tinselled show, and seeking to wean him from the cherished past. With these circumstances in mind, a strong case could be made, even on general grounds, for the genesis of *Fifine,* pivoting as it does on the theme of conjugal fidelity and infidelity, in a troubled mood of the poet's spirit.

But the argument does not rest merely on general grounds. Recent study of Browning's life has revealed that at the time of the writing of *Fifine* the poet was racked by an experience of a most poignant and personal character. I refer to Browning's proposal of marriage to Lady Ashburton and the revulsion of spirit that followed it. The influence of this episode on Browning's poetry was first pointed out by Professor DeVane.[18] He has shown how in "Daniel Bartoli," the poet, in allegorical disguise, recalls an unhappy event of his own life. Ten years after the death of his wife, a woman had, momentarily, come between him and her memory. It was but a passing shadow, dimming for a brief interval the light of spiritual communion between himself and his "moon of poets," as he had called Mrs. Browning. He, like the Duke in "Daniel Bartoli,"

> Found that the Present intercepts the Past
> With such effect as when a cloud enwraps
> The moon and, moon-suffused, plays moon perhaps
> To who walks under, till comes, late or soon,
> A stumble: up he looks, and lo, the moon
> Calm, clear, convincingly herself once more!
> How could he 'scape the cloud that thrust between
> Him and effulgence? . . .   (XVII. 279-86)

Yet this defection from constancy must have remained the most bitter memory of Browning's later life, since sixteen years after the incident he cannot recall it without evident anguish of spirit.

Even for the sake of a full understanding of his poetry, it is not without hesitation that one touches upon a reticence of

Browning's life. However, as Mr. DeVane has shown, in his sensitive as well as scholarly handling of this delicate theme, there is nothing in it that really detracts from the tradition of the poet's devotion to his wife. The story can be read in detail in the *Letters of Robert Browning,* collected by Mr. Thomas J. Wise.[19] While the Lady Ashburton episode may add a touch of natural human weakness to the portraiture of Browning, it does not mar the impression of a man honourable and sincere in all his ways. In the violence of his reaction, the poet was unjust to Lady Ashburton, perhaps inevitably so. Over against his representation in "Daniel Bartoli" of "a bold she-shape," the Delilah who ensnared him, should be set Henry James's kindly but discriminating portrait of Lady Ashburton in *William Wetmore Story and His Friends.*[20] The description is that of a high-spirited woman, gifted with beauty and fascination, whom wealth and position had combined to make a centre of universal admiration and somewhat of a spoilt darling of the gods. She was "a rich, generous presence that, wherever encountered, seemed always to fill the foreground with colour, with picture, with fine mellow sound," yet not, as James hints, without certain extravagances of temperament which called for "a kind of traditional charmed, amused patience" on the part of her friends. Whatever share these extravagances of temperament had in fomenting the quarrel between Browning and herself, Lady Ashburton is more to be pitied than blamed. Both parties seem to have been caught in an unfortunate coil of circumstances which left the scar of a painful memory on their lives.

The history of Browning's relations with Lady Ashburton is circumstantial evidence that, as Mrs. Orr conjectures, "some leaven of bitterness" was working within him when he wrote *Fifine.* If, as late as 1887, his disagreeable experience still rankled, when the poet made it the subject of a thinly veiled autobiographical confession in *Parleyings with Certain People of Importance,* how much more poignantly would it distress him in 1872. This, we should bear in mind, was shortly after he had made his rash proposal of marriage to Lady Ashburton and, in

Fifine at the Fair

the midst of a quarrel with her, was suffering the first pangs of remorse.

Fifine at the Fair was composed between December, 1871 and May, 1872.[21] The exact date of Browning's offer of marriage is uncertain, but his final break with Lady Ashburton evidently took place in the autumn of 1871. His correspondence, at the time *Fifine* was written, throws vivid light on a succession of unhappy incidents. In a letter to Edith Story of January 1, 1872,[22] he speaks of *Fifine* as being half-done and then goes on to refer, though somewhat obscurely, to his strained relationships with Lady Ashburton. On April 4, 1872, he wrote again to Edith Story,[23] giving her a full account of his proposal to Lady Ashburton; of the subsequent rupture of their friendship; of angry and recriminating letters that passed between them; of a last painful interview which probably took place during a brief visit of Browning to Lady Ashburton's home at Loch Luichart Lodge in October, 1871. This correspondence, surcharged with the bitterness of the poet's experience, reveals the distemper of his spirit during the months in which he was composing *Fifine*.

The connection between the personal background of Browning's life in 1872 and the theme and mood of *Fifine at the Fair* seems to me unmistakable. Not that the text of the poem is a direct transcription of his experience. Browning was much too near the distasteful circumstance of his relationship with Lady Ashburton to write of it in that way. But he could not compose a poem at such a time without having his imagination subtly shaded by the dark thought of his own lack of constancy to the memory of his wife. Though *Fifine* is not literally autobiographical, it has its inception, I believe, in this unhappy episode of Browning's life.

It is significant, in this connection, that the Prologue to *Fifine* contains very direct references to Mrs. Browning and that the Epilogue is practically addressed to her. In the Prologue, the sea, where the poet swims, represents a life emancipated through passion and thought; substituting for heaven, poetry. The air which sustains the butterfly—symbolic of Psyche, the soul—typifies a spirit element. From the sky, the poet's wife is watching as her husband leaves the solid and safe land, symbolizing the prosaic, unimaginative, though law-abiding routine of worldly existence. Later on in the poem, the sea becomes representative not so much of poetry as of the danger and instability of an experiment with fallible human nature when passion and imagination are unfettered. In particular, the imagery of swimming in the sea is used as an illustration of man's dealing with the false and shifting appearances of life, through which he learns to value the truth and permanence that reside in the heaven above him.

> Gain scarcely snatched when, foiled by the very
>   effort, sowse,
> Underneath ducks the soul, her truthward
>   yearnings dowse
> Deeper in falsehood! ay, but fitted less and less
> To bear in nose and mouth old briny bitterness
> Proved alien more and more: since each experience
>   proves
> Air—the essential good, not sea. . . .   (LXV. 1049-54)

The sea, also, typifies the roving of the imagination in the devious, perilous, and sophistical speculations of *Fifine*.

> All these word-bubbles came
> O' the sea, and bite like salt. The unlucky bath's
>   to blame.   (CXXXI. 2315-16)

But Browning could hardly play with this symbol, especially as it is developed throughout the course of the poem, without having his own recent venture in mind. Life, like an unstable element, in the person of Lady Ashburton had tempted him to leave his old moorings and explore a sea of fresh passion. "Frenetic to be free," he had trusted himself to a sea of change, allured by the specious bait of the liberation of the soul from form and convention. Yet, through it all, the soul of his wife, "which early slipped its sheath," is watchful of his experiment with novelty and temporary licence, guiding him till he rises into the true out of the false. So, he resumes his ordinary contacts with the world—regaining the secure shore—comforted by the thought of her spiritual presence.

Fifine at the Fair

>   Does she look, pity, wonder
>   At one who mimics flight,
>   Swims—heaven above, sea under,
>   Yet always earth in sight?   (Prologue, xix)

The body of the poem, with its convolutions of argument, is an example of Browning's immense intellectual vivacity and delight in casuistry. But here, too, the mood and theme of *Fifine* have a genesis in the Lady Ashburton incident. Though the poet speedily regretted his proposal of marriage, he could not forgive himself for being enticed into it. Wretched as the aftermath of disagreeable relations had been, this was not the chief element in his remorse. It was the realization that he was capable of being inconstant to the memory of his wife that caused his bitterest pang. In view of the high spiritual plane on which Browning had placed his union with Elizabeth Barrett, such a defection seemed to him actual disloyalty. His perception of this at the time of his vehement change of feeling must have been in the nature of a shock. That he, "Love's loyal liegeman once," who, "scorning his weak fellows, towered above inconstancy" and erected an altar in his heart to "the never-dying Past," should have been drawn to another woman, was a startling revelation of his own frailty and the subtlety of life's lure. He had been confident of the spiritual integrity of his connection with his wife and yet had fallen prone, a victim of "one shattering volley out of eye's black ball."[24] The humiliation of this unhappy incident and the disclosure to the poet of his human weakness must have led him to reflect deeply on the nature of such an experience. He would appreciate, as never before, the alluring way in which life presents new claims, and the potency of the glittering bait of sophistry, masquerading as truth, through which the world tempts the spirit to forgo an old allegiance.

In *Fifine,* Browning selects, not his own, but an extreme case of conjugal inconstancy. Don Juan is a philanderer who, in the sequel of the narrative, leaves his wife Elvire and hastens to an assignation with the gipsy, Fifine. It is characteristic of Browning that he prefers to present a thesis in its extreme guise. If evil, error, and sophistry are to be encountered, he must track them to their den and then, before dispatching them, give them a case, with all the intellectual acumen at his command. The choice of Don Juan, the arch-voluptuary, as the monologist in *Fifine* is typical of Browning's way of approach to a moral problem affording scope for a play of casuistry. He takes conjugal infidelity on its lowest terms as the starting-point of his poem. But the connection of the Don Juan of *Fifine* with the Don Juan of legend and drama is more formal than real. The discussion of the theme of the poem sweeps far beyond the range of the sensualist and mere man of pleasure, the Don Juan of popular tradition. The prototype of Browning's figure would have yawned prodigiously at the intellectual acrobatics and metaphysical subtleties of his namesake. As Stopford Brooke wittily remarks: "The Don Juan of the poem had much better have stayed with Elvire, who endured him with weary patience. I have no doubt that he bored Fifine to extinction."[25] The arguments of this prince of casuists are not those of an unbridled libertine seeking to condone his debauchery, but those of a man of sensibility, endowed with great gifts of thought and poetic feeling. As a matter of fact, Don Juan is but a stalking-horse for the reflection of the poet on the inconstancies of sex, leading up to a consideration of the Bohemian instincts of life in general, the relation of reality to illusion and of truth to falsehood. The dramatic element in *Fifine* is a shadow rather than a substance. Dowden, in common with Herford, Brooke, Leslie Stephen, and other able critics of *Fifine,* recognizes this when he writes: "The poet desires, as Butler in his 'Analogy' desired, to take lower ground than his own; but the curious student of man and woman, of love and knowledge—imagination aiding his intellect—is compelled, amid his sophistical jugglings, to work out his problems upon Browning's own lines, and he becomes a witness to Browning's own conclusions."[26]

The psychological connection between the happenings of Browning's life in the early eighteen-seventies and the subject-matter of *Fifine* is self-evident. In the light of his recent ill-judged proposal to Lady Ashburton, with the feeling that he had been false to the memory of his wife in the foreground of his consciousness, his mind was turning over in all its phases the problem of inconstancy as focused in sex relationships. The gipsy, Fifine, is not a gross creation. In earlier poems, such as *The Flight of the Duchess,* gipsies were to Browning symbols of detachment from formalism and convention, of the breaking forth of life into uncharted regions of freedom, of the craving of the spirit for liberation. Frequently in *Fifine,* the gipsy ceases to be a material woman[27] and becomes representative of life itself, with its siren arts, confusing the soul through the dazzling fence of sophistry pointed with truth and beguiling it into disloyalty to its own past. How close such allegory lies to the poignant experience of the gipsy lures of life that Browning had recently passed through in the Lady Ashburton episode! How vividly he would have in mind the cunning speciousness with which the Present intercepts the Past, and the power of sophistry wearing the mask of liberty "to cheat the eye with blear illusion, and give it false presentments"!

Of the many passages in *Fifine* where analogies may be traced between Browning's handling of his theme and the background of his life in 1872, one of the most striking is Don Juan's explanation of the momentary attraction of Fifine by an illustration taken from art. He compares his wife, Elvire, to a precious painting by Raphael which he values above all other treasures. But, having secured this matchless portrait, in the process of time his very permanence of possession dulls the edge of rapture. As Don Juan puts it:

> The Rafael faces me, in fine, no dream at all,
> My housemate, evermore to glorify my wall.
> (xxxv. 536-37)

Despite the beauty and uniqueness of the canvas that is his daily companion, his spirit chafes at being confined to a single object of contemplation which closes its circle of attainment.

> Then I resume my life: one chamber must not coop
> Man's life in, though it boast a marvel like my prize.
> (xxxv. 547-48)

So, in a mood of ennui and craving for novelty, "expectancy's old fret and fume," Don Juan turns from Elvire, his peerless Raphael, to Fifine, symbolized by Doré's last picture book. This, Don Juan argues, does not show any real lack of devotion to Elvire or imply that she is supplanted in his affections by Fifine. The gipsy is merely a fleeting, idle fancy. His relation to her is that of a man lured by a new and piquant fashion, something to quicken "novel hopes and fears" and combat the tediousness and monotony of life.

> So, any sketch or scrap, pochade, caricature,
> Made in a moment, meant a moment to endure,
> I snap at, seize, enjoy, then tire of, throw aside,
> Find you in your old place.... (XXXVI. 566-69)

Were a fire to break out in Don Juan's gallery, he would throw Doré's picture book to the four winds and risk life itself to save his Raphael from the flames.

Here, as elsewhere in *Fifine*—apart from the Prologue and the Epilogue—the analogy between Browning's experience and the illustrations of his poem is but a glancing one. To interpret the narrative as allegory and regard the meek and colourless Elvire as representative of Mrs. Browning, or the relation between Browning and Lady Ashburton as typified in the light-o'-love connection of Don Juan with Fifine, would be the height of caricature. Nor, in speaking of the distemper of the poet's spirit at the time he wrote *Fifine,* should we ignore passages of verse whose vivacity and even gaiety evince an artist's delight in the free play of his imagination. Yet it seems clear that the elaborate similes and metaphors of *Fifine,* reflecting from every conceivable facet the theme of the inconstancy of sex, are often linked in thought and mood with Browning's dark brooding over his recent innocent but bitterly regretted lapse from constancy. How could he pen the sophistical lines,

> Then I resume my life: one chamber must not coop
> Man's life in, though it boast a marvel like my prize,

Fifine at the Fair

without having his own yielding to such sophistry in the background of his mind?

Since the analogy is of a general character, it would be impracticable as well as tedious to trace all the threads of connection between Browning's personal experience and the intricate apologia that he puts into the mouth of Don Juan. Sometimes, as in the art illustration already considered, inconstancy is defended on the ground of Bohemian instinct, the vagrant impulse of the heart to break the bonds of convention and plunge into life's "adventure brave and new." This plea is involved in the gipsy motif of the poem and in many individual similes. Though Elvire is like the steady, daily light of the sun, Don Juan's attention is momentarily caught by the intermittent lights of night—a fenfire's dancing, the flash of a meteor, the rushlight of a peasant, the squibs set off by mischievous boys. So, for a brief interim, he wanders from his allegiance to Elvire, "chaste, temperate, serene," and prefers "what sputters green and blue, this fizgig called Fifine!"[28]

At times, the protean casuistry of Don Juan is reinforced by the argument that inconstancy is a justifiable experiment through which man acquires knowledge of life and insight into human nature. Elvire is like a steady-going bark transporting a mariner easily and safely over the sea of life. But a hazardous voyage of a temporary kind in the cockle-shell, Fifine, while the superior ship, Elvire, "refits in port," is a better test of seamanship. Through making an occasional trip of this nature, the adventurous sailor, "trusting to sea-tracklessness" and steering past rocks and shoals, comes into close contact with the forces of wind and wave and learns to understand their power.

Again, Don Juan takes a leaf from Plato's book and contends that a knowledge of Fifine may be a stepping stone to the appreciation of Elvire, since man, by means of imagination and faith, transmutes the imperfect and fragmentary reality within his grasp and from it reconstructs the perfect and ideal type. It is noteworthy that in all the multitudinous imagery of *Fifine*,

Elvire never ceases to be the peerless wife, and Don Juan's lapse from constancy is invariably represented as a transitory affair, a cloud that obscures for a moment the lodestar of his life.

In the Epilogue to *Fifine*, as in the Prologue, Browning speaks in his own person, and here the connection between the poem and the dark mood of the poet, induced by the distressing circumstances of his relations with Lady Ashburton, seems to me a very direct one. Browning pictures himself, in the Epilogue, as a householder sitting within the house of life in a discouraged and sombre mood.

> Savage I was sitting in my house, late, lone:
> Dreary, weary with the long day's work:
> Head of me, heart of me, stupid as a stone:
> Tongue-tied now, now blaspheming like a Turk;

Then, in a swift flash of intuition, he becomes conscious of the spiritual presence of his wife.

> When, in a moment, just a knock, call, cry,
> Half a pang and all a rapture, there again were
>   we!—
> "What, and is it really you again?" quoth I:
> "I again, what else did you expect?" quoth She.

Now the spirit of his wife summons him away from the melancholy and shadow-haunted house of his earthly life apart from her.

> "Never mind, hie away from this old house—
> Every crumbling brick embrowned with sin and
>   shame!
> Quick, in its corners ere certain shapes arouse! . . ."

But the poet is conscious of the drag-weight of the life he has been compelled to lead since the death of his wife; he is oppressed, not merely by loneliness, but by the distractions and worries that his intercourse with the world has involved him in. He hints at certain temptations which have assailed him and almost driven him to despair.

> "Ah, but if you knew how time has dragged, days,
>   nights!

Fifine at the Fair

> All the neighbour-talk with man and maid—such
> men!
> All the fuss and trouble of street-sounds, window-
> sights:
> All the worry of flapping door and echoing roof;
> and then,
> All the fancies . . . Who were they had leave,
> dared try
> Darker arts that almost struck despair in me?
> If you knew but how I dwelt down here!" quoth I:
> "And was I so better off up there?" quoth She.

Finally, Browning looks forward to ultimate reunion with his wife. Though—tired of waiting—he longs for immediate departure, leaving the body in a heap, the decencies of life must be observed. He must endure the remaining years of earthly separation from her "who long ago left his soul whiling time in flesh-disguise." Even the obsequies of death must be in accordance with social forms and proprieties, the solemn and often hollow conventions that the world imposes. But, after the harlequinade is over and earth's show breaks up, will dawn the liberation of truth, not of sophistry—of abiding reality, not of shifting appearance. In one of those flamelike bursts of emotion through which the poet is wont to voice the supreme conviction of his life and art, Browning anticipates the joyous freedom of the spirit, and the rapture of indivisible communion with the soul of his wife, forever blended with his soul in Love.

> "Help and get it over! *Re-united to his wife*
> (How draw up the paper lets the parish-people
> know?)
> *Lies M., or N., departed from this life,*
> *Day the this or that, month and year the so and so.*
> What i' the way of final flourish? Prose, verse?
> Try!
> *Affliction sore long time he bore,* or, what is it to
> be?
> *Till God did please to grant him ease.* Do end!"
> quoth I:

> "I end with—Love is all and Death is nought!"
> quoth She.

The poignancy and human interest of the Epilogue to *Fifine*, so unmistakably a cry from the poet's heart, are, I feel, heightened when we consider it in relation to the unhappy experience that Browning had just passed through in connection with his proposal of marriage to Lady Ashburton. While writing *Fifine*, he was still within the shadow of this distressing episode, and was regretting, in bitterness of soul, his defection from constancy to the memory of his wife. However bravely he might front the world, weariness and depression must have preyed on his inner spirit. His letters in the early months of 1872 show how perturbed he was by what he regarded as malicious gossip and distorted report concerning the relations between Lady Ashburton and himself. Is there not a reflection of this in the Epilogue when the poet complains of

> All the neighbour-talk with man and maid—such men!
> All the fuss and trouble of street-sounds, window-sights?

Then, at such a time, he must have been keenly conscious of the loneliness of his own hearth, haunted by ghosts of the past,

> All the worry of flapping door and echoing roof.

The way in which the world—in the person of Lady Ashburton—had lured him from entire devotion to his wife is, perhaps, in his mind when he writes:

> . . . Who were they had leave, dared try
> Darker arts that almost struck despair in me?

In the acute revulsion of feeling that swiftly followed his unfortunate proposal of marriage, Browning must have turned for comfort and forgiveness to the spiritual presence of his wife, renewing the full intimacy of the bond between them after his brief wavering in allegiance.

Fifine at the Fair

> When, in a moment, just a knock, call, cry,
> Half a pang and all a rapture, there again were we!

Finally, out of the dark mood that has its genesis in his personal history, the poet passes, with assurance sensitized by suffering, to an intuition of the sustaining might of Love as the sovereign principle of life, and a pledge of the spiritual communion between his wife and himself, over which Death has no power. It is characteristic that he voices this conviction through the lips of Mrs. Browning:

> "I end with—Love is all and Death is nought!"
> quoth She.

In a letter of August 19, 1871, to his friend Isa Blagden—six weeks before his last visit of a day to Lady Ashburton—Browning wrote of his wife: "All is best as it is, for her, & me too. I shall wash my hands clean in a minute, before I see her, as I trust to do."[29] The Epilogue to *Fifine* re-echoes this sentiment and is plainly linked in thought and feeling with the Lady Ashburton episode and its aftermath.

While I have tried to show that the theme and mood of *Fifine at the Fair* are coloured by a particular incident of Browning's life, there are, of course, many currents of influence in a poem of such complexity. The subtle casuistry of Don Juan is frequently related to the poet's intellectual agnosticism, his conviction that the mind of man is forever entangled in a web of sophistry and illusion. Knowledge, Browning tells us, is not golden, but lacquered ignorance. As a consequence, experiment with falsehood and evil by teaching the futility of knowledge has, at least, a negative value. It forces man to fall back on love for an explanation of life's mystery.

> . . . knowledge means
> Ever-renewed assurance by defeat
> That victory is somehow still to reach,
> But love is victory, the prize itself:
> Love—trust to![30]

The poet, on his intellectual side—especially in his later verse—has the temper of a casuist. This, in conjunction with his dramatic instinct, plays a large part in the elaborate case-making of *Fifine*. Only on his emotional side, through his conviction that the intuition of love grasps truth directly, does Browning escape from casuistry.

> Were knowledge all thy faculty, then God
> Must be ignored: love gains him by first leap.[31]

But the casuistry of *Fifine at the Fair* is a study in itself, involving a comparison of the poem with other casuistical writings of Browning. It, therefore, lies beyond the scope of this essay.

8

Browning's Casuists

A STUDY OF Browning's casuists *per se* may seem to lie quite apart from a consideration of his vital contribution to English poetry. In that conflict between imagination and intellect which was acute in Browning, his casuistic writings represent in the main the nadir of his poetic faculty. The dramatic and poetical unities of such masterpieces as *The Bishop Orders His Tomb at Saint Praxed's Church* and *My Last Duchess*, where character and incident, thought and emotion are adequately fused, are replaced by psychological analysis in which the understanding takes the bit in its teeth and makes the abstract play of the mind an end in itself.

A relative distinction should be made. The dearth of poetry is more extreme in *Mr. Sludge, "the Medium"* and *Prince Hohenstiel-Schwangau* than in *Bishop Blougram's Apology* and *Fifine at the Fair*. *Bishop Blougram's Apology* contains the fine imaginative passage beginning,

> Just when we are safest, there's a sunset-touch,
> A fancy from a flower-bell, some one's death,
> A chorus-ending from Euripides,

and the subtle introspection of *Fifine at the Fair* is often illumined by vivid imagery and lovely vistas of nature—poetic work of rare quality. But despite the welcome oases, there is much aridness in these casuistic monologues and a lack of the concrete elements of poetry. There are tracts of "grey argument" which, although they illustrate the fecundity of the poet's mind, make dry and tortuous reading.

Yet the casuistic poems of Browning are an integral product of his genius, and a knowledge of them is essential to the grasp of it. Viewed, not in isolation, but in relation to the central ideas and interests of his poetry, these frequently crabbed writings have a value out-reaching their intrinsic content.

The distinction of the finest poems of Browning lies in the fusion of aesthetic and dramatic gifts with the resources of a penetrating and richly endowed mind. They are the works of a poet who, to reshape Arnold's famous phrase regarding Burke, saturates poetry with thought. Their originality and incisiveness are bound up with their mental acumen, revealing as by a lightning flash the inner processes of character under the stress of a crucial situation. In the casuistic poems these intellectual qualities of sinewy thought and psychological insight are unfortunately divorced from the dramatic vision of man in action and from the imaginative and emotional bases of poetry. Yet they are, when servants rather than masters of poetic inspiration, attributes that give to Browning's verse much of its pith, fibre, and enduring place in literature. Even when they run amuck, as in the intricacies of *Prince Hohenstiel-Schwangau*, the poet's defeat and loss, like the failures of his hero Paracelsus, spring from the misuse of his strength.

It is, however, through their relation to Browning's philosophy of life that the casuistic poems are of special import. One phase of this—the cleavage between man's faculties of love and reason —they illustrate in a pre-eminent degree. In an attempt to vindicate his ethical convictions and to establish a firm basis for his religious faith, Browning is driven to place all stress on love, and by contrast to debase reason. The universal problems of sin and suffering and the particular doubts and difficulties of his age seem to him insoluble from the point of view of reason. His distrust of the capacities of man's mind is of a thoroughgoing character. He does not merely hold that knowledge is relative and limited. Reason is forever baffled in its search for truth, and its quest ends in the *cul-de-sac* of deception and illusion. Its futile groping is, to use the poet's figure in *The Ring and the Book*, like an arm thrust into water, deflected by the medium through which it passes and falling wide of what it seeks to grasp.

But Browning's emotional gnosticism is as unqualified as his intellectual agnosticism. He cuts the Gordian knot by exalting the heart above the head and by regarding love as infallible in its intuitive perception of truth.

> Wholly distrust thy knowledge, then, and trust
> As wholly love allied to ignorance!
> There lies thy truth and safety.[1]

In *Saul*, love in man's heart is an *a priori* evidence to David of the existence of a God of love. Thence there follow as corollaries Immortality, and a prophetic vision of a scheme of redemption in the Incarnation and Atonement of Christ. Once convinced of the impotence of reason, Browning makes it, in a left-handed way, support his concept of the supreme worth of man's moral struggle. Truth is concealed from the eyes of the intellect in order that the venture and trial of faith may be the more heroic.[2]

Browning's sceptical attitude towards reason in the interests of his ethics and religious belief has often been represented as individual and unique. But it is, rather, a specialized form of that way of retreat from apparently insuperable problems adopted by many of the great Victorians. Newman and Tennyson exhibit it as markedly as Browning. Arnold dallied with it in *Dover Beach*. He too felt the lure of that escape to the Ages of Faith which by blinding the eyes of reason would regain security of belief. Yet he could not forswear allegiance to "the high, white star of Truth." The "Victorian Compromise," manifest in other spheres, is nowhere else more strikingly illustrated than in the endeavour to withdraw religion from the realm of knowledge in order to obtain spiritual peace, though at a costly price.

A perception of the fallacy of Browning's abnegation of reason has led a number of modern critics to regard his philosophy of life as shallow, and vitiated by intellectual timidity. Such a judgment fails to reckon with the historical environment of the poet, or to understand the gravity and pressure of the problems he was facing. The wake of eighteenth-century Deism; the free-thinking and rationalistic tendencies engendered by the French Revolution; the Positivism of Comte; the advent of Higher Criticism, as a knowledge of the writings of Strauss and Renan seeped into England; the enunciation of the scientific theory of evolution with Darwin, Huxley, and Spencer as its high priests—confronted the mid-Victorians with religious difficulties which seemed to them insoluble. They were in a blind alley, and their only means of salvation appeared to be the abandonment of the dusty road of reason leading to the hold of Giant Despair in Doubting Castle, and a flight to the impregnable fortress of faith.

The extremity of that rejection of reason to which men were driven by the exigencies of the problems of the age is revealed in wide-flung ways. In the eighteen-fifties, during which Browning wrote the first of his great casuistic monologues, *Bishop Blougram's Apology,* Newman's *Lectures on the Present Position of Catholics in England* were printed. In these, Newman could so far juggle with his acute and powerful mind as to avow his belief in such churchly miracles as the liquefaction of the blood of St. Januarius and the motion of the eyes in pictures of the Madonna.[3] This *reductio ad absurdum* of reason is paralleled in scientific works of the decade. In *Omphalos: An Attempt to Untie the Geological Knot,* 1857, Philip Gosse, an able entomologist, gravely argued that God had planted fossils in the earth as a sort of gargantuan pious fraud. The divine purpose of the imposture, according to Gosse, was to give opportunity for faith to rise above the apparent confutation of the cosmology of Genesis in the testimony of the fossils. Men must still believe in the scientific accuracy of the biblical account of creation, despite the contradictory evidence of the senses and reason. God consequently becomes, as Kingsley put it in criticizing *Omphalos,* a *Deus quidam deceptor,* and the end justifies the means. Such shifts and straits of casuistry are a measure of the intellectual perplexities of the epoch. If Browning is at times enmeshed in their toils, his position can only be estimated fairly and judged sympathetically in the light of the historical background of his day.

I have dwelt on Browning's intellectual scepticism, because of its intimate connection with his casuistic poems. For a nescient theory of knowledge is the very soil in which casuistry breeds. If reason, self-tricked and deluded, is always involved in a "vile juggle," casuistry must be constantly attendant upon it and, indeed, inherent in its nature. Browning escapes the fogs of sophistry when he invokes the sunlight of love to dispel the mists that becloud the mind. The emotions of the heart are in intuitive touch with truth. But when the poet descends to the arena of reason, he is unavoidably entrapped in casuistry. Hence it becomes an interesting question, how far his hand is dyed by the medium in which he works. To what extent is he above his casuists, and to what extent is he at one with them? The arguments through which Bishop Blougram strives to justify his religious position have more than a superficial likeness to those used by Browning in his later poems to defend his own faith. Even that subtle sophist Don Juan, seems, at times, equipped with some of the choicest weapons from the poet's arsenal. It is difficult to avoid the conclusion that Browning's casuists are never really routed from the standpoint of reason. Here the poet's negative attitude towards knowledge sprains him. "Wisdom is justified of her children," and however gifted a man's intellect, he must have faith in reason in order to vindicate the ways of reason. It is only by recourse to the sovereign principle and virtue of love that Browning triumphs over casuistry. He carries the case to a higher tribunal, but he does not defeat the sophist on the latter's chosen ground.

While Browning's intellectual agnosticism enters as an important element into his casuistic monologues, it is not, of course, a complete explanation of their genesis. This is decidedly complex. Sir Leslie Stephen[4] has stressed the poet's psychological bent, passion for case-making, delight in the adroit play of the mind, love of the odd and bizarre, as factors having a bearing on his casuistic writings. He has also, in common with Professor Jones, emphasized the ethical necessity felt by Browning of justifying his optimism in face of the ills of the universe. If his casuists, though in a lesser degree than his criminals, exemplify low and base traits of human nature, the poet is impelled to depict them in order to prove that evil is "stuff for transmuting," and to reconcile its existence with the purposes of God for man. Even while exposing the Jesuistry of his sophists, he strives, in the spirit of the dying Paracelsus,

> To trace love's faint beginnings in mankind,
> To know even hate is but a mask of love's,
> To see a good in evil, and a hope
> In ill-success; to sympathize, be proud
> Of their half-reasons, faint aspirings, dim
> Struggles for truth, their poorest fallacies,
> Their prejudice and fears and cares and doubts;
> All with a touch of nobleness, despite
> Their error, upward tending all though weak,
> Like plants in mines which never saw the sun,
> But dream of him, and guess where he may be,
> And do their best to climb and get to him.   (V. 873-84)

A comprehensive review of Browning's dealings with casuistry would involve a study of a large portion of his poetry, embracing selections from his early, middle, and late writings. *Sordello*, 1840, bristles with casuistry. The prudential maxims of Chiappino in *A Soul's Tragedy*, 1846, anticipate the worldly wisdom of Bishop Blougram and Prince Hohenstiel-Schwangau. The special pleadings of Fra Lippo Lippi, Andrea del Sarto, and Cleon in *Men and Women*, 1855, and of Caliban in *Dramatis Personae*, 1864, are frequently of a sophistical nature. The elements of casuistry in *The Ring and the Book*, 1868-69, are manifold, and have been made the theme of an extensive treatise.[5] *Aristophanes' Apology*, 1870, is a network of casuistic argument. The thinly veiled portrait of Disraeli in the Parleying with "George Bubb Dodington," 1887, is twin brother to that of Napoleon III in *Prince Hohenstiel-Schwangau*.

Browning's Casuists

There are, however, four works which, through their concentration on the problems of casuistry and their skill in depicting it, may be regarded as the most important writings of Browning in this vein. These are *Bishop Blougram's Apology,* 1855, *Mr. Sludge, "the Medium,"* 1864, *Prince Hohenstiel-Schwangau,* 1871, and *Fifine at the Fair,* 1872. It is my purpose in this essay to make some reference to the connection of these poems with personal interests of Browning linked with contemporary happenings; but I wish to consider them, particularly, in their relation to his philosophy of life—more specifically that agnostic theory of reason which in part involves him in the casuistry of his own imaginative creations.

The range of the four monologues is striking. They represent casuistry in the various spheres of religion, spiritualism, politics, and sex in its bearing on the bond of marriage. Their inception illustrates a tendency, most marked in the later writings of Browning, to find a point of departure for his poems in some actual person or event. None of the principal characters of these monologues is purely fictitious. Bishop Blougram, Mr. Sludge, and Prince Hohenstiel-Schwangau have their historical genesis in their respective linkings with Cardinal Wiseman, Daniel Home, and Napoleon III. They are, consequently, in touch with men and movements of the Victorian era. The monologist in *Fifine at the Fair,* the semi-historical Don Juan, is a character already famous in legend and literature; and the poem is deeply coloured by an unfortunate incident in Browning's life, his proposal of marriage to Lady Ashburton in 1871.

I shall discuss the four casuistic monologues in their chronological order.

Browning told Sir Charles Gavan Duffy that Bishop Blougram was intended to suggest Cardinal Wiseman, the first Roman Catholic Archbishop of Westminster.[6] The appointment of this prelate in 1850, in conjunction with a papal bull dividing England into ecclesiastical districts, roused a storm of controversy. There are in *Bishop Blougram's Apology* several references, under a thin dramatic disguise, to incidents in Wiseman's career. In a broader sense, it is evident that the poet had also in mind the general drift towards Roman Catholicism of the extreme wing of the Oxford Movement. Its great central figure, Newman, is in his thought as well as Wiseman.

Browning's reaction to the tenets of Roman Catholicism as proclaimed by Wiseman and Newman may be described as critical but not bigoted. Various factors determined his attitude. The poet's family traditions were Nonconformist. So far as he can be claimed by a religious party, his affiliations lie with the Evangelicals rather than with the Broad or High Churchmen.[7] In *Christmas-Eve,* 1850, he declares his own preference for a simple and unritualistic type of service. Yet it is evident that his conception of Christianity soon evolved beyond the narrow bounds of Puritan Nonconformity. By the time he wrote *Bishop Blougram's Apology,* his spiritual horizons had been widened both by his cosmopolitan experience and by the natural development of a reflective and gifted intellect. Moreover, he is strikingly English in his individual way of dealing with religious problems. His approach to them is linked with typical modes of thought or spiritual insights traceable throughout his poetry. A discerning critic has said: "It is not as a creed, still less as a body of religious opinion, that Christianity attracts Browning. It is as a living experience that its spell is potent."[8]

Though Browning's outlook on Roman Catholicism is in certain respects that of the average English Protestant, and while he can jibe in execrable verse at the folly of being

> manned by Manning, and new-manned
> By Newman and, mayhap, wise-manned to boot
> By Wiseman,[9]

his criticism is mollified by the breadth of his religious thought and its independent character. When John Forster and Sir Charles Gavan Duffy spoke of *Bishop Blougram's Apology* as an attack upon the Roman Catholic faith, the poet protested, maintaining that the work was not a satire, and that he had been generous in his treatment of Cardinal Wiseman.[10] Later on, "the great good old Pope" of *The Ring and the Book* is portrayed as the acme of human wisdom and spiritual insight. His utterances represent the highest reach of Browning's own faith and the most complete expression of his philosophy of life.

I turn now to the particular consideration of the casuistry of *Bishop Blougram's Apology* in its relation to the basic dualism of the poet's thought—a gulf between love and reason involving a profound distrust of the latter faculty. I have drawn attention to the fact that an agnostic rejection of knowledge is the seedling of casuistry, and raised the question, how far is Browning himself caught in the sophistry he is probing? I have also pointed out that the Victorian Compromise, through which belief was preserved at the expense of reason by confining religion to the sphere of faith and the intuitions of the heart, overleaps the boundaries of denominational allegiance. The Roman Catholic, Newman; the Broad Church Anglican, Tennyson; the Dissenter, Browning, in whose veins ran the blood of Puritan ancestors—adopt a position, in this regard, fundamentally akin. There is, consequently, in the realm of reason, an intrinsic bond of sympathy, conscious or unconscious, between Browning and the creation of his brain, Bishop Blougram. It was, undoubtedly, a recognition that the poet's renunciation of reason in the interests of faith was not far removed from the Roman Catholic credo, which led Wiseman, when reviewing *Bishop Blougram's Apology* in the *Rambler*,[11] to write: "Though much of the matter is extremely offensive to Catholics, yet beneath the surface there is an undercurrent of thought that is by no means inconsistent with our religion; and if Mr. Browning is a man of will and action, and not a mere dreamer and talker, *we should never feel surprise at his conversion.*"

There are two main threads of casuistry running through the arguments of Bishop Blougram. The first is primarily ethical, bearing on the conduct of life. The second is primarily intellectual, bearing on the issues of faith and doubt. The Bishop bases part of his defence on the contrast between the futility of abstract idealism and the success of a prudent and practical adaptation of one's talent and outlook to the environment and capacities of a workaday world. Browning, himself, had a keen sense of the necessity of making a fruitful use of the means and possibilities of man's earthly lot. All poetry, he once wrote to Ruskin, is the problem of "putting the infinite within the finite."[12] In *Pauline, Paracelsus,* and *Sordello,* he grappled with this problem in the sphere of life. The heroes of these poems are men of genius, and the crux of their difficulties lies in reconciling the inexhaustible cravings of the spirit with the conditions and limitations of a finite world. Browning wrestles with this moral paradox as strenuously as Jacob with the angel and, in the main, successfully. He does not, like Bishop Blougram, conclude that the urgency of working within the cabin confines of earthly experience justifies an acceptance of worldly standards. A man should not spurn the actual, but neither should he be content with it. He must constantly strive to press beyond it and to lift it up towards the light of the ideal. The ethical convictions of Browning are the core of his philosophy, and on moral grounds, *per se,* he is rarely, if ever, entangled in casuistry.

When, however, we turn to that argument of Bishop Blougram which is primarily intellectual, revolving about the issues of belief and doubt, it may be queried whether Browning ever thoroughly disengages himself from the speaker's casuistry. The Bishop declares that he casts in his lot with the adherents of faith on account of its utilitarian value. He then goes on to suggest that the inability of reason to attain religious truth or to solve the problems of the universe may be preordained in order that men may rely entirely on faith. Difficulties of belief from the standpoint of intellect are like breaks in the mountain path of life, but, the Bishop speculates,

> What if the breaks themselves should prove at last
> The most consummate of contrivances
> To train a man's eye, teach him what is faith?
> And so we stumble at truth's very test! (ll. 205-8)

If this comparison were simply an illustration of the relativity of human knowledge which leaves scope for faith, it would not,

Browning's Casuists 139

in itself, involve an agnostic attitude towards reason. But Bishop Blougram pushes his argument further. He widens the chasm between belief and reason in two directions. The maximum of belief is represented by an absolute form of it in Roman Catholicism, the maximum of agnosticism by a complete intellectual scepticism. The broader and deeper the abyss between belief and reason, the greater is the challenge to faith, and the more signal its triumph when it leaps the gulf. "Let doubt occasion still more faith!" exclaims the Bishop, and again:

> With me, faith means perpetual unbelief
> Kept quiet like the snake 'neath Michael's foot
> Who stands calm just because he feels it writhe.
> (ll. 666-68)

On this ground the poet, with Newman in his mind, makes Blougram defend the most preposterous of churchly miracles—the liquefaction of the blood of St. Januarius at Naples, and the motion of the eyes of the Madonna in the Roman States.[13] The extreme irrationality of these miracles is but a foil for the unqualified exhibition of faith in its unreasoning acceptance of the supernatural.

Although Browning would scout the crass materialism of such miracles, it is indisputable that his agnostic abnegation of knowledge entangles him, personally as well as dramatically, in the casuistry of *Bishop Blougram's Apology*. This is especially evident in his later writings, where his rejection of reason is drastic, and all worth is centred in faith motivated by love as a solvent of life's problems. He, too, along with Bishop Blougram, tries to turn his rationalistic scepticism to moral advantage, by making the incapacity of reason a challenge to the daring venture of faith in the blackness of night environing the intellect. He, too, fixes a great gulf between the intuitions of the heart and what are regarded as the phantoms of the mind. It is, therefore, not surprising to find that Bishop Blougram is, at times, the mouthpiece of Browning's inmost religious convictions. The Bishop's argument that a searing vision of God's omnipresence would blind man on earth, and that the existence of evil is necessary if the world is to be a place of probation and testing, is a familiar tenet of the poet's ethics. In the *apologia* for Christianity put on Blougram's lips, the correspondence of dramatic and personal thought is still more striking. Who can doubt that Browning is voicing his own belief when the Bishop asserts:

> It is the idea, the feeling and the love,
> God means mankind should strive for and show
>   forth
> Whatever be the process to that end,—
> And not historic knowledge, logic sound,
> And metaphysical acumen, sure!
> "What think ye of Christ," friend? when all 's
>   done and said,
> Like you this Christianity or not?
> It may be false, but will you wish it true?
> Has it your vote to be so if it can?   (ll. 621-29)

The elements of truth in these words are apt to cloak the Achilles' heel of the statement, but the criticism of "historic knowledge, logic sound" in connection with the evidences of Christianity, is based on that distrust of reason which is the root of casuistry. And Browning is as deeply involved in this sophistry as his Roman Catholic prelate. In his later writings, where his intellectual agnosticism is most pronounced, he becomes extremely sceptical of any approach to religious truth through the exercise of reason. As I have elsewhere stated, in laying exclusive stress on love, he is inclined to regard the revelation of Christianity, not merely as historically unproven, but as embodying a narrative of events absolutely inconceivable from the point of view of intellect.[14]

As a result of his rationalistic scepticism, Browning is unable to refute the casuist on the battle-ground of reason. But in *Bishop Blougram's Apology,* as elsewhere, he rises above casuistry through recourse to the cardinal virtue of love, in whose light doubts dissolve as mists in the sun. The Bishop is an adherent of belief, but he is not himself a believer at heart. His decision to embrace Roman Catholicism is based on utilitarian grounds. Faith has positive value; it works; it produces practical results in the sphere of life. Over against such prudential motives, Browning places the intuitive witness of the heart to the validity of the fundamental truths of religion. The existence of a loving and self-sacrificing God, which is the core of Christian revelation, is attested by evidences deeper than rational proof. Its guaranty lies in faith inspired by love in the soul of the individual, in transfigured lives, in the spiritual experience of humanity. Bishop Blougram acknowledges that Luther's fire of religious conviction is far superior to his own cold, formal, and calculating acceptance of belief as an instrument of worldly policy.

> Believe—and our whole argument breaks up,
> Enthusiasm's the best thing, I repeat; . . . .
> Why, to be Luther—that's a life to lead,
> Incomparably better than my own.   (ll. 555-56, 568-69)

In such lines the poet voices his own ideals. As Leslie Stephen says in his article on Browning's casuistry: "No poet is more sensitive to the beauty of the heroic and unselfish impulses or provides them with more impressive utterance. His sympathy is with the vivid spontaneous intuitions, which disperse the sophistries, and can on occasion override the commonplace rules of conventional morality."[15]

Certain conclusions may now be drawn from the first of the four important poems in which Browning comes to close grips with casuistry. By transferring the argument of *Bishop Blougram's Apology* to his own chosen ground, the poet wins what may be called a Pyrrhic victory. He triumphs, yet surrenders the outposts of intellect to the casuist. In the realm of love the hollowness of the Bishop's sophistry is exposed, but in the realm of knowledge, Browning is, in a sense, fighting with his own shadow. The dialectics of Blougram are never pierced by the sword of reason.

In *Mr. Sludge, "the Medium,"* Browning has delineated the meanest and most contemptible of his casuists. The notorious career of the prototype of Sludge, Daniel Home, has been sketched in Mr. Wyndham's entertaining biography.[16] As is well known, an attendance at a seance of Home's resulted in a decided difference of opinion between Browning and his wife. He was repelled by the Medium's trickery, while she was disposed to credit the veracity of his communications. The violence of Browning's reaction, in which he showed his antipathy to Home, was due in part to his contempt for such crass exhibitions of spiritualism, and in part to his indignation that his wife had been the victim of a gross imposture. He could hardly write a poem in which the American charlatan served as a model without a measure of personal animus. Yet *Mr. Sludge, the "Medium,"* is far from being a diatribe or even a polemic aimed at spiritualism. Browning's interest in the psychology of the Medium and his experiences outweighs any element of vindictiveness. There is also a catholic charity in the poet's philosophy of life. No creature, however mean, is without a case or a cause that has not latent in it a germ of truth, even though encrusted by error. As a poet who believes profoundly in the omnipresence of spirit, Browning discerns in the corrupt and debased spiritualism of Sludge a dim groping for the loftiest of realities. Sludge, like Saul, is also among the prophets, and gold occasionally glints through the dross of his casuistry. In his oracular mood, he can even become the mouthpiece of some of the poet's deep convictions. As Professor Herford has commented: "Sludge is clearly permitted, like Blougram before and Juan and Hohenstiel-Schwangau after him, to assume in good faith positions, or at least to use, with perfect sincerity, language, which had points of contact with Browning's own."[17]

When Sludge professes to abandon subterfuge and "vomit truth," he introduces two main arguments as a semi-serious defence of his practices. The first is based on his claim to be in his fantastic way a "seer of the supernatural." He appeals to the witness of the Bible and "history with its supernatural element" as attesting God's miraculous intercourse with humanity. Then he maintains that, since religion is all or nothing and spirit interpenetrates life at every point, no being or incident is too small or trivial for God's use as a channel of divine revelation.

Out of his very insignificance and the freakish oddities of the phenomena of spiritualism, Sludge strives to conjure evidence that he is in intimate and unique touch with the invisible world. There must be

> Strict sympathy of the immeasurably great
> With the infinitely small, betokened here
> By a course of signs and omens, raps and
>   sparks. . . .   (ll. 1070-72)

At this point, the Medium reinforces his argument by emphasizing the doctrine of special providences. He meets the objection that "Sludge seems too little for such grace," by the plea that he is of all-importance to himself. If nothing is too minute for God's oversight, is he not justified in discerning in incidents trivial to others but of personal concern to himself, miraculous acts of divine intervention? Is it more incredible that God should select Sludge as a *via media* of spiritual revelation, than that he should single out this world from millions of others to be the home of Adam, with all the consequences that flowed from the creative fiat? "There's a special providence in the fall of a sparrow," but this leads Sludge, unlike Hamlet, not to defy but to accept augury. He will still continue to

> Look, microscopically as is right,
> Into each hour with its infinitude
> Of influences at work to profit Sludge.   (ll. 958-60)

The second main argument through which Sludge defends himself is of a different order. It centres on an exposition of the nature of truth. Pitched in a lower key, Sludge's *apologia* echoes the special pleading of that master casuist Francis Bacon in his essay "Of Truth." It also has correspondences with Emerson's essay "Illusions." Under the conditions of human life, Sludge declares, men are unable to bear a revelation of truth in its absolute and pristine essence. An apperception of truth, naked and undisguised, would depress men by its constant disclosure of the relative failure of their lives, of how continually they are balked by hindrance and disappointments. A quest of knowledge in the sheer interests of truth unbares the complete futility of reason and ends in the impasse of intellectual agnosticism. Truth is involved in self-mockery.

> What knowledge, sir,
> Except that you know nothing? Nay, you doubt
> Whether 't were better have made you man or
>   brute,
> If aught be true, if good and evil clash.
> No foul, no fair, no inside, no outside,
> There's your world!   (ll. 1385-90)

But when truth is gilded with flattering illusion, men are led on like children in pursuit of a bauble, and their hope and optimism sustained. What matter if delusion enters in, since the deception makes life workable and inspires men with faith in the supernatural. Sludge claims that he transfigures the world by investing it with a miraculous gleam, even though his juggle with it is on the low level of the trickery of the clown in the circus. If illusion has both utilitarian and mystical values in heightening the well-being of life, then,

> Don't let truth's lump rot stagnant for the lack
> Of a timely helpful lie to leaven it!   (ll. 1305-6)

The Medium compares his deception in a general way with the function of the imagination in literature. Poets are not content with bare facts. They invent and give free rein to fancy as Homer did in telling the story of the siege of Troy. Even in "plain prose" such "dealers in common sense" as historians do not limit themselves to facts. Their narratives or biographies are coloured by their subjective impressions. They are, at best, imaginative reconstructions of truth. Sludge claims that his fictions are akin to those of men of letters. He carries the process of illusion one step further and acts the books they write. Error itself bears testimony to the veracity it shadows. Just as "there is some soul of goodness in things evil," so Sludge avows:

> I'm ready to believe my very self—
> That every cheat's inspired, and every lie
> Quick with a germ of truth.   (ll. 1323-25)

Browning's Casuists

Although this exposition of the nature of truth in *Mr. Sludge, "the Medium"* revolves about a more abstract problem than the religious issues of *Bishop Blougram's Apology*, it is evident that in both monologues Browning is in part involved in the casuistry of his poetic creations. And the source of his entanglement is basically the same, namely, his sceptical attitude towards knowledge. As certain of Bishop Blougram's arguments are paralleled in passages of verse where Browning is voicing his own credo, so Sludge's sophistical defence is echoed in various personal utterances of the poet. In his elaborate introduction to the narrative of *The Ring and the Book*, Browning grapples with the problem of the relation of truth to imaginative works of literature. There is much in his plea for the function of the imagination in art, as fusing the live soul of the poet with the inert stuff of fanciless fact, which is just and sound. Yet in dealing with this subtle question, it is clear that his distrust of reason, at times, entraps him. He resorts to a casuistic definition of truth strikingly similar to the sophistry put on the lips of Sludge. If human knowledge is illusory, man must content himself on earth, in the sphere of intellect at any rate, with a semblance of truth. The poet does not entirely confine himself to the assertion that an alloy of imagination must be mingled with the native gold of truth to make it malleable. He goes further and maintains that deception must be intermixed with truth in order to adapt the latter to the imperfect probationary character of man's destiny in this world. There must be

> No dose of purer truth than man digests,
> But truth with falsehood, milk that feeds him now,
> Not strong meat he may get to bear some day.   (I. 825-27)

The imagination, according to Browning, is midway between love and reason in its relation to truth. It is not, like love, in intuitive and immediate contact with truth, but neither is it absolutely cut off from it, like reason. "Art may tell a truth obliquely," and therefore has an advantage over reason. By breaking up the white light into prismatic colours adapted to man's feeble vision, it approximates truth, even though comprising an element of illusion. But human reason striving to face the white light directly is blinded, and the result is the nescience of intellect. At the close of *The Ring and the Book,* the conclusions of Browning regarding the futility of any perception of truth through the instrumentality of reason are unqualified in their pessimism. The inference that the poet draws from the drama of passion and tragic incident he has been depicting is

> This lesson, that our human speech is naught,
> Our human testimony false, our fame
> And human estimation words and wind.   (XII. 838-40)

The bearing on the casuistic monologues of these conceptions of love, reason, and imagination, embraced in Browning's philosophy of life, may now be summed up. In the sphere of love the poet rises quite above casuistry. In the sphere of reason he is obviously entangled in it. In the sphere of the imagination, owing to the middle position that faculty occupies between love and reason in its relation to truth, his attitude with regard to casuistry is wavering and difficult to define. Browning, in his personal utterances, is on common ground with Sludge in recognizing the presence of an element of illusion in art. But Sludge emphasizes the negative implications of this. He dwells on the inventions of poetry and the imaginative reconstructions of history in order to bolster his gospel of deceit. Browning, on the contrary, when he casts aside his dramatic disguise, stresses the positive function of the imagination as a mediator between truth in its absoluteness and the limited capacities of man to apprehend it. Art, to use his image again, is like a prism transmitting to humanity the light of truth, broken and softened, yet as near its dazzling essence as the sight of man can bear. A conviction of the efficacy of the mediation of the imagination is inwrought in the noblest intuitions and judgments of artists and philosophers. It is in accord with their lofty insights, and not on the low level of the casuistry of a Sludge, that Browning writes in *Easter-Day* of gleams of heaven and earth

> Made visible in verse, despite
> The veiling weakness,—truth by means

> Of fable, showing while it screens,—
> Since highest truth, man e'er supplied,
> Was ever fable on outside. (XXVIII. 922-26)

Yet the form of Browning's statement in *Easter-Day,* with its introduction of the concept of fable, shows how difficult it is to separate the skeins of truth and error in dealing with the imaginative faculty. Through a subtle twist of casuistry, the mediation of the imagination in art may be represented as leading to delusion and falsehood, rather than enabling man to grasp that relative degree of truth which is adapted to the finitude and imperfection of his earthly nature. " Art may tell a truth obliquely," as Browning puts it, but this indirection of method seems to poise the imagination delicately on a tight rope between reality and fantasy. Intermingled with the poet's fine *apologia* for his artistic handling of the story of *The Ring and the Book* are assertions which skate on the verge of casuistry.

> Fancy with fact is just one fact the more; . . . . (I. 464)

> Is fiction which makes fact alive, fact too?
> The somehow may be thishow. (I. 705-6)

In Browning's later poems, where his distrust of any faculty except love to be in contact with truth is most marked, there are passages reminiscent of Sludge's casuistry in the sphere of the imagination as well as in that of the intellect.

Prince Hohenstiel-Schwangau is Browning's most extensive study of the political casuist. The Prince as an opportunist in affairs of state has his literary prototype in Chiappino and his literary successor in George Bubb Dodington. The actual genesis of the character is, however, historical. The model of Prince Hohenstiel-Schwangau is Napoleon III; as Dodington, though more indirectly, reflects the career of Disraeli. Browning never shared the enthusiasm of his wife for Louis Napoleon and always regarded him as a political adventurer. His attitude was critical and at times contemptuous, but it may be described as judicial rather than acutely hostile. It was not marked by that personal animus he felt for Daniel Home. As a consequence he gave Napoleon credit for a certain measure of accomplishment, even though he considered his career, in the main, to be a failure. *Prince Hohenstiel-Schwangau* was composed shortly after the French emperor's fall at Sedan, and Browning's final estimate of the man is well summed up in the letters he wrote about this time to Isabella Blagden and Edith Story. On December 29, 1871, Browning wrote to Miss Blagden:

> By this time you have got my little book and seen for yourself whether I make the best or worst of the case. I think in the main, he meant to do what I say, and, but for the weakness, grown more apparent in these last years than formerly, would have done what I say he did not. I thought badly of him at the beginning of his career, *et pour cause;* better afterward on the strength of promises he made, and gave indications of intending to redeem; I think him very weak in the last miserable year.[18]

In a similar vein, Browning wrote to Edith Story, on January 1, 1872, regarding the connection of Prince Hohenstiel-Schwangau with Napoleon III.

> ... I don't think, when you have read more, you will find I have "taken the man for any Hero"—I rather made him confess he was the opposite, though I put forward what excuses I thought he was likely to make for himself, if inclined to try. I never at any time thought much better of him than now; and I don't think so much worse of the character as shown us in the last few years, because I suppose there to be a physical and intellectual decline of faculty, brought about by the man's own faults, no doubt—but I think he struggles against these; and when that is the case, depend on it, in a soliloquy, a man makes the most of his good intentions and sees great excuse in them—far beyond what our optics discover![19]

The Prince's long and tortuous self-defence is based on the admission that he is not one of those great and inspired men "whose master-touch not so much modifies as makes anew." His work has been not to overthrow an old or to bring into being a novel order of things, but to strive through twenty years to stabilize and maintain the tottering edifice of society as he found it.

> A conservator, call me, if you please,
> Not a creator nor destroyer: one
> Who keeps the world safe.   (ll. 298-300)

Such a policy, though prudential and opportunist, has been in accord with the needs of a transitional epoch. Hohenstiel-Schwangau confesses that he has merely retraced the imperfect line of the past, here and there making the crooked straight, the roughness smooth. But by such patchwork he claims that he has simplified the task of the great man who, when the time is ripe, will arrive to create new conditions of life and reshape society "from round to square."

Various casuistic arguments are introduced by the Prince in support of his makeshift course of action. If the exigencies of the age require the preservation of the old order, is he not justified in refraining from attacking what is out of joint in it, since such an assault might lead to social anarchy? Who will quarrel with evil if good comes out of it? He acknowledges that in the past he has had high ideals and aspirations. Here Browning has in mind the services of Napoleon III to the cause of Italian freedom. In the finest poetical passage of *Prince Hohenstiel-Schwangau,* the fallen emperor's thoughts turn back to Italy and the noble vision of liberation he has cherished.

> Ay, still my fragments wander, music-fraught,
> Sighs of the soul, mine once, mine now, and mine
> For ever! Crumbled arch, crushed aqueduct,
> Alive with tremors in the shaggy growth
> Of wild-wood, crevice-sown, that triumphs there
> Imparting exultation to the hills!   (ll. 834-39)

But such dreams have faded, and he is now "pedestalled on earth" which he finds is not air. The generous enthusiasms of the soul have been replaced by utilitarian and materialistic aims. Experience has taught him that it is imperative in an age like his to satisfy the bodily needs of men, and to abandon the vain attempt to enkindle them through lofty ideals. Consequently, he has given them cheap bread by means of free trade. While the cravings of the spirit may have free play in an after life, the fleshy wants of the body, such as food, health, and rest, are primary on this earth. Nature teaches that men are united by a satisfaction of their bodily necessities, but thrust apart by the divergence of their intellectual and spiritual qualities. Therefore the "Saviour of Society" claims that he has held the old order of things together by concentrating his efforts on the gratification of the needs of men's bodies rather than of their souls.

Into the midst of the sophistical pleas of Prince Hohenstiel-Schwangau, Browning suddenly interjects a sketch of an ideal career of Louis Napoleon as it might have been had he lived up to the best that was in him. Here the role of casuistry is played by "Sagacity," and the thinly disguised Napoleon is represented as turning a deaf ear to the prudential maxims of Sagacity and following the light of the ideal. By availing himself of a device almost unique in art, the poet paints two portraits, one of which is a criticism on the other. It is clear that Browning is temperamentally antipathetic to such a character as that of Napoleon III. Throughout his poetry he approves of bold, decisive courses of action; and his heroes are men and women who act in the light of ideal principles and honest convictions, scorning worldly consequences. For timorous, prudential, time-serving policies he has little patience or tolerance. The procrastinating lovers in *The Statue and the Bust,* who in order to preserve their social respectability abstain from translating their impulses and desires into action, even though such action would have been the fruition of an unlawful love, are unhesitatingly condemned.

> Only they see not God, I know,
> Nor all that chivalry of his,
> The soldier-saints who, row on row,
> Burn upward each to his point of bliss.[20]

While Browning gives his shadowy representative of Louis Napoleon a case and provides him with ingenious arguments, he leaves us in no doubt regarding the hollowness of Hohenstiel-Schwangau's casuistry.

Fifine at the Fair is the greatest of Browning's casuistic monologues. It is by far the most poetical of the four works I am considering, and it plumbs the intricacies of casuistry in masterly fashion. Though the importance of this poem would justify full exposition, I have already (in the preceding essay) indirectly dealt with many of the casuistic elements involved in this monologue. In order to avoid repetition, I shall limit myself to a brief outline of the central problems of casuistry in *Fifine,* referring the reader to the longer treatment of this theme.

The monologist in *Fifine* is the arch-voluptuary Don Juan. But his personality undergoes a sea-change in the poet's hands. Milton's Satan in *Paradise Regained* is not more unlike Satan in *Paradise Lost* than Browning's Don Juan is unlike the Don Juan of Molière and Byron. The indulgence of the passions of sense, which is the principal motif of the traditions and legends that cluster about Don Juan, is a mere point of departure in *Fifine.* The liaison with the gypsy is kept in the background. It is not the experience of sensuality, but the intellectual sophistry through which a libertine may strive to extenuate his philandering, that is the central theme of the poem.

The casuistry of Don Juan revolves about the problem of sex in relation to the bond of marriage. This particular setting of the monologue is deeply coloured by a personal element. In my preceding essay on *Fifine,* I have discussed fully the bearing of Browning's unfortunate proposal of marriage to Lady Ashburton and its bitter aftermath on the contents and spirit of the poem.

Numerous threads of casuistry are woven into the complex fabric of *Fifine.* The first and most important of these is intimately blended with the general setting of the monologue. Fifine and her gypsy tribe are Bohemians. They symbolize a roving, independent type of life. Their freedom is linked by Browning with those instincts of the human spirit which chafe at the barriers of the finite moulds and orthodox institutions of society. If the spirit cannot satisfy its aspirations through legitimate channels, it may seek to escape even at the risk of violating the conventional precepts of morality. This innate craving of the human spirit for liberty is the basis of Don Juan's sophistical argument that momentary defection from constancy to his wife Elvire is justified. Even though Don Juan has a peerless wife, there must be some enticement to gratify "expectancy's old fret and fume." The crystallization of any relationship, however precious, involves a limitation and confinement of the spirit. As Don Juan carefully explains, his fleeting passion for Fifine cannot be compared in worth or depth with his habitual love for Elvire. But his indulgence in a passing fancy for the gypsy banishes ennui, quickens "novel hopes and fears," and combats the tediousness and monotony of life.

A second favourite casuistic argument of Don Juan is equally inwrought in the fabric of *Fifine*. It is based on the contention that, since human life is a state of probation, experiment and practice with evil are necessary to the understanding and evaluation of good. The probationary character of life is vividly exemplified by the symbolism of the sea. Similes and metaphors linked with the sea are pervasive in *Fifine,* and many of them are of great poetic beauty. In my separate treatment of *Fifine*, I have pointed out how such imagery as the swimmer struggling with the treacherous sea; or the contrast between the safe voyage in a superior ship, symbolic of Elvire, and the daring voyage in a cockle-shell craft, symbolic of Fifine, are used to reinforce various sophistical arguments.

Despite the importance of the imagery of the sea, it is far from exhausting the store of simile and metaphor with which the poet endows Don Juan, as his supple brain plays about the crux of the interrelationships between good and evil, truth and falsehood, in a fallible and imperfect world. As an absolute idealist, Browning believes that the existence of evil and falsehood has to be reconciled with the divine plan for the universe. Therefore by penetrating beneath their appearances to reality they must be made to yield their ultimate contribution to goodness and truth. By giving a casuistic twist to this conviction, Don Juan argues that a man must be actually involved in the toils of evil and falsehood before he can appreciate what goodness and truth are. Through intercourse with Fifine he professes to show that elemental flame may spring from straw and rottenness as well as from gums and spice. His temporary commerce with one of the baser forms of evil will finally teach him

> That, through the outward sign, the inward grace allures,
> And sparks from heaven transpierce earth's coarsest covertures,—
> All by demonstrating the value of Fifine!
> (xxviii. 336-38)

Finally, Don Juan stresses the illusory character of life, and from this conjures a score of casuistic arguments. Fifine and her tribe are actors, but their frank acknowledgment that they play parts has the grace of sincerity. The mimicry of the circus performers is "honest cheating." The rest of humanity are actors on the stage of life, but they do not openly avow their roles. They deal with illusion and falsehood, yet pretend that they are in direct contact with truth. At this juncture, Don Juan's illustrations drawn from the practice and love of miming become comprehensive in their range. The Pornic Fair widens into the Venetian carnival and that, in turn, into the pageantry and masquerade of life. While listening to the music of Schumann's "Carnival," Don Juan imagines himself ensconced on a pinnacle in the vicinity of St. Mark's Church, whence he gazes on the masqueraders far below in the streets of Venice. The scene as viewed from this dizzy height appears monstrous and incomprehensible. But when he descends from his "pinnacled pre-eminence" to the streets and mingles with the revellers, incongruities diminish, and nearness to the masks enables him to discern some traces of the elemental humanity beneath each of them. This imagery is used to emphasize the distinction between an absolute point of view which might be that of the spirit world, and a relative point of view which must be that of our mortal condition. In this earthly sphere, men can only struggle towards truth by traffic with the evil and falsehood environing them, till they learn to pierce through such semblances to essential reality. In the long run "evil proves good, wrong right, and 'howling' childishness." Consequently, Don Juan maintains, we should accept worldly standards, come to close grips with life, and not criticize it from the standpoint of an abstract idealism.

> ... I found
> Somehow the proper goal for wisdom was the
>   ground
> And not the sky,—so, slid sagaciously betimes
> Down heaven's baluster-rope, to reach the mob of
>   mimes
> And mummers. ...   (CVIII. 1866-70)

The casuistry of *Fifine at the Fair* is so protean that it is difficult to determine at what points Browning is personally entangled in its sophistry and at what points he is above it. In no other monologue is there such a range of casuistic argument. The vistas of *Fifine* are as shifting and kaleidoscopic as the sea-scapes introduced by way of illustration. The protagonists of the poem are often symbolic. As I have written above,[21] frequently in *Fifine*, the gypsy ceases to be a material woman and becomes representative of life itself, with its siren arts, confusing the soul through the dazzling fence of sophistry pointed with truth and beguiling it into disloyalty to its own past. Yet in *Fifine at the Fair,* as elsewhere in the casuistic monologues I have been dealing with, clearly the poet is himself ensnared by his intellectual agnosticism. The general picture of life drawn in *Fifine* is not merely that of a sphere of being in which man's knowledge is relative and imperfect, but of a state in which truth is hidden from the mind, and basic elements of falsehood and illusion are engrained in the very faculty of human reason. What men deem to be the gold of knowledge is in reality but lacquered ignorance. It is impossible to escape the conviction, if such a point of view be accepted, that the mind of man must ever be haunted by casuistry, since it works with deceptive materials and its conclusions always fall wide of the truth.

It is noteworthy that in *Fifine at the Fair*, as in *Bishop Blougram's Apology* and other monologues, Browning invokes the testimony and assurance of love in order to rout casuistry. The defeat of knowledge forces him to turn elsewhere for an explanation of life's mystery. The heart is appealed to in order to controvert the evidence of the head.

> . . . knowledge means
> Ever-renewed assurance by defeat
> That victory is somehow still to reach,
> But love is victory, the prize itself:
> Love—trust to![22]

In the Epilogue to *Fifine*, the final apostrophe to love has a peculiar depth and poignancy. It is linked with Browning's passionate conviction of the supremacy of love as revealed in the enduring tie between his own spirit and that of his wife. The waters of this monologue, we must recall, have been troubled by the poet's brooding on what he regarded as a momentary lack of constancy to the memory of Mrs. Browning. But in the Epilogue, he leaves the dark house of sophistry where he has been lingering, and closes the most intellectually sceptical of his poems with the triumphant ejaculation put on the lips of his wife: " 'I end with—Love is all and Death is nought!' quoth She."

The general relation of Browning's philosophy of life to his casuistic monologues may now be summed up. The poet on his intellectual side—particularly in his later verse—has much of the temper of a casuist. This is due, as has been stressed, to his lack of faith in reason. Such an attitude is not purely individualistic. A distrust of knowledge is reflected in the writings of many of the great Victorian men of letters, and might almost be said to be inwrought in the spirit of the age. Yet on his emotional side, Browning is untroubled by the sophistries that beset the intellect. The intuitions of the heart are undimmed by the mists of falsehood and illusion darkening the mind. Hence love is the solvent of casuistry, since its perception of truth and contact with reality are instinctive and unerring.

9

Browning's Conception of Love as Represented in "Paracelsus"

THE IMPORTANCE of *Paracelsus*, as containing an initial but surprisingly mature statement of Browning's outlook on life, and a significant expression of his artistic interests and intellectual convictions, has been generally recognized. Though the poem was composed in his twenty-third year, Browning may be said to have established definitely in it the basis of his reflective thought on the fundamental problems of humanity. Few writers have oriented themselves so completely at such a youthful age. While further elaborated in his later works and given a different setting, practically all of the leading and controlling ideas of his poetry are present in *Paracelsus*. As Stopford Brooke states it: "When *Paracelsus* was published in 1835 Browning had fully thought out, and in that poem fully expressed, his theory of God's relation to man, and of man's relation to the universe around him, to his fellow men, and to the world beyond."[1]

In particular, *Paracelsus* is noteworthy through its emphasis of what has been called "the richest vein of pure ore in Browning's poetry," namely, the poet's view of the nature and function of love.

The primary truth or essential thought underlying Browning's presentation of the career of the Renaissance scholar and physician is indicated so plainly, that it is impossible to mistake it. Through his exclusive devotion to the pursuit of knowledge, Paracelsus leaves love out of his scheme of life. On account of this tragic error he is brought to the verge of ruin, despite the splendid endowment and magnificent aspiration of his genius. Two principles, knowledge and love, are constantly contrasted throughout the course of the poem, and the ambitions of two individuals, Paracelsus and the poet Aprile, represent the quest of these great ideals. But while the main thesis of the poem, that love must be added to knowledge in order to secure a harmonious development of life and attain its true goal, is sufficiently plain, the precise significance and full import of Browning's conception of love, as set forth in *Paracelsus*, are by no means so self-evident.

For instance, it has been generally assumed that there is a single and unified view of love running through *Paracelsus* from start to finish. Is this the case? Is Aprile, with his ardent longings and impassioned visions, an adequate embodiment of Browning's notion of love as expressed throughout the entire poem? More particularly, is the idea of love, as expounded in the speech of the dying Paracelsus in the fifth canto, identical with that put on the lips of Aprile in the second canto? It is, of course, obvious that Aprile is introduced as a foil to Paracelsus, and that in a general way he typifies the votary of love, as Paracelsus the seeker after knowledge. Moreover, so far as the two characters and their ambitions illustrate the pursuit of love and knowledge, each is the complement of the other, and the fusion of their aims would lead to a true understanding and adequate fruition of life.

> *Paracelsus.* Love me henceforth, Aprile, while I learn
> To love; . . . .
> I too have sought to KNOW as thou to LOVE—
> Excluding love as thou refusedst knowledge.
> Still thou hast beauty and I, power.
>
> Die not, Aprile! We must never part.
> Are we not halves of one dissevered world,
> Whom this strange chance unites once more? Part?
>   never!
> Till thou the lover, know; and I, the knower,
> Love—until both are saved.   (II. 618-26; 633-37)

Yet, while the force of these passages is admitted, is it possible to show that the contrast between Paracelsus and Aprile is consistently maintained in the details of the poem? Is the fundamental error of Paracelsus due to a failure to grasp the particular conception of love represented by Aprile and his aspirations? Is Aprile's own downfall to be attributed primarily to a neglect of knowledge, or is it the result of an imperfect comprehension of the full truth concerning the nature of love?

There has been a divergence of critical opinion regarding the emphasis to be placed on the part played by Aprile in the poem, and its contribution to the final "attainment" of Paracelsus.

Edward Dowden, who thinks that the whole scene in the house of the Greek conjurer at Constantinople "leaves a painful impression of unreality," writes as follows of Aprile: "The lover here is typified in the artist; but the artist may be as haughtily isolated from true human love as the man of science, and the fellowship with his kind which Paracelsus needs can be poorly learnt from such a distracted creature as Aprile."[2]

One of the most interesting and able attempts to show that Browning's delineation of Aprile embodies the central teaching of the poem regarding the nature of love, was made by Josiah Royce, in an article entitled "The Problem of Paracelsus," published in *The Boston Browning Society Papers*.[3] I shall quote from Professor Royce's article the more freely, in that I differ from his main conclusion, that the key to the problem of Paracelsus is to be found in the second canto of the work. It is, I shall try to show, by comparing the second with the fifth canto, and by recognizing that there is a complex rather than a uniform representation of love involved, that the apparent inconsistencies of the poem can be explained.

After stating that the whole tragedy of *Paracelsus* turns explicitly upon the poetic antithesis between "loving" and "knowing," Royce points out that Browning meant much more by this than "the comparatively shallow and abstract platitude that the intellect without the affections is a vain guide in life." The words love and knowledge, he says, are used, both in *Paracelsus* and in

Paracelsus

the poet's later works, "in a pregnant sense." In an analysis of the character of Paracelsus, which lays great stress on Browning's fidelity to his sources, Professor Royce classifies the hero of the poem as an "empirical mystic," who, in order to confirm his higher intuitions, strives to find in the outward facts of the physical world a revelation of the ultimate meaning of the universe. Aprile, on the other hand, is a poet, who seeks in the inner shrine of the heart an unfolding of God's purposes and the clue to the mystery of life. It is the divergence in the types represented by the two men and, above all, the difference between the places where they have sought for a manifestation of the divine order, that Royce regards as disclosing the sense in which Browning uses the terms "knowing" and "loving." "The antithesis between 'knowledge,' as the occultist conceives it, and 'love,' as the poet views it, is the contrast between looking in the world of outer nature for a symbolic revelation of God, and looking in the moral world, the world of ideals, of volition, of freedom, of hope and of human passion, for the direct incarnation of the loving and the living God."

In support of this view Professor Royce refers to the fact that in *Reverie* and other poems, Browning makes a similar distinction between knowledge and love. "Mind in survey of things," according to Browning, discerns in the external order of the universe the existence of "power," but no clear evidence of a moral purpose at work. But in the inner world and in those human relationships where the intuitions of the heart have free scope, the goodness and providence of God are apprehended as a manifestation of love by the seeker after love.

That Browning does frequently link the perception of power in the outward order of the universe with knowledge, and seek for a revelation of the moral qualities of God in love as a divinely inspired virtue animating the soul of man, is indisputable. Nor can it be doubted that this particular antithesis between the spheres of knowledge and love enters as an element into *Paracelsus*. It is, however, I believe, strictly a subordinate element. It does not, for one thing, explain the failure of Aprile. Nor does it take into account the striking differences between the conception of love in the second and the fifth divisions of the poem. Throughout his article, Professor Royce, as it seems to me, has overstressed Browning's faithfulness to the exact type of character represented by the historical Paracelsus. On the other hand he has not given sufficient weight to more immediate sources of inspiration connected with the poet's relationship to the Romantic Movement, and the artistic and ethical qualities of his genius.[4]

An investigation of any of the leading ideas of *Paracelsus* must begin with the recognition of the essential connection in theme and spirit between *Pauline, Paracelsus,* and *Sordello,* published in the years, 1833, 1835, and 1840, respectively. All of these poems are occupied with character, as exhibited in thought, feeling, and motive, rather than in outward event. Though there is a certain gradation in the degree of their subjectivity, historical environment and circumstance are everywhere subordinate in these three works to "the incidents in the development of a soul," depicted as they arise within the inner world of man's spiritual being. Moreover, as has been noted by various critics, the characters delineated in this group of poems are of the same general type. They are all endowed with the infinite aspiration and towering ambitions of genius, and their problem lies in the difficulty of reconciling the inexhaustible demands and cravings of the spirit with the finite conditions and limitations of life. The dramatic tension of this conflict is portrayed in *Pauline, Paracelsus,* and *Sordello* as giving rise to successive experiences of aspiration and failure followed by renewed striving. Through the fluctuation of these spiritual vicissitudes the deeper meaning of life is gradually discerned. Poetry, to quote Browning to Ruskin once more, is the problem of "putting the infinite within the finite."[5] It is this problem, in the sphere of life, that is the crux of the three studies in the development of a soul, which constitute the most significant work of Browning in the early stages of his poetical career. In keeping with the genius of a poet who has taken

> for a worthier stage the soul itself,
> Its shifting fancies and celestial lights,

Paracelsus

the approach to the study of *Paracelsus* must be made from within rather than from without. That is to say, the interpretation of the dominant ideas of the poem must be sought through their connection with Browning's own individuality and the artistic and ethical influences formative of the spirit of his poetry, rather than in an ostensible machinery of historical event.

There are two characteristic attitudes of Browning's mind, or, perhaps it might be said, dispositions of his spirit, which are constantly reflected in his poems.

A deep conviction of the infinite potentialities of the soul, its transcendental origin and immortal destiny, is a primary element in his self-consciousness. Linked with this is a belief that the purpose of life is a continuous striving to surpass the limitations imposed upon the soul by the finite conditions of time and sense.

> . . . life is—to wake not sleep,
> Rise and not rest, but press
> From earth's level where blindly creep
> Things perfected, more or less,
> To the heaven's height, far and steep. . . .[6]

Browning's perception of the inexhaustible capacities of the soul has its source in part in the prodigality of his own intellectual and spiritual powers. It also has its roots in the romantic traditions and enthusiasms he inherited from that group of English poets whose works are aglow with the hopes and impulses of the revolutionary epoch. Browning, as has been said, "carried with him something of Byron's energy, Keats's artistic skill, Shelley's ideal passion, and Wordsworth's transcendentalism, into the orderly, scientific age which succeeded the romantic period."[7] In particular, the torch of Browning's poetic inspiration was kindled from the pure and luminous flame of Shelley's ethereal genius. In the soaring aspiration and spiritual ardour of Shelley, his thirst for the infinite, his quest of an ideal beauty, his ceaseless endeavour to transcend the finite barriers of life, are winged seeds of thought and emotion which bear fruit in the imagination of Browning.

But while the mood of romantic aspiration and an intense consciousness of the boundlessness of personality enter vitally into Browning's poetry, there is a complementary truth which has an important place in his view of life and is an equally significant element in his thought. The world to Browning, as to Keats, is "the vale of Soul-making," and, in this moulding of souls, the finite as well as the infinite has a positive part to play. The limitations imposed on man by the imperfect conditions of his earthly existence are a school of discipline intended to serve the end of spiritual growth. To refuse to use the instrumentalities of life, faulty though these may be, and to disregard its laws, is to scorn the means through which the spirit is nourished and enabled to elicit the divinity that lies within it. To attempt to overleap the finite or to neglect the claims of the material and temporal realities of life, is to evade life's test and to fall into the error of spiritual abstraction. While placing the goal beyond all limited accomplishment, the soul must learn to make a fruitful use of the means and possibilities of man's earthly lot. Thus, while, from one point of view, life must be an unceasing aspiration in pursuit of an infinite ideal, from another it must be a continuous stooping to a world of weakness and finitude.

A perception of this latter truth, with its corresponding attitude of a wise acceptance of the working conditions and restricted powers of life, is the counterpoise to that mood of passionate aspiration and unfettered idealism, spurning the clogs of sense, wherein Browning is confessedly the inheritor of the mantle of Shelley and his fellow romanticists. The sources of the second disposition of Browning's thought and feeling, where he parts company with Shelley, lie, in a measure, in certain robust elements, both physical and psychical, in his nature. Bodily vigour, with its accompaniment of a rich sensory organization, made him appreciate "the value and significance of flesh" and gave him a firm grip on the concrete and tangible, as opposed to anything partaking of the character of spiritual asceticism. This physical tendency is reinforced by intellectual and emotional qualities. In Browning's minute observation, his delight in subtle analysis, his

Paracelsus

keen perception of the manifoldness of life and the distinctness of its various forms, he manifests, even in the service of ideal ends, an individualizing temperament akin in method if not in aim to the critical and scientific realism of his day.

But Browning's recognition of the necessity of stooping to the finite must also be attributed in large part to his religious consciousness, particularly his appreciation of the fundamental truth revealed through the Christian doctrine of the Incarnation. This is especially apparent in the way he stresses the natural and human, as well as the mystic and divine, aspect of personality.

The two dispositions of Browning's inner being prevent him from attempting to cut the Gordian knot of life's mystery by ignoring its complexity, or by doing violence to the integrity of personality by overlooking one of its dual elements. The incidents in the development of a soul, with which he is essentially concerned, centre about the paradox that man is a being in whom the claims and purposes of the finite and infinite, body and soul, flesh and spirit, time and eternity, meet and must each receive due recognition.

While the interplay between the two habitual attitudes of Browning's spirit may be traced throughout his poetry, it is especially pivotal in *Pauline, Paracelsus,* and *Sordello.* The heroes of these poems are unmistakably of the romantic type. They are all characterized by a restless and eager self-consciousness, unsatisfied longings, infinite desires, an unmeasured hunger for perfection, that impel them to press on beyond the limits of the finite. In their indomitable aspiration, lofty idealism, and unclouded vision of absolute spiritual values, they represent the incarnation of romantic traditions and impulses, which are an elemental part of Browning's own genius.

But Browning, like Goethe, was able from the standpoint of a dual consciousness to overlook and diagnose the perils of romanticism, even while it struck responsive chords within his being. Throughout *Pauline, Paracelsus,* and *Sordello,* he has probed with an unsparing hand the cancer of romantic egoism, with its passionate, unbridled impulses of limitless self-assertion, its scorn of all relative accomplishment, and its tendency to seek refuge in vague abstractions. It is a disdain for the finite, a refusal to stoop to the necessary conditions of life, a negation of the actual rather than the ideal side of man's nature, that constitute the fallacy and account for the imperfect insight of these gifted though tempest-tossed men of genius—children of the heaven-storming Titans—whom Browning has so vividly depicted in his earlier poetry.

Such being the general setting of *Paracelsus,* I proceed to a discussion of Browning's conception of love, as set forth in the second and fifth divisions of the poem.

In the second canto of *Paracelsus,* love is revealed as embodied in the person and ideals of the poet Aprile. Here, as Professor Royce has pointed out, the fact that Aprile has the artist's vision of beauty and seeks a manifestation of the divine import of life in the world of human emotions, enters into Browning's thought in regarding him as an embodiment of the principle of love. Yet Aprile is not merely a poet, but a particular type of poet, and represents very definite impulses and sympathies in Browning's nature. In no part of *Paracelsus* is Browning's kinship with that early nineteenth-century group of English romanticists, of whom Shelley may be considered an outstanding representative, more strikingly apparent than in the episode of the meeting between the Renaissance scholar and the Italian artist in the house of the Greek conjurer at Constantinople. The very creation of Aprile is undoubtedly to be traced to the influence of the personality and writings of Shelley upon Browning. Just to what extent the latter was indebted to certain elements in *Prometheus Unbound, Alastor,* and *Adonais* for the suggestion of the character of Aprile must be a matter of conjecture. But it seems unmistakable that he had Shelley vividly in mind in his portraiture of the spiritually impassioned seeker after absolute beauty, "who would love infinitely and be loved." The limitless aim, the eager craving after emotional experience, the exquisite sensitiveness, the single-hearted impulsiveness of Shelley, are reflected in Aprile. Shelley, like Aprile, eagle-winged in aspiration, had been dazzled by a vision of the infinite, and his lofty conception of love remaining

Paracelsus

merely nebulous, too often tended to dissipate itself in dreams and abstractions.

The genesis of Aprile is indicative of the type of love embodied in his person and utterances throughout the second canto of *Paracelsus*. It is, as a matter of fact, one form of that ideal of romantic love for the notion of which Browning is primarily indebted to Shelley and to Shelley's spiritual master, Plato. It was inevitable, in view of his literary traditions, that Browning should be profoundly affected by that great conception of love, which has played so important a role in English poetry. In *Pauline,* Browning's first printed work, Shelley and Plato are apostrophized as the teachers and seers who have moulded the thought and captivated the imagination of the youthful hero. The influence of Plato's view of love, as enunciated in the *Symposium* and *Phaedrus,* might be illustrated from a large number of Browning's poems. Such a love lyric as *Cristina* is based on a belief in reminiscence and the transcendental nature of love, ideas steeped in Platonic mysticism. Again, in *Easter-Day,* the ascension of the soul above the sphere of finite existence to a divine love is in harmony with Plato's notion of man's quest of a perfect and eternal archetypal loveliness, but dimly foreshadowed in the perishable forms of earth. This view of love is in keeping with the first of the two characteristic dispositions of Browning's mind and heart previously referred to, the spirit of romantic ardour and illimitable aspiration, which is so significant an element in his genius.

The fine opening passages of the second canto of *Paracelsus,* where Aprile reveals his "mighty aim" and "full desire," portray love in the loftiest vein of romantic idealism. The love of the poet Aprile might be defined in the very words of Plato as "the desire of generation and production in the beautiful." Aprile would woo the loveliness of life through the medium of the creative genius of the artist. He yearns to reveal and transfigure the beauty of the natural world by reclothing it in the glorious forms of art. Thus his works would remain in the sight of all men, as pledges of the love which existed between himself and the beautiful. But, desiring to grasp the whole sum and absolute essence of beauty, he cannot rest content with any finite manifestation of it. From art to art Aprile's vision of love leads him on in ecstatic contemplation of a bewildering wealth of beautiful forms.[8]

The way in which the love of Aprile rises from the material to the spiritual, and from the finite to the infinite, is illustrated by the order in which the various artistic forms become the object of his desire. He begins with sculpture, the most essentially imitative of the arts, the art that clings closest to earth. From sculpture he passes to painting, art in two dimensions, the more imaginative and less material of the spatial arts. But, having reached this stage, Aprile would "throw down the pencil as the chisel" and ascend to the more spiritual region of poetry. Finally, "to perfect and consummate all," he rises above poetry to the sphere of music, the most subtle and least corporeal of the arts. Music to Browning is always a symbol of the infinite, the art in which, above every other, the soul may aspire towards the spiritual, eternal, and divine. Thus the hero in *Pauline* speaks of

> music which is earnest of a heaven
> Seeing we know emotions strange by it,
> Not else to be revealed, ...   (ll. 365-67)

So, in *Paracelsus,* "even as a luminous haze links star to star," Aprile would

> supply all chasms with music, breathing
> Mysterious motions of the soul, no way
> To be defined save in strange melodies.   (II. 477-79)

Yet love cannot rest even here. The sum of earthly beauty is unable to satisfy it. In God alone does the divine craving of love, the deepest impulse of the soul, find the adequate object of its desire. So Aprile, having striven, in fancy, to embrace the whole universe of finite beauty through the mediation of all the arts, longs at length to pass beyond this, and to dwell in mystic intercommunion with the perfect love of God.

> I have gone through
> The loveliness of life; create for me

Paracelsus

>   If not for men, or take me to thyself,
>   Eternal, infinite love!   (II. 484-87)

Few poets have represented love in its romantic and transcendental aspect so superbly as Browning. His perception of the insurgent vehemence and boundless vision of love, as a supreme spiritual principle, blends in repeatedly with his conviction of the ceaseless progress towards an infinite ideal. The poet's treatment of love from this point of view has received general recognition. "Of all the passions," writes Professor Alexander, in his summary of Browning's philosophy, "none so reaches out towards the infinite as love. For Browning, then, as well as Plato, love both symbolizes and arouses that thirst for the infinite which is the primary need of humanity. There is something mystic and transcendental in the power of love."[9] In a similar vein Professor Herford says: "Browning as the poet of Love is thus the last, and assuredly not the least, in the line which handed on the torch of Plato. The author of the *Phaedrus* saw in the ecstasy of Love one of the avenues to the knowledge of the things that indeed are. To Dante the supreme realities were mirrored in the eyes of Beatrice. For Shelley Love was interwoven through all the mazes of Being; it was the source of the strength by which man masters his gods. To all these masters of idealism Browning's vision of Love owed something of its intensity and of its range."[10]

But while the portrayal of love as a mystic, transcendental, and romantic passion, is very frequent in Browning, does it embrace his complete view of the nature of love, particularly as set forth in the poem of *Paracelsus*? Through the self-revelation of Aprile, Paracelsus realizes his fatal mistake in leaving love out of his scheme of life:

>   I learned my own deep error; love's undoing
>   Taught me the worth of love in man's estate, ...
>   (V. 854-55)

Is it, however, a failure to grasp the specific conception or aspect of love represented in the aims of Aprile, that is the fundamental error of Paracelsus?

A comparative study of Browning's delineation of Paracelsus and Aprile forces home the conviction that, despite the distinction between the objects of their pursuit, the resemblances between them are more basic than the differences. Though the one seeks knowledge, the other love as revealed through beauty, both are idealists and transcendentalists, with a thirst for the absolute, an unquenchable desire to surpass all finite limitations, a vision of perfection which forbids them to rest content with any finite attainment. As Paracelsus aspires and fails, so Aprile aspires and fails. To preserve the formal identification of the characters with the principles of knowledge and love, Browning, in places, attributes the failure of Aprile to a neglect of knowledge. But, in reality, Aprile's example is a warning to Paracelsus because there is an underlying similarity in their aspiration and failure. In common with Paracelsus and Sordello, Aprile is perplexed and baffled through his incapacity to "fit to the finite his infinity." Wishing to possess all, "to thrust in time eternity's concern," he clings to the bare form of the infinite and loses himself in dreams and abstractions. If he strives to break the spell that binds him and to single out one individual shape of loveliness, "and to give that one entire in beauty to the world," immediately other shapes come crowding thick upon him, and his will is paralysed.

> And did not mist-like influences, thick films,
> Faint memories of the rest that charmed so long
> Thine eyes, float fast, confuse thee, bear thee off,
> As whirling snow-drifts blind a man who treads
> A mountain ridge, with guiding spear, through
>   storm?   (II. 602-6)

An unwillingness to subdue his nature to the conditions imposed by life, or to work out his destiny in and through the necessarily imperfect circumstances of his earthly lot, is recognized by Aprile as the source of his downfall.

> Knowing ourselves, our world, our task so great,
> Our time so brief, 't is clear if we refuse
> The means so limited, the tools so rude

> To execute our purpose, life will fleet,
> And we shall fade, and leave our task undone.
> (II. 497-501)

The failure of Aprile is, in itself, an indication that Browning has not set forth his full conception of the nature of love in the second canto of *Paracelsus*. Apart from teaching the general worth of love, it is difficult to see how such a type of love, as is represented in the person and quest of Aprile, could have proved the salvation of the Renaissance hero of Browning's poem. The errors of Paracelsus are those of a transcendentalist and idealist blinded by a vision of the absolute, refusing to stoop to the weakness and finitude of life. Yet it is precisely the romantic and transcendental characteristics of love, regarded as the unceasing pursuit of an ideal of perfection and an infinite spiritual aspiration, that are embodied in the poetical imaginings of Aprile. Such a portrayal of love is in keeping with the romantic origins of the figure of Aprile, and an expression of that side of Browning's genius which is in sympathy with the impulses and traditions of romanticism. Since, however, it presents an aspect of love that is akin in spirit to the uncompromising idealism, passion for the absolute, and soaring aspiration of Paracelsus, it cannot, except by a *tour de force*, be regarded as supplying a corrective for the error of that character. While Browning makes a general distinction between knowledge as the aim of the Renaissance scholar, and love as the artist's passion for the beautiful, the contrast between Paracelsus and Aprile is not consistently maintained in the details of the two opening cantos of the poem. It is hard to escape the conviction that Aprile fails, not from a lack of knowledge, but because he, like Paracelsus, has spurned the finite conditions of life.

It seems, therefore, unmistakable that Browning's portrayal of love in the spirit of romantic idealism, in the second part of *Paracelsus,* involves the poem up to this point in a measure of self-contradiction. If the presentation of love throughout *Paracelsus* must be considered as all of one piece, the difficulty extends itself to the entire work.

It is, however, not in the second, but in the fifth canto of the poem that Paracelsus realizes most fully the causes of his failure, and obtains his deepest insight into the nature of love. A comparison between Browning's treatment of love in these two parts of the narrative is illuminating. In the last words of the dying Paracelsus, love is conceived of in a way that cannot be regarded as a mere reiteration or enforcement of that romantic ideal of love embodied in the impassioned reveries of Aprile.

The fact is that Browning's representation of love, both in *Paracelsus* and in other poems, is a complex one. As Browning portrays love with all the energies of his being, and the full resources of his genius, it is inevitable that love should be in his poetry a highly organized and manifold concept. In particular, it reflects the two fundamental dispositions of his spirit already alluded to, and the artistic and religious influences entering into his life and work. The counterpart of Browning's mood of aspiration, as has been noted, is his recognition of the necessity of stooping, in the spirit of humility and self-sacrifice, to the finite limitations of life. The sources of this disposition lie largely in Browning's profound appreciation of the central truths of the Christian faith.

Consequently, Browning has given in the final canto of *Paracelsus,* not a romantic or Platonic, but a Christian representation of love.

Such a delineation of love is indeed foreshadowed in Aprile's confession of his failure at the close of the second part of the poem. Could he live again, he tells Paracelsus, he would not spurn the finite or reject the imperfect means at his disposal. Rather he would strive to give some partial representation of beauty to the world, even though this were but a fragment or a trifle, "one strain of all the psalm of the angels," as a pledge of the infinitude of beauty beyond. While still inspired by a consciousness of an ultimate goal of perfection, he would be content to achieve on earth a portion of that infinite good, which should be a prophecy of the whole. Aprile's final desire is to unite himself and his art with common life, and to set it forth in

Paracelsus

beauteous hues. Such a willingness to work within the bounds allotted to humanity, he perceives, is not inconsistent with the highest aspiration. To stoop to the weakness and lowliness of his brother men would not, as he mistakenly had thought, involve a sacrifice of his divine calling. His would be the self-same spirit, but "clothed in humbler guise":

> As one spring wind unbinds the mountain snow
> And comforts violets in their hermitage.   (II. 570-71)

That Browning is here representing Aprile's error as due to a failure to grasp that conception of love which may be regarded as pre-eminently Christian, is made explicit in lines added by the poet, in one edition of *Paracelsus,* at the end of Aprile's dying speech:

> Man's weakness is his glory—for the strength
> Which raises him to heaven and near God's self
> Came spite of it. God's strength his glory is,
> For thence came with our weakness sympathy,
> Which brought God down to earth, a man like us!

The final attainment of Paracelsus, as portrayed in the fifth canto, is an expansion of the idea of love set forth in these lines. It is a description of love which, without direct Christian reference, is permeated by Browning's religious sympathies. Love is here, not a romantic passion for a transcendent ideal of absolute beauty, but a divine condescension to human imperfection, and a tender compassion for mortal frailty. Love stoops to conquer, triumphs in the midst of conflict and suffering, and wins its way from weakness to strength. Such a love breaks down the overweening pride of Paracelsus, his self-sufficient individualism, his scorn of the limitations of life, and unites him in bonds of sympathy with his brother men. In the light of this vision of love he realizes the cause of his failure:

> In my own heart love had not been made wise
> To trace love's faint beginnings in mankind,
> To know even hate is but a mask of love's,
> To see a good in evil, and a hope

> In ill-success; to sympathize, be proud
> Of their half-reasons, faint aspirings, dim
> Struggles for truth, their poorest fallacies,
> Their prejudice and fears and cares and doubts;
> All with a touch of nobleness, despite
> Their error, upward tending all though weak,
> Like plants in mines which never saw the sun,
> But dream of him, and guess where he may be,
> And do their best to climb and get to him.
> All this I knew not, and I failed. (V. 872-85)

Love teaches Paracelsus no longer to despise the past, or to close his eyes to God's plan of a gradual evolution and progressive unfolding of the divine purpose from age to age. In his previous disregard of these truths Paracelsus may be said to prefigure that lack of sympathy with human weakness, and that abstract idealism, so typical of the revolutionary and romantic epoch at the dawn of the nineteenth century.

> I saw no use in the past: only a scene
> Of degradation, ugliness and tears,
> The record of disgraces best forgotten,
> A sullen page in human chronicles
> Fit to erase. I saw no cause why man
> Should not stand all-sufficient even now, . . .
> I would have had one day, one moment's space,
> Change man's condition, push each slumbering claim
> Of mastery o'er the elemental world
> At once to full maturity. (V. 812-24)

Through his deeper insight into the character of love, Paracelsus discerns it as an immanent principle dwelling even in "life's minute beginnings," and incarnating itself at every stage of the evolutionary process. Viewed in the light of love, the struggles and imperfections of the past are fraught with value and significance and consecrated by human endeavour.

> Not so, dear child
> Of after-days, wilt thou reject the past . . .

Paracelsus

>   nor yet on thee
> Shall burst the future, as successive zones
> Of several wonder open on some spirit
> Flying secure and glad from heaven to heaven:
> But thou shalt painfully attain to joy,
> While hope and fear and love shall keep thee
>   man. (V. 826-37)

Thus the poem of *Paracelsus* closes, not with Aprile's resplendent vision of "eternal, infinite love," but rather with love in its humblest manifestations, "human at the red-ripe of the heart."

> . . . love—not serenely pure
> But strong from weakness, like a chance-sown plant
> Which, cast on stubborn soil, puts forth changed
>   buds
> And softer stains, unknown in happier climes;
> Love which endures and doubts and is oppressed
> And cherished, suffering much and much sustained,
> And blind, oft-failing, yet believing love,
> A half-enlightened, often-chequered trust:—. . . .
>   (V. 698-705)

> . . . Love still too straitened in his present means,
> And earnest for new power to set love free. (V. 859-60)

To sum up the conclusions derived from a study of Browning's *Paracelsus*, it seems evident that a complex rather than a single and uniform conception of love is involved.

In the second canto, love, typified in the person and ambitions of the artist Aprile, is depicted in its romantic aspect, as a struggle to reach heights unattainable on earth. Love is revealed as a principle of infinite aspiration involving the pursuit of an ideal of perfection. Such a portrayal of love is in harmony with the Shelleyan origins of the character of Aprile, and is a reflection of Browning's own romantic traditions and sympathies. It is also in keeping with Browning's innate transcendentalism, and his perception of the inexhaustible energies and unlimited scope of personality.

While the conception of love in the fifth division of *Paracelsus* is complementary rather than antithetical to that set forth in the second canto, it cannot be regarded as of identical character. In the words of the dying Paracelsus, love is represented from another point of view, as a principle of self-surrender and a strength that stoops to weakness. Love is conceived of here, not as a transcendent aspiration, but as a condescension of the divine to the human, and a wise acceptance of the limited means and opportunities of life. As opposed to the emptiness of an abstract intellectual ideal, love binds together the claims of the spirit and the flesh and "shows a heart within blood-tinctured, of a veined humanity."[11] Such a portrayal of love is an expression of the spirit of the Christian *Magnificat,* rather than of romantic or Platonic idealism, and it manifestly has its sources in Browning's deep religious convictions, above all his appreciation of the supreme truth revealed through the doctrine of the Incarnation.

Since love is the richest and most highly organized concept in Browning's poetry, the twofold strand in his delineation of it is, as I have stated, a natural consequence of the two fundamental attitudes of his soul: those of aspiration towards the ideal and of stooping to the real. These provinces of Browning's feeling are in large part rooted in the two great moulding influences that enter into his life and poetry, his artistic inheritance of the traditions of English romanticism, and his religious legacy of the spirit and tenets of evangelical Christianity.

While the romantic elements in Browning's treatment of love have been very generally recognized, a like stress has not been placed on that aspect of his conception of love which is represented in the fifth part of *Paracelsus.* Yet it might readily be shown, by reference to a large number of Browning's poems, that his delineation of love from this point of view is as vital and characteristic as his portrayal of it in the spirit of romantic idealism. To select a single example among many, the beautiful love lyrics placed at the end of each parable in *Ferishtah's Fancies* all centre about love as manifested in its pre-eminently human aspect. It is the thought of love stooping to finite imperfection, "not serenely pure, but strong from weakness," love refusing to spurn the body or despise the world in the interests of an ascetic ideal of spirituality, that forms the chorded refrain of these exquisite snatches.

In particular this conception of love is intimately related with Browning's perception of its supreme revelation in the person of Christ. "Such ever was love's way: to rise, it stoops," is the characterization of the nature of love Browning places on the lips of St. John in *A Death in the Desert*; and in *Saul* and *An Epistle of Karshish*, the Incarnation is represented as the Divine Love that for man's sake became poor and of low estate.

>'T is the weakness in strength, that I cry for!
>   my flesh, that I seek
>In the Godhead![12]

>The very God! think, Abib; dost thou think?
>So, the All-Great, were the All-Loving too—
>So, through the thunder comes a human voice
>Saying, "O heart I made, a heart beats here!
>Face, my hands fashioned, see it in myself!
>Thou hast no power nor mayst conceive of mine,
>But love I gave thee, with myself to love,
>And thou must love me who have died for thee!"[13]

10

The Forgeries of Thomas J. Wise and Their Aftermath

THE RECORDS of literary forgery, however unsavoury, will always have a certain historical and psychological interest. The misdoings of Ireland, Collier, Chatterton, and De Gibler reveal a perverse ingenuity and a mental sophistry which in their exhibition have somewhat of the lure of detective stories and may serve "to point a moral, or adorn a tale." From the point of view of the eminence of the works concerned, the Shakespeare fabrications of Ireland and Collier are the most notorious in English literature. Yet if extent of fraudulence, long continuance in its crooked practices, subtlety and audacity of procedure are taken into the reckoning, our own time has produced a forger who surpasses all his predecessors. It is this man's deceit and its aftermath, since others guilty or innocent have been entangled in his coils, that is the subject of this chapter.

There are three books, printed at five-year intervals, which may be regarded as forming a trilogy centring on the manifold activities, praiseworthy or culpable, of that great English bibliographer and prince of literary forgers, Thomas J. Wise. These and their dates of publication are: John Carter and Graham Pollard, *An Enquiry into the Nature of Certain Nineteenth Century Pamphlets*, 1934; Wilfred Partington, *Forging Ahead: The True Story of the Upward Progress of Thomas James Wise*, 1939; and Miss Fannie E. Ratchford, *Letters of Thomas J. Wise to John Henry Wrenn: A Further Inquiry into the Guilt of Certain Nineteenth-Century Forgers*, 1944. A revised edition of Mr. Partington's *Forging Ahead* entitled *Thomas J. Wise in the Original Cloth* was published in 1947.

The Forgeries of Thomas J. Wise

The essay which follows is a transcript of an article of mine published in the *Journal of English and Germanic Philology,* July, 1945. The only changes I have made are the insertion of a short passage in the text based on my independent research, and a slight correction, referred to in a note, for which I am indebted to Mr. Partington's recent work.

While Carter and Pollard have contributed further data regarding the forgeries of Thomas Wise in *The Firm of Charles Ottley, Landon & Co.: Footnote to an Inquiry,* 1948, centring on Wise's audacious invention of a non-existent publishing house on whom he foists his spurious printings of several poems of Swinburne, these findings lie outside the scope of my article, and I have preferred to reproduce it substantially in its original form.

Although no formal accusation was made against Wise by Carter and Pollard, his guilt was proven in their acute *exposé.* The imposture of more than fifty spurious "first editions" of selections from the works of important nineteenth-century authors was unmasked. Amongst these were writings of Wordsworth, Tennyson, Dickens, Thackeray, the Brownings, Swinburne, George Eliot, William Morris, R. L. Stevenson, and Rudyard Kipling. The shock of this initial disclosure may be recalled by way of retrospect. Wise's services to English letters and far-flung literary connections; his eminent position as the foremost bibliographer of his time; the fame of his magnificent Ashley Library; the numerous honours conferred upon him, made his subtle yet pervasive frauds, extending over many years, almost inconceivable.

Wilfred Partington's *Forging Ahead,* in part a biography of Wise, supplied additional evidence of the extent of his fraudulent practices.

The genesis of Miss Ratchford's work lies in the relationships between Thomas J. Wise and John Henry Wrenn, one of the foremost of American book collectors. It was due to Wise's invaluable aid that Wrenn was enabled to accumulate that fine collection of rare books, many of them first editions, which has now a permanent home in the Wrenn Library at the University of Texas. During the course of their long association Wise wrote numerous letters to his American friend. These have been ably edited by Miss Ratchford, the librarian of the Rare Books Collections at Austin, in this volume, consisting of prefatory material, pages 3-114, and the text of the letters, pages 117-557.

While the letters of Wise to Wrenn are, in a sense, the *raison d'être* of Miss Ratchford's book, two thirds of her prefatory essays, pages 37-111, have little to do with them. They centre upon an attempt to prove a charge so sensational and arresting that it overshadows what is ostensibly the primary theme of her work. The sub-title of the volume, *A Further Inquiry into the Guilt of Certain Nineteenth-Century Forgers*, strikes the key-note of these essays. Miss Ratchford strives to show that the guilt of the production and provenance of the spurious pamphlets, hitherto regarded as wholly that of Wise, was shared by a group of conspirators. Amongst these she implicates Sir Edmund Gosse, Buxton Forman, and indirectly the publishing firm of Richard Clay and Sons. In view of the prominence of the men arraigned, Miss Ratchford's accusation is a veritable bomb-shell thrown into the world of letters, and her arguments challenge close scrutiny.

Bearing in mind what has been written, the purpose of my essay is twofold. So far as Thomas Wise is concerned, his guilt needs no further demonstration. But in the 460 pages of Wise's letters to Wrenn, with whom as a book collector he was so closely associated, there are intimate glimpses of his activities which throw additional light on his methods and the complex strands of his personality. Certain references culled from my own correspondence with Wise during the time when his forgeries were exposed by Carter and Pollard may also be of interest. The first part of this essay will therefore deal with Thomas Wise. In the second part I plan to consider the charge that a group of men were involved in the forging of spurious editions. More particularly, it is the implication that the distinguished *littérateur* Sir Edmund Gosse was one of these conspirators that will be my primary concern.

While as consecutive reading the mass of bibliographical detail in Wise's letters to Wrenn will only appeal to the specialist, an impressionistic survey of them is keenly interesting. They disclose in the first place the paradoxical character of Wise. His friendship for Wrenn was genuine, and he secured for him many a scarce and precious book at moderate prices. Yet he had no compunction in planting on his co-worker a complete series of his own forgeries, introducing them to him with the utmost cunning and duplicity. The glittering bait of the spurious editions was dangled before Wrenn's eyes with all the artifice employed by an expert angler when inducing a fish to rise to the fly and executing a skilful strike. It seems clear that to Wise a sheer love of the game of intrigue, the pleasure of the egoist in outwitting his fellow-men, was as potent a motive as putting money in his purse.

The letters written to Wrenn are, in the second place, a revelation of the prodigious bibliographical knowledge of Wise, conjoined with striking limitations in his intellectual and artistic outlooks. His enthusiasm is concentrated on book collecting. Throughout this voluminous correspondence there is hardly a word of appreciation regarding the contents of the works that pass through his hands. The rarity, the format, the cost constitute his latest find "a beautiful book," but there is no hint on his part of any genuine interest in the literary merits of the masterpieces which come within his purview. If the market price of an unpublished manuscript of a great poet can be enhanced by withholding it from the world for a long period of time, Wise has no scruples. In the midst of his exciting discoveries of Swinburne treasures at "The Pines," he writes: "These pamphlets are really good things, and I mean to maintain their monetary value. I am able to control them, and shall assuredly do so. They are a beautiful and unique series of books, and shall in no way be spoiled. They are not going to be included in Swinburne's works for many years. This is arranged for in the fees I have paid as royalty."[1]

The letters of Wise which will most attract the general reader are those recording his experiences at "The Pines." His delving into Swinburne manuscripts with the zest of a man who has unearthed a gold mine; his relations with Watts-Dunton and Edmund Gosse; his fight to ward off competing book-dealers, one of whom he brands as "that rascal," are vividly described. Although he lacks aesthetic sensibilities, Wise has a full-blooded interest in human nature. He revels in anecdote, and his letters kindle at this juncture.

The prefatory essays of Miss Ratchford's book are a valuable and illuminating comment on the letters which she edits. She is thoroughly conversant with every detail of the voluminous bibliographical data concerned. As librarian of the Rare Books Collections at the University of Texas she has had access to sources which enable her to annotate the Wise letters, and often to supply fresh and pertinent information and illustration. Her book reveals painstaking and scholarly research, and the handling of her wealth of material is incisive and sensitive. As an intimate record of a fascinating chapter in the history of Anglo-American bibliography, and as a self-disclosure of the outward activities and inward psychology of Thomas Wise, Miss Ratchford's volume is an important contribution.

So much has been said of late regarding the misdoings of Wise, that there is a danger of forgetting the indebtedness of England to a man who almost single-handed held his own against wealthy competitors from overseas, and secured for her the permanent possession of many genuine and choice first editions and association volumes of eminent poets and prose writers. The Ashley Library, now housed in the British Museum, is an enduring monument to Thomas Wise, a great bibliophile, and this fine achievement should not be obscured by his unhappy swerving from the path of honesty.

Nor ought certain endearing human qualities of Wise to be ignored. He had a genius for friendship, and, as many a university man in England and America could testify, was always ready to place his knowledge and the resources of the Ashley Library at the disposal of any young scholar. If a personal reference may be pardoned in order to illustrate his kindness, the writer of this essay is amongst those who have enjoyed his hospitality and been aided by him. My correspondence with Mr. Wise continued in the years when he was under fire, and he discussed the Carter and Pollard book with me. Although he never admitted his guilt, his letters throw interesting sidelights on his reactions at this critical time. In common with many of Wise's friends, I urged him to vindicate his good name even at the expense of his reputation as an expert bibliographer. Naturally, as is now evident, he could not do this and was forced to seek refuge in evasive excuses. On January 7, 1935 he writes: "The advice you offer regarding the C. and P. Book is identical with that given me by many other friends, and has already been adopted. I am afraid you have not seen my letters and those of Mr. Maurice Buxton Forman in the Times Lit. Sup. last July. In these letters a full and definite statement was made, and surely nothing further can be necessary." As a glance at the reproduction opposite page 39 of Miss Ratchford's book will reveal, Thomas Wise even sent me the proof sheets of his introduction to *A Browning Library,* in which he tells of his discovery, "somewhere about 1885," of the purported Bennett cache of the Reading edition of Mrs. Browning's *Sonnets from the Portuguese.* It has always seemed to me an illustration of the curious twist in his mind that he should have given me, and I have no doubt in the beaten way of friendship, the proof sheets of the most notorious cock-and-bull story he ever told.

The involvement of Wise in the fabrication of spurious editions was, as has been stated, fully established in Carter and Pollard's *Enquiry* of 1934. But the sub-title of Miss Ratchford's book, *A Further Inquiry into the Guilt of Certain Nineteenth-Century Forgers,* breaks new ground. If her findings are valid, a group of men, including an eminent bibliophile, and a literary critic and essayist of international repute, must be branded as participants in Wise's fraudulent practices. These startling and dramatic charges have stirred up controversy. The *New York Times Book*

Review of December 17, 1944 contained an able review of Miss Ratchford's work by David Randall. An article by John Carter, entitled "Thomas J. Wise and His Forgeries," was printed in the *Atlantic Monthly,* February, 1945. While referring to several of Randall's and Carter's conclusions, I shall in the main avoid touching on ground that they have already covered. With the exception of brief allusions to Buxton Forman and the firm of Richard Clay and Sons, my exclusive concern will be the question of the innocence or the guilt of Sir Edmund Gosse in the light of Miss Ratchford's charges, and some independent evidence which seems to me of importance.

Miss Ratchford's case against Buxton Forman is a strong one, and it has been substantiated by Carter's article in the *Atlantic*. There is a document in the library of Mr. Carl H. Pforzheimer, one of America's foremost book collectors, which, to quote Carter's words, "convicts Wise in his own handwriting of the responsibility for one of the forgeries and includes Forman in the responsibility." He was undoubtedly a confederate of Wise, though, as Carter says, "the degree and nature of his complicity in the affair as a whole remain speculative."[2] The use of the press of Richard Clay and Sons to print many of the spurious editions evokes suspicion, but it seems likely that Wise was in collusion with some subordinate in the firm, and that the publishers themselves were innocent.

Sir Edmund Gosse, a great biographer and essayist, is beyond comparison the most distinguished of the men who are accused by Miss Ratchford. Consequently, her statements regarding him must be carefully examined and analysed. Circumstantial evidence can often be a tricky thing, and attention should be drawn at the outset to general considerations which make the guilt of Gosse seem very improbable. His high public position as librarian to the House of Lords, his literary eminence, impressions of the integrity of his character as derived from his life and writings, must be taken into the reckoning. More specifically, his frequent criticism of Wise's carelessness and lack of scrupulousness in the editing of manuscripts should be borne in mind. As contrasted

The Forgeries of Thomas J. Wise

with Wise he had little to gain from these forgeries; and it is to be noted that when Wise was driven to bay and tried to implicate Buxton Forman, he never hinted that Gosse had any part or lot in the forging of the spurious pamphlets.

Apart from mere conjecture, Miss Ratchford's indictment of Sir Edmund Gosse is based entirely upon two pieces of evidence. The first is a marginal emendation of a word in the proof sheets of the fabricated edition of Mrs. Browning's *The Runaway Slave at Pilgrim's Point,* which she maintains is in Gosse's handwriting. The positive identification of a single word of seven letters seems to me most dubious, particularly as the final *s* in it resembles Gosse's initial rather than his customary terminal *s*.[3]

Miss Ratchford's second piece of evidence is much more important, and it does involve puzzling aspects. It has to do with Gosse's famous narrative in which he told the world the story of the way in which Mrs. Browning first showed her husband the manuscript of the *Sonnets from the Portuguese.* In the concluding sentences of this account, he goes on to sponsor the forged Reading edition of the *Sonnets* by a circumstantial statement of the manner in which they were published in 1847. This tale, originally printed by Gosse in his introduction to Dent's edition of the *Sonnets* in 1894, was repeated by him verbatim in *Critical Kit-Kats,* 1896, 1902, and 1914.

Gosse declares that Browning told the story which he relates, eight years before his death, to a friend, with the understanding that it should not be divulged during the poet's lifetime. So long as this mysterious friend was surmised to be Thomas Wise, the fictitious elements in the narrative were readily explainable. They were believed to have been implanted in Gosse's mind by Wise in order to bolster his account of the discovery of the Reading edition of the *Sonnets from the Portuguese.* But, as Miss Ratchford has pointed out, Wise was a young man of twenty-two in 1881, "eight years before Browning's death," and he did not meet the poet until 1886. Moreover, in 1927, Gosse wrote a letter to Mr. J. R. Burton averring that it was to himself Browning told the story he had printed in 1894.[4] In the light of this letter it is necessary to scrutinize anew the narrative published in *Critical Kit-Kats* and elsewhere, and to dismiss the assumption that it originated *in toto* from a report conveyed by Wise to Gosse of an interview he had with Browning.

There are clearly two strands in Gosse's pronouncement. The main body of his account deals with the circumstances and environment linked with the original showing of Mrs. Browning's sonnets to her husband. The only demonstrable fictitious element in this portion of the narrative is the statement that this disclosure was made at Pisa in 1847 instead of at Bagni di Lucca in 1849. On the other hand the sentences at the end of the account are devoted to the description of the printing of the Reading edition of the *Sonnets from the Portuguese* in 1847 through the instrumentality of Miss Mitford. This incident is entirely fictitious. It is I think evident from the text that Gosse does not mean to imply that this part of his tale comes from the lips of Browning; and in his letter to Mr. Burton in 1927 he only refers to "the story regarding the authorship of these poems" as being told him by the poet.

Miss Ratchford in her book makes little or no distinction between the two strands of Gosse's narrative, but seems to regard the whole of it as having its genesis shortly before the publication of Dent's edition of Mrs. Browning's sonnets. As she writes: "It is of no small importance that when he rushed the story into print it was new to Gosse, that it was still warm and glowing with romantic surprise when he gave it to the public in November, 1894."[5] This statement, however, must be qualified, since I have recently received a letter from Miss Ratchford in which she says that she does not doubt that Gosse heard from Browning himself the true story of his first sight of the *Sonnets from the Portuguese* in manuscript. But she maintains that in this earlier part of the account Gosse deliberately substituted Pisa for Bagni di Lucca and the year 1847 for 1849, in order to fit in with the fictitious story of the circumstances connected with the publication of the Reading edition of the *Sonnets* and to collaborate with Wise in his forgery. It can at any rate be readily proven that while the portion of Gosse's narrative concerned with the printing of the Reading pamphlet was indeed new to him in 1894, the main body of his account antedates this and, with the exception of the Pisa error, is based on an actual statement of Browning.

When Buxton Forman penned his half-veiled sceptical comment on the Reading edition in "Elizabeth Barrett Browning and Her Scarcer Books: A Bio-Bibliographical Note," 1896, he wrote of Gosse's story: "It is not expressly stated that Browning told the mysterious friend of Miss Mitford's part in the matter; and there are other friends of the poet to whom that part of the story is new."[6] How new it was is demonstrated by the fact that when Gosse published the private catalogue of his library, which went to press in November, 1893, he never mentions the Reading pamphlet of 1847, but specifically describes Mrs. Browning's *Poems,* 1850, as "the first [edition] in which the *Sonnets from the Portuguese* appeared."[7]

The major division of Gosse's narrative is, however, of much earlier origin. The proof that the substance of his story, with the exception of the Reading addendum, is derived from Browning is circumstantial. It has generally been assumed that the account given by F. J. Furnivall in 1890 of the way in which Browning first saw the *Sonnets from the Portuguese,* which was also based on a personal statement of the poet, is more accurate in its details than that of Gosse. Furnivall refers to Browning's discovery of the *Sonnets* as follows: "Spying about, he saw a tiny roll of paper on her looking-glass or table, pounst on it, and said, 'What's this?' unrolling it the while. 'Only something I wrote about you, and you frightened me from showing it to you,' said she. And in her next edition the *Sonnets from the Portuguese* were printed."[8] In Gosse's version, on the other hand, Mrs. Browning entered the breakfast room and, "while her husband stood at the window watching the street," she "pushed a packet of papers into the pocket of his coat," told him to read it, and then "fled again to her own room."[9] Commenting on the discrepancy between these two versions of the manner in which the poet became aware of the existence of his wife's sonnets, Carter and Pollard write: "The picture of Browning *finding* them, rather than of her *offering* them, could not fail to impress as being more true to life than Gosse's version."[10] But there is irrefutable evidence that it is Gosse who is true to life here, and Furnivall who is in error. In a letter written by Browning to Julia Wedgwood in November, 1864, the poet relates how his wife first showed him her sonnets, and then adds: "How I see the gesture, and hear the tones,—and, for the matter of that, *see the window at which I was standing* [italics mine], with the tall mimosa in front, and little church-court to the right."[11] Since the letters of Browning to Julia Wedgwood were not published until 1937, and it is Gosse alone who has recorded the significant detail of the poet's standing at the window, this in itself is sufficient evidence that his account is derived from Browning.

The one palpable error in the first part of Gosse's narrative is his assertion that Mrs. Browning showed her sonnets to her husband in the spring of 1847 at Pisa. The letters of Browning to Leigh Hunt in 1857, to Julia Wedgwood in 1864, and to Peter Bayne in 1881, prove that it was at Bagni di Lucca in 1849 that this disclosure took place. It has generally been assumed that this error originated at the time that Gosse wrote his account in 1894. Since the date of 1847 fits in so precisely with the fictitious story of the printing of the Reading edition of the *Sonnets from the Portuguese* in the same year, two explanations have been suggested. Critics who believe in Gosse's innocence surmise that the fable of the *Sonnets* being first shown to Browning at Pisa was implanted in Gosse's mind by Wise as well as the fiction of the printing of the *Sonnets* at Reading in 1847. On the other hand Miss Ratchford, as has been noted, regards the mention of Pisa instead of Bagni di Lucca as a deliberate alteration on the part of Gosse in order to convince the public that Wise's forgery was a genuine first edition.

It is clear, however, that the Pisa mistake was made some years before 1894. In his life of Browning, published in 1890, William Sharp writes: "It was here, in Pisa, I have been told on indubitable authority, that Browning first saw in manuscript those "Sonnets from the Portuguese" . . . which no other woman than his wife could have composed." A few sentences further on, Sharp comments: "It is pleasant to think of the shy delight with which the delicate, flower-like, almost ethereal poet-wife, in those memorable Pisan evenings . . . showed her love-poems to her husband."[12] The general though not exact correspondence with Gosse's account, since Sharp speaks of the *Sonnets* being revealed to Browning in the evening, not in the morning, is evidence that the outlines of the story were known by certain people at least as early as 1890. In particular, the fact that Sharp as well as Gosse makes the mistake of regarding Pisa instead of Bagni di Lucca as the place of the original showing of the *Sonnets,* indicates the likelihood of his "indubitable authority" being Edmund Gosse.

Since Gosse was entirely ignorant before 1893 of the existence of the Reading edition of the *Sonnets from the Portuguese,* he could not in 1890 have purposely substituted Pisa for Bagni di Lucca in order to give an air of authenticity to the forgery. Nor if, as seems probable, the fabricated Reading edition was printed around 1893-94 would Wise have any interest in giving birth to the Pisa story in 1890.[13] The conclusion which seems to me most likely is that the confusing of Pisa with Bagni di Lucca was due to a lapse of memory on the part of Gosse. What possible reason would he have for deliberately making this alteration in 1890? He may have been misled to some extent by his knowledge of a passage in a letter written by Elizabeth Barrett to Browning on July 22, 1846: "You shall see some day at Pisa what I will not show you now. Does not Solomon say 'there is a time to read what is written.' If he doesn't, he *ought.*"[14] May it not have been the erroneous idea that the *Sonnets from the Portuguese* were first shown to Browning at Pisa which suggested to Wise the possibility of forging a fictitious 1847 edition of them? I shall return to this point later.

Although these considerations seem in themselves to demonstrate that Gosse's mistake was unintentional, there is one argument against this conclusion to be considered. Gosse in his letter to J. R. Burton in 1927, when referring to that part of his account in *Critical Kit-Kats* which had to do with the circumstances linked with the revealing of the *Sonnets from the Portuguese,* declares that the poet's statement to him was made "seriously and explicitly" when he "was taking notes" of his speech. Miss Ratchford regards this as evidence that any varying from actuality in Gosse's narrative was intentional on account of his collusion with Wise. We know, to quote Wise's own words, that "in 1881 Browning was telling and partly dictating to Gosse the story of his life, and this story, up to and not beyond Browning's marriage on September 12, 1846, was printed by Gosse in the *Century Magazine,* December 1881." But was Gosse, despite his assertion in the letter of 1927, taking careful notes of the details of the disclosure of the *Sonnets from the Portuguese* several years after Browning's marriage? There is a curious vagueness in this letter concerning the time he heard this tale. In the opening sentence he writes: "Mr. Robert Browning told me (I think in the year 1887) the story regarding the authorship of those poems which I have told in my *Critical Kit-Kats* and elsewhere." In the third sentence he adds: "The only correction of my account which I can make is that perhaps the conversation was later than 'eight years before' Mr. Browning's death." How much weight can we attach to the meticulous accuracy of his note taking of a story which he confesses might have been related to him by Browning any time between 1881 and 1887?

It is important to recall in connection with these lapses of memory that Gosse was never an exact scholar, and could be proverbially careless in matters of detail. The numerous factual inaccuracies of his life of Gray and of *From Shakespeare to Pope* provoked the stinging indictment of Churton Collins in the *Quarterly.* In the fine objective study of *The Life and Letters of Sir Edmund Gosse* by Evan Charteris, this weakness is frankly discussed, although the whole portrait is that of an honourable man incapable of forgery. As Charteris sums it up:

> It would be of interest to fathom the causes of his carelessness. Even to the profane it is clear that Gosse was hasty and impulsive,

and once armed with an *a priori* notion was tempted to regard too uncritically all facts which fitted. It has been seen that, in a letter to Stevenson, he declares that a sustained exercise of thought was a thing unknown to him. This, without being literally true, points to a certain lukewarmness in research and a certain distaste for collecting all the factors of a problem. He had the impatience of the imaginative man. He possessed the dangerous boon of a powerful but not always accurate memory, and he trusted it with the eager alacrity of a poet. . . . He never had the discipline of examinations and "schools," no don had drilled his mind, he was pitchforked into the world; he awoke at a bound, he careered at his own will in the fields of literature. His knowledge was wide and stimulating but it was not minute. His mind was vividly alert but not meticulous. He had "emulation," but with him it was not "the scholar's melancholy."[15]

I have suggested that Gosse's initial mistake in regarding Pisa instead of Bagni di Lucca as the place where Mrs. Browning first showed the manuscript of the *Sonnets from the Portuguese* to her husband, may have put into Wise's head the scheme of forging a spurious edition of them. This error, as the passage cited from Sharp's *Life of Browning* reveals, was in circulation at least as early as 1890. In view of Browning's enthusiasm when he read the *Sonnets,* it would seem strange, if this took place in 1847, that they were not published until 1850. It must have appealed to the inventive brain of Wise as a golden opportunity to fabricate an 1847 edition which would fit in so naturally with the story of the disclosure of the *Sonnets* at Pisa in the spring of that year. This would also lead Gosse to regard the Reading pamphlet as authentic when Wise showed it to him, and to credit Wise's tale of the circumstances of its publication. Gosse loved a romantic episode in which he scented literary possibilities. He was careless in factual matters, and never had the critical acumen of the exact scholar. Being already convinced that the *Sonnets from the Portuguese* were revealed to Browning at Pisa in 1847, and having a copy of the Reading edition of 1847 before his eyes, he was predisposed to accept Wise's version of the way in which the pamphlet had been printed and to tack this on as an addendum to the original story he had heard from the lips of Browning.

In the most lengthy *apologia* that Thomas Wise ever wrote, printed in *The Times Literary Supplement,* May 24, 1934, there are paradoxical strands interwoven. So far as his own defence is concerned the *apologia* is ridiculously lame. Yet in the course of it he exonerates Edmund Gosse, an old and cherished friend for whom he had genuine respect. Here for once I am convinced he is telling the truth. In the first place he accounts for the substitution of Pisa for Bagni di Lucca by attributing it to an initial mistake of Gosse. He then ascribes any confusion of statement on the part of Gosse regarding the time of the first printing of the *Sonnets* to the facts that Gosse had the 1847 book in front of him, the genuineness of which he had no reason to suspect, and the date of 1847 in his mind. What Wise of course does not state is that his own cunning machinations fostered these errors, and that he had implanted in Gosse's mind the fabulous anecdote of the publication of the *Sonnets* in 1847 through the agency of Miss Mitford. It is fully understandable how the impressionable Gosse, chock-full of Victorian sentiment, would seize the opportunity of relating the story told him by Browning, perhaps with a touch of romantic embellishment, in conjunction with the dramatic announcement of the discovery of a precious first edition of the *Sonnets from the Portuguese,* which he in all innocence accepted as genuine.

The relationships between Thomas Wise and Edmund Gosse as revealed in their correspondence militate against the idea that there was any collusion of the two men in the fabrication of spurious editions. Wise's attitude is inclined to be deferential, and he accepts with meekness Gosse's frequent criticisms of his carelessness and lack of scrupulousness in the editing of manuscripts. As Partington comments: "Again and again Gosse vehemently protested against Wise's habit of rushing pieces of poetry and prose to the printer to turn into privately printed first editions, without saying anything about their origin, or where they had appeared serially, or giving them proper editorial treatment."[16] There is no hint anywhere in this correspondence that Gosse suspected Wise of forgery, but circumstantial evidence to the contrary. In his article in the *Atlantic,* 1945, already mentioned, John Carter has cited two letters, one written by Wise to Gosse in 1896 and the other by Gosse to Wise in 1927. In these letters there are allusions to four works which are forgeries of Wise, but the text of the letters shows that Gosse is entirely ignorant of their lack of genuineness. These two letters, as it seems to me, are in themselves convincing evidence of Gosse's innocence.

It is of significance to note that Wise deluded Gosse, in the letter of 1896 cited by Mr. Carter, precisely as he deceived Wrenn in a letter of November 24, 1899. Both letters deal with printings of Ruskin's works which are forgeries. Wise writes to Gosse in 1896:

It may interest you to know that the copy of "Leoni" I sent you was formerly the property of Fredk. Crawley, Mr. Ruskin's old factotum, now living at Oxford upon a pension of £100 a year allowed him from Brantwood. I looked him up in 1889 when I was hunting all around for material for my Ruskin Bibliography. I bought from him all the relics he had—books, letters, sketches, among other things this tract.

In 1899, Wise wrote to Wrenn:

The foregoing is a list of a most interesting series of Ruskin rarities of which I have the refusal.

They belong to Mr. Frederick Crawley, to whom many of the letters in my series of privately printed Ruskin letters were addressed. He had them all, of course, from Mr. Ruskin himself. I have the offer of them at £50.0.0. for the lot. This is an extremely reasonable price, and I think you will do well to buy them.[17]

The discussion of an absorbing theme of Miss Ratchford's book has left little space for comment on the excellence of many aspects of her work. While the writer of this essay believes her charge against Gosse to be unfounded, it is difficult to disentangle all the filaments of Wise's tortuous web. His notorious career has inevitably cast a shadow of suspicion on men who were his close friends and associates. Miss Ratchford's sincerity and freedom from ex-parte argument are self-evident, but her case against Sir Edmund Gosse is not substantiated.

11

Browning Studies in England and America, 1910-1949

THE PUBLICATION of Griffin and Minchin's *The Life of Robert Browning* in 1910 is a convenient point of departure for a concise review of significant historical and critical studies of the poet and his work that lie within the compass of our own era.

While the time is now ripe for a new life of Browning, Griffin and Minchin's book remains up to the present, within its limits, the standard biography. In its aim and scope their work is historical rather than critical. In this respect it differs from the biographies of Browning written by Chesterton, Dowden, and Herford. It is more closely allied to Edmund Gosse's *Personalia* and Mrs. Orr's *Life and Letters of Robert Browning*. Estimated as an historical survey, its fullness, accuracy, and objectivity entitle it to the first place amongst the biographies of the poet.

Since 1910, however, there has been a considerable addition to the data linked with Browning's life and the sources and genesis of his poems. There have also been a number of valuable critical studies of his poetry. This fresh material is of sufficient importance to enlarge our perspective of the poet and his contribution to English literature. The material is at present widely scattered, and in order to synthetize it two major works of Browning scholarship are imperative: first, a new life of the poet; and, second, a book on the historical background and literary criticism of his *magnum opus, The Ring and the Book*. In the meantime it may not be inexpedient to take stock of the more important contributions to Browningiana between 1910 and 1949.

My survey makes no pretence to inclusiveness. In order to keep it within due limits, I confine it to Browning studies in England and America and omit comment on such excellent French works of biography and criticism as those of Berger, De Reul, and Hovelaque. Even with this reservation, a review within the scope of an essay must be selective rather than comprehensive. In *A Browning Handbook* Professor William Clyde DeVane has assembled and arranged all of the essential data available up to 1935 concerning each of the poems of Browning. This difficult task, involving wide reading and diligent research, has been so well performed that his book has become an indispensable tool of modern Browning scholarship. In particular it has paved the way for the writing of a new life of the poet, and a definitive work on *The Ring and the Book*. Few, if any, pertinent facts regarding Browning's life and poetry known before 1935 have escaped Mr. DeVane's scrutiny; and the critical balance and acumen of the *Handbook* are as admirable as its fidelity. Yet, since Mr. DeVane's method, involving an analysis of every individual poem, is necessarily discursive, room may be left for a general summary, however imperfect, of recent additions to Browningiana. Some of these are factual discoveries, and others are writings of a biographical or critical nature illustrating trends of scholarly research between 1910 and 1949.

Since historical and critical studies of Browning and his poetry depend to a greater or less extent on source material, I shall begin by considering additions to this after 1910.

The canon of Browning's poetry has been slightly enlarged. The "Centenary Edition" of 1912 and the *New Poems* of 1914, both edited by Sir F. G. Kenyon, contain altogether twenty-nine poems of Browning not included in earlier editions. These, however, are not of outstanding quality; and, with the exception of a few *juvenilia,* almost all of them had been printed before in magazines.

The recent discovery by Professor Donald Smalley that an anonymous article printed in the *Foreign Quarterly Review,* July, 1842, was written by Browning is a find of considerable interest, since up to the present his essay on Shelley has been regarded as his only piece of critical writing in prose. The text of the article has been reprinted and edited with introductory chapters and notes by Mr. Smalley in a book entitled *Browning's Essay on Chatterton*, 1948. Mr. Smalley points out that this sketch of the poet Chatterton is of particular importance as an early example of Browning's special pleading and of his departure from historical fact in the portrayal of character. The poet's subjective bias in favour of Chatterton results in an *apologia* that diverges from the truth of history, and is coloured throughout by his imaginative and emotional creative faculties. With this in mind, Mr. Smalley regards the essay as throwing much light on the whole series of casuistical monologues afterwards written by Browning and also on the method he pursues in his central masterpiece, *The Ring and the Book*. The drag-net is a wide one; and while agreeing with many of the writer's conclusions, I feel that in his natural enthusiasm for his discovery he sometimes overstresses its significance. His analysis of the three basic motifs of Browning's special pleading in the Chatterton essay is, however, acute and illuminating. The book as a whole is the work of a well-informed scholar and an able critic.

By far the most important addition to source material since 1910 has been the publication of numerous letters of Browning and his wife to various correspondents. Four collections may be stressed as rich in information and significance. These are: *Letters of Robert Browning to Miss Isa Blagden*, edited by A. Joseph Armstrong, 1923; *Elizabeth Barrett Browning: Letters to Her Sister, 1846-1859*, edited by Leonard Huxley, 1929; *Letters of Robert Browning*, collected by Thomas J. Wise and edited by Thurman L. Hood, 1933; *Robert Browning and Julia Wedgwood*, edited by Richard Curle, 1937.

The bulk of the letters of Browning to Isabella Blagden cover a period of twelve years from 1861 to 1872. With the exception of the poet's love letters to Elizabeth Barrett they are his most important correspondence. Their primary interest is, however, biographical rather than literary. Since on pages 63-64 of this book, in the essay entitled "Our Lady of Bellosguardo," the nature and contents of these letters are discussed, I refer my readers to that passage.

Mrs. Browning's letters to her sister, Henrietta, extend from 1846 to 1859. These record numerous incidents of her life in Italy, her devotion to her husband, her loving solicitude for her young son. They are an intimate and affectionate family correspondence enhanced by the charm and vivacity of Elizabeth Browning's writing, and are a valuable supplement to the two volumes of her letters published by Sir F. G. Kenyon in 1897.

The majority of Thomas J. Wise's large collection of Browning letters published in 1933 had already been printed privately under the title, *Letters of Robert Browning to Various Correspondents*. These were accessible to Griffin, and he made extensive use of them in his life of Browning. The collection in its final form, edited by Mr. Hood, is wide in range, containing letters of Browning written to numerous people from 1830 to the year of his death, 1889. They may be said to fall into three main divisions: first, family correspondence, such as the letters of the poet to his sister, Sarianna, and to Pen and Fannie Browning; second, letters to intimate friends in England and Italy, such as Isabella Blagden and the Story family; third, letters to various correspondents in the large circle of Browning's literary and social *milieu*, including many men of note in the Victorian age, such as Carlyle, Tennyson, Leigh Hunt, Edmund Gosse, Dr. Furnivall, and Sir Frederic Leighton. Here are printed the poignant account of his wife's death that Browning wrote to his sister; the smaller portion of his letters to Isa Blagden, 26 as compared with 116 published in the collection edited by Dr. Armstrong; the letters to Edith Story dealing with the unhappy incident of Browning's relations with Lady Ashburton; his quarrels with Austin and Fitzgerald; the explanations of difficult passages in his poetry pried from him by Furnivall, who, as high priest of the Browning Society, was frequently constrained to consult the Oracle in order to answer the queries of the poet's devotees. Summed up as a whole, the Wise collection contains more biographical than critical or literary information. The letters are concerned with Browning's life in the world of men and affairs rather than his inward thoughts or a discussion of his poetry.

The thirty letters written by Robert Browning to Julia Wedgwood from 1863 to 1870 differ in character from the collections I have been reviewing. In certain of their interests they are more akin to the poet's letters to Elizabeth Barrett. Julia Wedgwood, though a blue stocking, was a woman of decided intellectual force. Her passion for introspection drew from Browning an answering revelation of the workings of his mind; and her trenchant criticism of *The Ring and the Book* struck fire in response. From the point of view of the literary critic, the Julia Wedgwood correspondence is of particular value. It also supplies information regarding Browning's tour in southern France in 1864, and important data concerning the composition of *The Ring and the Book*.

To complete my survey of collections of Browning letters since 1910, reference should be made to the printing in 1935 of *Twenty-two Unpublished Letters of Elizabeth Barrett Browning and Robert Browning, Addressed to Henrietta and Arabella Moulton-Barrett*. These date from October 2, 1846 to June 24, 1855. They dovetail with the letters written by Elizabeth to Henrietta included in the collection edited by Huxley in 1929, and supply additional details of the lives of the Brownings in Italy.

Letters to Browning and his wife are frequently as important from the point of view of source material as those written by them. Three collections of them are derived from that great store of Browning *memorabilia* which the indefatigable zeal of Dr. A. J. Armstrong has amassed at Baylor University.

The first of these is a selection from approximately one hundred letters of Landor to Browning that have been preserved at Baylor. They were printed in 1932 in the *Baylor Bulletin*, in "Baylor University's Browning Interests," Series V, and afterwards included in H. C. Minchin's charmingly written book, *Walter Savage Landor*, 1934. The letters of the aged Landor reveal the staunch and endearing qualities of Browning's friendship. Abandoned by his family and relatives, poor and ill, he found in Browning a friend who was ever helpful and sympathetic.

The second collection of this material is *Intimate Glimpses from Browning's Letter File,* published as Series VIII of "Baylor University's Browning Interests" in the *Baylor Bulletin,* 1934. It contains a large number of letters, but few of particular value. The most interesting are those which have to do with the proposed installation of the poet as Lord Rector of various Scotch universities.

The most important of these three collections is *Letters from Owen Meredith to Robert and Elizabeth Barrett Browning,* edited by Aurelia Brooks and J. Lee Harlan, Jr., 1937. There are sixty-two letters of Robert Lytton in this collection and nine letters of Browning. They were written, with the exception of a few brief later notes, between 1853 and 1864, and contain many references to the Browning *milieu* in Italy. Some of these should be read in conjunction with the Isabella Blagden letters, since a devoted friendship for Isa was a bond between the Brownings and Lytton. In the sphere of literature Lytton's attitude towards Browning is that of a disciple, but in his correspondence with Mrs. Browning there is a greater warmth and intimacy of friendship. The belief in spiritualism which Lytton shared with Elizabeth, in contrast to the scepticism of her husband, is amply reflected in his letters. They also contain much discussion on literary matters, including frequent allusions to such poems as *Aurora Leigh* and *Lucile.*

One valuable manuscript of source material in addition to these collections of letters has come to light since 1910. I deal with it separately on account of its unique nature. Amongst the numerous Browningiana sold at the Sotheby auction in 1913 was a series of 56½ pages octavo of autograph notes written by Elizabeth Barrett to Browning in 1845. These are notes of appreciation and criticism on the manuscripts of *Dramatic Romances and Lyrics, Luria,* and *A Soul's Tragedy,* which Browning had given to her for reading and review. In response, she suggests a considerable number of minor alterations in words, phrases, and rhythms of twelve of the twenty-one poems in *Dramatic Romances and Lyrics,* and in the two dramas.

When Sir Frederic Kenyon edited the *New Poems* in 1914, he wrote an interesting account in his preface of these letters or jottings. Through some oversight, he was not shown that portion of the manuscript which contains the comments on *The Flight of the Duchess.* Fortunately, this material has since been examined and reviewed by Professor Edward Snyder. He points out that the eleven pages of Elizabeth Barrett's notes on *The Flight of the Duchess* include more suggested revisions than the combined number of proposed changes in the other poems of *Dramatic Romances and Lyrics* annotated by her. An article in *QR,* 1937, "New Light on the Brownings," by Edward Snyder and Frederick Palmer, Jr., sums up the result of this investigation.

The influence of Elizabeth Barrett, both before and after her marriage, on the poetry of Browning, is of importance. Consequently, these 56½ pages of annotation are illuminating. The acumen of the criticism as well as Browning's personal regard for the writer are evidenced by the fact that only four of the seventy-three alterations proposed in the text of *The Flight of the Duchess* were rejected. The likelihood of a touch of autobiography entering indirectly into this poem has been reinforced by our knowledge of Elizabeth's painstaking comment on it.

In turning from source material to historical and literary studies of Browning since 1910, it seems necessary to chart a method of procedure. Although it is somewhat difficult to draw lines of demarcation, the numerous books and articles written may be classified under three headings: first, those which deal in a general way with the life and poetry of Browning; second, those which involve a consideration of some particular aspect or interest of his work; third, those which are concerned with individual poems. I shall follow this order in my review.

Under the first heading it is, again, difficult to draw a dividing line between biography and criticism, but a certain distinction may be made between writings that include a decided biographical element and those whose intent is primarily critical.

The initial work of value after 1910, of a semi-biographical character, is *The Early Literary Career of Robert Browning,* by Thomas R. Lounsbury, 1911. This book gives an account of the literary career of Browning from the publication of his first poem in 1833 to his marriage and departure for Italy in 1846. It traces the growth of the young poet's reputation, with special reference to the favourable reception of *Paracelsus* by English reviewers and well-known men of letters. This was followed by the arrest and decline of that reputation caused by the failure of *Strafford* and the succeeding dramas as acting plays, and above all by the publication of *Sordello.* Browning was caviare to the majority of reviewers and the reading public for many years afterwards. His poems became a byword for difficulty and obscurity. Lounsbury's analysis of the weaknesses of Browning's dramas as plays for the stage is acute. The biographical element in his account of them was supplemented by the publication of *The Diaries of William Charles Macready, 1833-1851,* edited by William Toynbee, 1912. Lounsbury's criticism of *Sordello* is in the main pertinent, although he fails to do justice to the beauty and distinction of individual passages in that craggy and tortuous work. He writes with grace and incisiveness as well as with soundness of judgment, and his book is a contribution to modern Browning scholarship.

Miss Lilian Whiting's *The Brownings: Their Life and Art,* 1917, and Osbert Burdett's *The Brownings,* 1928, as their titles indicate, deal with the lives and poetry of Browning and his wife in conjunction.

The worth of Miss Whiting's book should not be underrated, nor should the extravagance of her enthusiasms blind the reader to the reliability of her facts. She knew Florence intimately and was a close friend of Pen Browning and his wife. Amongst her other friends were many members of the Browning circle in Italy, such as Kate Field, Edith Story, Mrs. Bronson, and Madame Pasquale Villari (Linda White). She was thus able to record interesting reminiscences of the lives of the two poets which would otherwise be lost. One instance of the factual value of Miss Whiting's book is that she was the first to correct the erroneous story that Mrs. Browning showed her husband the manuscript of the *Sonnets from the Portuguese* at Pisa in 1847. Through information derived from Pen Browning she pointed out that this disclosure was made at Bagni di Lucca in 1849. And thereby hangs a tale, for the proof of the wrong dating of this incident was destined to be a central piece of evidence in Carter and Pollard's exposure of Thomas Wise's most famous forgery, the Reading edition of the *Sonnets from the Portuguese,* purporting to have been printed in 1847.

Osbert Burdett's book on the Brownings is ably and attractively written. It blends biography and criticism, weaving the latter about the interrelationships of the Brownings, in accordance with the plan of the work "to tell the story in which each took part, and to consider the writings of both mainly in so far as they contribute to it." Pages 116 to 208 are devoted to "the love letters," and Burdett's running comment on these is excellent. A rapid survey of the early lives of Robert Browning and Elizabeth Barrett stresses certain common elements in their heredity and religious environment. His book centres on the union of the two gifted poets, different in genius and temperament but attuned in spirit, and the interplay of their lives, fraught with personal and artistic consequences, is well delineated. The closing chapters comprise a brief summary of the widowed years of Browning, revealing how memories of his wife and her spiritual influence are still potent in his poetry, *The Ring and the Book* being a striking example. Burdett's study of the Brownings is to be commended for its sympathetic appreciation and sound critical analysis.

The booklet, *Some Memories of Robert Browning,* by Fannie Barrett Browning, 1928, deserves passing mention. In a simple and unaffected way, the poet's daughter-in-law writes of some intimate personal memories. Her touching account of Browning's last illness and death may be compared with "The Diary of Miss Evelyn Barclay" (printed in "Baylor University's Browning Interests," Series V in the *Baylor Bulletin,* 1932). Miss Barclay, a family friend, was staying at Pen's residence, the Palazzo Rezzonico in Venice, at the time of the poet's death.

The Family of the Barrett, by Jeannette Marks, 1938, is a large volume of some 700 pages. It is based on a thorough examination of the records of Jamaica in order to trace Edward Moulton-Barrett's family background, and also that of Browning's grandmother, Margaret Tittle. Despite the tribute due to so much patient research, it is a question whether the findings of the book justify such labour. Miss Marks stresses the contrast between the important position of the Barretts in the West Indies and the humble station of the Tittles. She also maintains that, some generations back, there was an infusion of Creole, in the sense of negroid, blood, into the Tittle ancestry of Browning. These facts have some significance as a partial explanation of the hostility of Edward Barrett to any alliance between his daughter and Robert Browning.

In summing up contributions to Browning bibliography since 1910, reference may be made to the correction of several errors. The monograph of Frederick A. Pottle, *Shelley and Browning: A Myth and Some Facts,* 1923, disproves the accounts of Sharp and Mrs. Orr of the way in which Browning became acquainted with the poetry of Shelley. Pottle proves that Browning's first knowledge of Shelley's verse was through the reading of a copy of his lyrics entitled *Miscellaneous Poems,* published piratically by William Benbow in 1826.

I have already alluded to the correction of the mistake that Mrs. Browning first showed her husband the manuscript of the *Sonnets from the Portuguese* at Pisa in 1847. In addition to Miss Whiting's statement, the printing of letters of Browning to Leigh Hunt and Julia Wedgwood reveal that this disclosure took place at Bagni di Lucca in 1849.

In two articles in *MLN,* 1928, reprinted in this book, I have corrected Mrs. Orr's errors regarding Browning's vacation tours in France in 1862 and 1864, as well as her mistaken account of the way in which the poet received the Secondary Source of the old Roman murder story that is the theme of *The Ring and the Book*.

In the sphere of literary criticism, as distinct from biography, there has been no outstanding book written on the poetry of Browning as a whole since 1910, though several works are worthy of comment. The first of these is *Robert Browning*, by William Lyon Phelps. This was originally printed in 1915, but in the "new edition" of 1932 the book was enlarged with additional chapters. Phelps's work contains excellent interpretations of many of Browning's best-known poems. It is to be commended for its clearness of exposition and vivid illustrations. It is popular in a good sense. Phelps was a distinguished teacher rather than a scholar; and his book, though stimulating in its vitality, is not a work of original and penetrative critical insight. The review of *The Ring and the Book* is ably written, but the notion that the Old Yellow Book was discovered by Browning in 1861 rather than 1860 is I believe contrary to fact.

The second work of general literary criticism I shall consider is *One Word More on Browning*, by Frances Theresa Russell, 1927. This is a book of uneven quality. Mrs. Russell's criticism, as has been said, "is fresh and stimulating." It is also provocative, and some of her judgments, particularly those on *The Ring and the Book*, seem to me wide of the mark. Her vivacity and enthusiasm are reminiscent of Chesterton's discussion of Browning's poetry, but like Chesterton she tends to indulge in violent paradoxes which blur the nuances of actuality. Yet such chapters of her work as Browning's "Flair for Feelings," "His Pungency and Wit," "His Saving Grace of Pessimism," contain much that is of value as a personal and unconventional reaction to the poet's writings. The book is an impressionistic study of Browning's poetry coloured by Mrs. Russell's temperament and prejudices, but not lacking in keenness of observation and a saving modicum of intellectual grip. I will reserve comment on its most controversial chapter, "Gold and Alloy," until my review of writings centring on *The Ring and the Book*.

A third work of merit in the field of literary criticism is *Browning: Background and Conflict,* by F. R. G. Duckworth, 1931. The book is divided into two sections. In Part I, "Background," the author evaluates estimates of Browning's poetry in three separate periods, namely, the years 1850-59, 1890-99, and 1920-29. The first of these decades he finds "on the whole inimical to the poet"; the second is that in which "his reputation came to its zenith"; the third is one of varied estimates, but represents, in the main, a decline in Browning's fame from the peak of the second decade. A survey of these periods leads Mr. Duckworth to the conclusion that "in each decade the critics had tended, in different degrees, to be blind to those very qualities in Browning's poetry on which they might have been expected to dwell with the most insistence."[1] He admits that his study is carried on within narrow limits and, as a matter of fact, he leaves out of the reckoning the period in which were written such lives of Browning as those of Chesterton, Dowden, Herford, and Griffin, and Hodell's fine work on the Old Yellow Book.

Part II, "Conflict," is the most important section of Duckworth's book. It pivots on the paradox that the decade of 1920-29, despite its interest in psychology, ignored the chief of Browning's virtues—the acuteness of his psychological insight. In his chapters entitled "The Outward Man," "Time and Eternity," "Mysticism," and "The White Light," Duckworth proceeds to stress the evidence of psychological conflict in the life and poetry of Browning. The analysis is a valuable one, although psychology abstracted from other factors is partial in its insight and conclusions. His handling of this theme should be compared with the more philosophical approaches of Jones, Pigou, Stopford Brooke, and Herford to the same central problem. As the titles of his chapters "Time and Eternity" and "Mysticism" indicate, Duckworth is aware of the metaphysical issue. Yet the earlier writers I have mentioned have the advantage of being more fully oriented in Browning's religious backgrounds; and their broad study of this crux, the adjustment of man's infinite spirit to a finite world, on the basis of his philosophy of life seems to me more fruitful than psychological analysis. All poetry, Browning wrote to Ruskin, is the problem of "putting the infinite within the finite";[2] but to represent his difficulty as almost solely due to an inner conflict in his mind is to minimize the whole play of environmental influences on his poetry which are as important as those bound up with his individual personality.

Duckworth's chapter on "The White Light" is the best in his book; and the contrast which Browning felt between his wife's direct poetic expression and his own oblique dramatic method is ably illustrated. It is an omission that no reference is made to *Numpholeptos,* since that poem, in allegorical guise, reads almost like a commentary on Browning's words in a letter to Elizabeth Barrett: ". . . your poetry must be, cannot but be, infinitely more to me than mine to you—for you *do* what I always wanted, hoped to do, and only seem now likely to do for the first time. You speak out, *you,*—I only make men and women speak—give you truth broken into prismatic hues, and fear the pure white light, even if it is in me, but I am going to try. . . ."[3]

Limitations of space preclude more than passing mention of such excellent essays in the sphere of literary criticism as "Robert Browning and Elizabeth Barrett Browning," by Henry Jones; "The Brownings," by Oliver Elton; "The Reputation of Robert Browning," by D. C. Somervell. Sir Henry Jones's article in *The Cambridge History of English Literature,* 1916, contains a masterly analysis of the dramatic element in Browning's poetry. Oliver Elton's essay in his *A Survey of English Literature,* 1920, emphasizes the realism of Browning's portrayal of character and situation. His comments on the poet's metres, grammar, and diction are of value, and the review as a whole is fresh and stimulating. D. C. Somervell's monograph in *Essays and Studies,* 1929, dwells on the enduring legacy of Browning to English poetry.

Indirectly connected with the province of literary criticism are three able articles by Maurice Browning Cramer: "Browning's Friendships and Fame before Marriage (1833-1846)," *PMLA,* 1940; "What Browning's Literary Reputation Owed to the Pre-Raphaelites, 1847-1856," *ELH,* 1941; "Browning's Literary Reputation at Oxford, 1855-1859," *PMLA,* 1942. The first of these articles modifies Lounsbury's picture of the indifference or hostility encountered by the poet after the publication of *Strafford* and *Sordello.* Through reference to individual opinions rather than reviews, Cramer shows that Browning had a group of admirers, small but distinguished, and that their appreciation gave him a place in inner literary circles. In the second and third articles, Cramer dwells on the enthusiasm of the Pre-Raphaelites for his poetry, and points out that their influence won for him a steadily increasing reputation amongst Oxford students.

I come now to the second main heading of my review, books or articles written after 1910 dealing with particular aspects of Browning's work. The material here is so voluminous that I can only select a number of studies based on central interests of his poetry.

On the technical side, H. H. Hatcher's *The Versification of Robert Browning,* 1928, is the standard work. It contains an analysis, arranged in catalogue form, of the metres used by the poet. It also draws attention to the rapidity of his composition, and reveals how loath he was to revise any of his writings.

The classical themes and sources of some of Browning's poems have been made the subject of considerable study. Amongst the best accounts of the poet's use of the classics are: "Browning's Ancient Classical Sources," by Thurman Los Hood, *HSCP,* 1922; "The Classical Poems of Robert Browning," by Edmund D. Cressman, *CJ,* 1927; "Browning's *Aristophanes' Apology,*" by Frederick Monroe Tisdel, *UMS,* 1927; "A Parleying with Aristophanes," by Donald Smalley, *PMLA,* 1940. Hood's scholarly article is thorough in its listing and elucidation of Browning's frequent allusions to Greek writers. It also distinguishes between the original and intermediate sources of his knowledge of the classics. Cressman analyses about twenty poems on classical themes. Tisdel comments on "the great mass of minute classical reference" crowded into *Aristophanes' Apology,* but regards this learning as the acquisition of a poet rather than of a profound scholar. As a catalogue of the books in Browning's family library reveals, the apparent erudition of the poems dealing with his favourite authors, Euripides and Aristophanes, was derived from the intensive study of a few works of reference rather than a wide range of reading. Smalley points out that while Browning made liberal use of sources, his own poetic theories colour *Aristophanes' Apology*. In particular he represents the dramatic ideals of Euripides as expressive of his own standards and aims in poetry.

Little of significance has been written on the general subject of Browning's art since 1910. C. N. Wenger's *The Aesthetics of Robert Browning*, 1924, though not a definitive book on this important theme, has the merit of emphasizing the connection between the poet's conception of art and his philosophy of life. A more specialized study, G. H. Palmer's "The Monologue of Browning," *HTR*, 1918, is an admirable discussion of his familiar vehicle of artistic expression. Palmer stresses the importance of the poet's development of the dramatic monologue in making it a mirror not of a single mood, but of a total complex individual.

As was to be expected, much has been written recently on Browning's religious beliefs and philosophy of life, but little of it is of permanent worth. John A. Hutton's *Further Guidance from Robert Browning in Matters of Faith*, 1929, is an addendum to his former treatise on this theme. This book centres on *Ferishtah's Fancies* and is in large part a paraphrase of its arguments.

Two essays by H. B. Charlton, "Browning's Ethical Poetry," *BJRL*, 1942, and "Browning as Poet of Religion," *BJRL*, 1943, are written with insight. Charlton traces the evolution of the poet's religious convictions and his philosophy of life, as revealed in his work, up to the climax of the Pope's soliloquies in *The Ring and the Book*, and the final utterance of personal faith in the *Epilogue to Asolando*. At the same time he regards the increasing involvement of Browning in religious and philosophical problems as detrimental to his poetic genius.

In my article, "Browning and Higher Criticism," *PMLA*, 1929 (see pages 19-51 of this book), I have considered the poet's attitude towards an important modern movement, historical and critical, of religious thought.

As a complement to Sir Henry Jones's representation of love as the supreme motive of Browning's art, it is instructive to read Louis Wann's fine article, "Browning's Theory of Love," *Personalist*, 1925. In contrast to Sir Henry's concentration on love as a universal principle, with its supreme expression the love between God and man, Wann dwells on the poet's delineation of love between man and woman. He finds that sixty-four poems of Browning deal with sex-love. These divide into poems culminating in the success of love, the realization of the ideal, and those which end in frustration and non-attainment. Wann admirably illustrates the place in soul development that Browning allots to failure in love, in harmony with his characteristic philosophy of life:

> Ah, but a man's reach should exceed his grasp,
> Or what's a heaven for?

Our modern *penchant* for imagery and symbolism is exemplified in several interesting and original writings on such aspects of Browning's poetry. One of the best of these is "Touch Images in the Poetry of Robert Browning," by John Kester Bonnell, *PMLA*, 1922. In this article, Mr. Bonnell draws attention through copious citation to the frequency of tactile images in his verse. He stresses "the peculiar strength, variety, and fineness of the poet's sense of touch." He links this with Browning's love of sculpture and architecture; and refers to the incident of his passion for modelling in the studio of W. W. Story during the winter of 1862, which made his wife whimsically expostulate that he cared for nothing but clay, "poor lost soul."

A recent study, of an arresting and stimulating character, is *Browning's Star-Imagery* by C. Willard Smith, "Princeton Studies in English," no. 21, 1941. Mr. Smith has made a thorough and painstaking investigation of the symbolic meanings of Browning's star-imagery. He has shown how constantly the poet linked stars with the ideas of resolution, aspiration, hope, intellectual and poetic decision. Differences of opinion are more apt to arise in connection with Smith's convictions regarding the structural functions of Browning's star-imagery than with his explanation of the symbolism involved. A single detail of poetic design, even though a favourite one, is a slim basis to be considered a guide to the organic structure of the writings of such a catholic intellectual and imaginative genius. The findings of such an excursus stand in constant need of correction in the light of that richer and more fruitful insight only to be gained by a comprehensive study of the content, development, and outline of Browning's poetry. Nevertheless the book contains sound and scholarly discussions of such themes as the relation between the poet's references to the stars and his general vision of light, the associate images linked with the stars, the dominance of star-symbolism in certain writings of Browning and its subordination in others.

I come now to the last division of my survey, namely, books and articles written on single poems of Browning.

If an evaluation may be made of the relative worth of contributions to Browning studies since 1910, it seems to me that the work which has been done on *The Ring and the Book* is of primary importance. No biography of Browning in this period equals in historical merit that of Griffin and Minchin; and the best literary and philosophical estimates of his poetry are still those of Jones, Stopford Brooke, Dowden, Herford, and Symons. In connection with *The Ring and the Book,* however, what has been written after 1910 compares favourably both in variety and in significance with the historical and critical work of any previous period.

It will be convenient to consider the contents of the books and articles concerned with Browning's *magnum opus* under four headings: Source Material; Genesis and Composition; Summaries of Reviews; Interpretations.

Up to 1910 only three versions of the Roman murder story on which *The Ring and the Book* was based were known to exist, namely, the Old Yellow Book, the Secondary Source, and the Casanatense document. In 1939 a new Italian account, contemporary with the events narrated, came to light. An English translation of this, prefaced by an introductory survey of its contents, was printed as "Baylor University's Browning Interests," Series XI in the *Baylor Bulletin,* 1939 (see pages 95-104 of this book). This find led to the discovery by Miss Beatrice Corrigan of several other hitherto unknown accounts of the Franceschini case. Photostats of these have been procured from the Italian libraries in which the manuscripts have been preserved, and the work of translating these new versions has been nearly completed. Although the recently found manuscripts are only association documents, since none of them probably were read by Browning, they enlarge our knowledge of the notorious career, trial, and execution of Guido, and they throw valuable incidental light on the poet's handling of his theme.

On account of Mrs. Orr's mistake in the dating of an important letter and the inferences she drew from this, the story of Browning's composition of *The Ring and the Book* was badly confused. In two articles, originally printed in *MLN,* 1928 (see pages 75-94 of this book), I have corrected her errors regarding the poet's itineraries in France in 1862 and 1864, the dates of the preliminary composition of *The Ring and the Book,* and the manner in which he received the Secondary Source. The publication of the correspondence between Browning and Julia Wedgwood, edited by Richard Curle, 1937, has supplied a good deal of additional data concerning the early and later stages of the composition of *The Ring and the Book.* This has been noted by Paul A. Cundiff in his article, "The Dating of Browning's Conception of the Plan of *The Ring and the Book," SP,* 1941. It is now possible, for the first time, to reconstruct the whole picture of the genesis and composition of the poet's masterpiece.

The correspondence between Robert Browning and Julia Wedgwood has a broader interest in connection with *The Ring and the Book* than the information it gives regarding its composition. When Miss Wedgwood received from the poet in 1868-69 the various instalments of his new work, she wrote letters in response frankly stating her impressions of it. These are sometimes laudatory but frequently critical, the views of a woman of keen intellect though coloured by a dogmatic temperament and feminine prejudices. It is of particular interest to note that both her praise and her criticism anticipate the comments of Victorian reviewers on Browning's *magnum opus*. She admires the characters of Pompilia, Caponsacchi, and the Pope. On the other hand she is repelled by the realistic portrayal of the sordid and brutal crimes of Guido and his band of cut-throats. She protests that there is far too much of the element of evil in the poem, and that the environing atmosphere of blackness is more than the small white central figure of Pompilia can bear. Her second major criticism is that Browning is "so strongly and so incompletely dramatic."[4] This she regards as a strange mixture; and she complains that he never varies the dialect of his poem, but makes his characters talk, even when they are as simple and illiterate as Pompilia, in his own idiom. Browning, in reply, vigorously defends himself on both counts. He effectively answers the criticism of the darker elements in his narrative by pointing out his realistic fidelity to life; and he pillories Julia Wedgwood's somewhat sentimental idealism. In answering Miss Wedgwood's second criticism Browning is less convincing. He argues that "Italian ignorance" is "quite compatible with extraordinary insight and power of expression,"[5] and as a consequence the speeches of Pompilia in *The Ring and the Book* are on the whole in accord with those she might have uttered. He also refers to the right of the poet to idealize character. Yet he minimizes the extent to which his own thought and idiom of language enter into the poem.

Three articles merit comment under the heading of Summaries of Reviews: "The Early Vogue of 'The Ring and the Book,' " by Helen P. Pettigrew, *Archiv,* 1936; "Browning and the Victorian Public in 1868-69," by B. R. McElderry, Jr., *RSSCW,* 1937; and "Victorian Evaluation of *The Ring and the Book*" also by Mr. McElderry, in the same journal, 1939. Mrs. Pettigrew's study, as she states it, "undertakes to compile and analyze British opinion as expressed in reviews, in private letters and in diaries, during the instalment publication (1868-1869), during the nineteen years following, and at the time of Browning's death in 1889." Her summary of early reviews reveals that the initial enthusiasm with which the first instalment of *The Ring and the Book* was greeted was modified as the succeeding volumes appeared. Praise and adverse criticism were about equally distributed. As time went on, however, the balance swung towards the side of disapproval or mere formal tribute, till, she concludes, "a later generation, daunted by the obvious length and complexity, seem more and more to have let *The Ring and the Book* lapse into reverent neglect."

Mr. McElderry, in his first article, regards Mrs. Pettigrew's findings as correct. He feels the assumption "that publication of *The Ring and the Book* in 1868-69 rescued Browning from neglect and established him as a major Victorian poet" is far from true. He accounts for the early enthusiasm of the reviewers by the fact that the poet's reputation had been gradually growing before 1868, suggesting that the reviewers wished to atone for former neglect. Their praise, however, was soon qualified. McElderry maintains that the favourable criticism of the Victorians was largely based on their sentimental appreciation of the characters of *The Ring and the Book,* more particularly, Pompilia, Caponsacchi, and the Pope. This was a palliative that enabled them to swallow their repugnance for the theme of the story. Moreover if the accusation of adultery was frequently introduced in the course of the narrative, it was clear that Pompilia and Caponsacchi were guiltless. Virtue, in a spiritual sense, was triumphant. Apart from this "sentimental appreciation," unfavourable criticisms on artistic grounds were frequent. The length of the poem, its tortuousness, complexity of structure, and involved syntax were attacked.

McElderry's second article on *The Ring and the Book* is mainly an expansion of the first. He cites extracts from various reviews dealing with the form, subject-matter, style, character studies, and the moral lessons or "message" of the poem. The ethical teaching won the approval and admiration of most of the reviewers, as well as the delineation of the virtuous characters, but there were many adverse judgments on the other points. McElderry concludes that, on the whole, the tributes paid by Victorians to *The Ring and the Book* register "a personal triumph rather than an artistic one."

There is yet opportunity for a comprehensive study comparing and contrasting the Victorian evaluation of Browning's poem with that of post-Victorian times. Since *The Ring and the Book* is the most massive, if not the most important, contribution to Victorian poetry, and since more has been written on it than on any other single work of the era, such a study would throw interesting light on shifting standards and currents of literary criticism from the eighteen-seventies down to our own day.

Under the heading of Interpretations, I include books and articles written on the larger aspects of *The Ring and the Book* within the period of my survey. In this connection I wish to acknowledge my indebtedness to the excellent summary and critical review of this material up to the year 1935 in W. C. DeVane's *A Browning Handbook*. My comment will necessarily be briefer than his and less adequate, save that I carry the survey up to 1949.

If the publication of Griffin and Minchin's *Life* may be regarded as a point of departure for a review of modern historical studies of Browning, in like manner Charles W. Hodell's classic work, *The Old Yellow Book,* 1908, is a point of departure for a consideration of more recent critical studies of *The Ring and the Book*. As an appendix to his translation of the Old Yellow Book, Professor Hodell wrote a fine general appreciation entitled "The Making of a Great Poem: An Essay on the Relationships of The Ring and the Book to the Old Yellow Book." Although this essay, printed in 1908, antedates the period of my survey, it has had such influence on succeeding studies that reference must be made to it.

Later writers, in their zeal for disproving Browning's alleged fidelity to the text of his Roman murder story, have failed to do justice to Hodell's conception of the relation of the poet's *mag-*

num opus to its primary source. Hodell is far from regarding *The Ring and the Book* as anything in the nature of a literal transcript. He stresses the way in which Browning transmutes his crude materials by the play of his creative imagination. Yet there is, undeniably, some inconsistency in Hodell's position. "His thinking," as DeVane puts it, "is always bolder than his conclusions."[6] In a portion of his essay which he calls "Browning's Fidelity to the Fact of His Source-Material," he points out justly enough how closely the poet followed the Old Yellow Book in many particulars. At the same time he recognizes that "the passion of the story, as Browning has conceived it, the spiritual meaning of the tragedy—all the real poetry—are created by the Poet."[7] But he immediately adds: "They are created, however, in strict accordance with the detail fact in the Book. In few cases, indeed, does the Poet violate the ascertained fact of his sources, even in his freest range of creation." In similar vein, after dwelling on Browning's transfiguration of Pompilia, he is impelled to write that the poet "has added the important features of her characterization without transgressing the definite limits of fact."[8] This attitude of regarding the handling of incident and character in *The Ring and the Book* as ideal yet compatible in almost every detail with factual veracity is one that the poet himself was apt to assume. It is too extreme and frequently contrary to actuality. The fallacy inherent in it has been made the target of later criticism, which has centred particularly on Browning's representation of his heroine, Pompilia.

Sir Frederick Treves's *The Country of "The Ring and the Book,"* 1913, is the first work of importance on Browning's masterpiece to be published after 1910. It is written with charm and literary distinction; and the accurate tracing of the locale of the poem as well as the picturesque descriptions of the stretch of valley and hill between Florence and Rome make it a valuable association volume. The book is divided into three parts: "The Story," "The Country of the Story," and "The People of the Story as They Appear in the Poem." In Treves's narrative there is less shading of distinction than in Hodell's work between the

Pompilia of history and the heroine of *The Ring and the Book*. As he writes in his preface: "Few need to be reminded that the story is true, and that the poet follows the ancient record with as much exactness as the limner of a missal copies a passage of Holy Writ." In this respect Treves's work is uncritical, but in reviewing the story he corrects several errors in Browning's sources reproduced in *The Ring and the Book*. Through a scrutiny of Italian Registers of Baptism he proves that Guido's age at the time of his death was forty, not fifty as is stated in the Secondary Source. He cites from Registers of Marriage to show that Pompilia and Guido were married on September 6, 1693, not in December of that year. He also draws attention to Browning's mistaken assumption, based on a misinterpretation of an allusion in the Old Yellow Book, that the Comparini had a home in a suburban villa on the outskirts of Rome, as well as a house in the Via Vittoria.

A. K. Cook's *A Commentary upon Browning's The Ring and the Book*, 1920, is an excellent work. The critical judgments in the introductions and appendices are original and, in the main, sound. The scholarly annotation of the poem is admirable, and has made this book the standard commentary. Cook follows Hodell in stressing Browning's creative genius, but he does not maintain that this is in accord with unswerving fidelity to historical fact. In discussing the poet's portrayal of Caponsacchi and Pompilia,[9] he even asserts that "the charm and the nobility of the finely contrasted characters of the hero and the heroine were entirely his creation." Yet Cook's position is still conservative in contrast to the radical conclusions of later critics such as Judge Gest and Mrs. Russell. He admits that readers of the Old Yellow Book will be struck by a discrepancy between its characterizations and those of *The Ring and the Book*. "They will not, I think, discover a 'true St. George' and an absolutely blameless heroine in the Caponsacchi and Pompilia who appear there." But he feels that even in the reading of the Yellow Book our impression of them is favourable. Caponsacchi is depicted as "humane, manly, resolute, adventurous." He speaks the truth "without reserve" and in defiance of consequences, although he lacks the "spiritual exaltation and enthusiasm" with which he is endowed by Browning. Pompilia is not without blemish. Under the stress of suffering and of terrible circumstances, "a weakness and timidity which the poet veils betrayed her into subterfuge and falsehood." Cook evidently does not believe her guilty of a liaison with Caponsacchi; and thinks that most readers of the Book will share Browning's conviction of her innocence.

On the vexed question of the genuine or spurious nature of the letters alleged to have been written by Pompilia, Cook, although with some hesitation, seems inclined to agree with Browning that they are forgeries. He admits that Pompilia's declaration on oath that she could not write is false, but concludes "if we are driven to disbelieve it, it becomes, not certain indeed nor even in my judgment at all probable, but at any rate not impossible that she wrote those letters."[10]

The next work of significance I shall comment on in this section of my survey is *The Old Yellow Book, Source of Browning's The Ring and the Book: A New Translation with Explanatory Notes and Critical Chapters upon the Poem and Its Source*, by John Marshall Gest, 1925. Judge Gest, as was to be expected, approaches his subject from a trained jurist's point of view. He wishes to evaluate the actual facts and legal evidence of the Franceschini case. But he also has somewhat of the advocate's zeal, since he is provoked by Browning's devastating criticism of the lawyers in *The Ring and the Book*. This he feels is at variance with truth; and as a member of the legal profession he defends these seventeenth-century representatives of it. As a consequence, his analysis of the discrepancies between Browning's poem and its sources is much more drastic than that of Cook. He is severe in his censure of the poet's caricature of the prosecuting and defending advocates who took part in the trial of Guido. "These men," he writes, "were experienced and zealous lawyers, whose conduct of the case, in the performance of their official duties, merited the highest praise, while Browning's travesty of their arguments and his contemptuous ridicule of the men themselves, in which he is echoed by all his unthinking followers, deserve serious condemnation."[11]

Judge Gest differs widely from Mr. Cook in his estimates of the historical Pompilia and Caponsacchi. Cook minimizes the discrepancy between Browning's portraiture and that of the Old Yellow Book: Gest widens it into a gulf. He regards the love letters as genuine, and is convinced that Pompilia had guilty relations with Caponsacchi. He sums up his conclusions by writing: "Pompilia was an ordinary girl, deprived of advantages in childhood, with sufficient good looks to attract, and insufficient character to resist temptation, and with instincts stronger than her principles. The victim of an unhappy marriage, she is an object of compassion rather than of admiration. Caponsacchi was a frivolous young fellow, on the lookout for adventure, light in thought and unscrupulous in action."[12] Gest is on relatively secure ground when he attacks the theory that *The Ring and the Book* is a photographic reproduction of history. The limitation of his work, and it is a serious one, is that he has little conception of the right of a great poet to reshape and transfigure his crude materials through the alchemy of his creative imagination. His censure of Browning is equally applicable to Shakespeare, if the measuring rod of such matter-of-fact legalistic criticism is valid in art.

In previous comment on Mrs. F. T. Russell's *One Word More on Browning,* 1927, I reserved its central chapter, "Gold and Alloy," dealing with *The Ring and the Book,* for consideration in this portion of my review. Mrs. Russell takes her cue from Judge Gest, but she is more polemic in the expression of her opinions. Her journalistic style and love of paradox militate against the weighing of her statements. In her criticism of Browning's lack of fidelity to his sources she quite overshoots the mark. She refers to his "headstrong emotionalism," to his "iridescent fancies," and ignores the large element of realism, and indeed of factual truth, to be found in *The Ring and the Book.* Her assertion that 10 per cent would be a liberal estimate of the motivation the poet drew from his sources, while 90 per cent of it is sheer fiction, is typical of Mrs. Russell's exaggeration.

The title of this chapter, "Gold and Alloy," is of course suggested by the famous opening metaphor of Browning's poem which has so sorely puzzled commentators. Mrs. Russell maintains that the poet's "concluding process was a complete reversal from that described in his own metaphor." The alloy that was removed after the fashioning of the Ring was she asserts the "pure crude fact," not the fiction of his imagination. Without accepting Mrs. Russell's theory, it must be admitted that Browning's metaphor contains an element of ambiguity if not of positive error. Attempts to interpret it have been so numerous that they might in themselves be made the subject of a complete essay. Without pretence to solve the crux, I might suggest that all art involves the transition from a lower to a higher truth through the media of interpretative imagination. A photograph is more literally, but less essentially true than a painting. In a sense there is always repristination in art, since truth is recaptured on a loftier height. Browning seems to have something like this in mind in *The Ring and the Book* when he writes:

> Fancy with fact is just one fact the more;.... (I. 464)

> Is fiction which makes fact alive, fact too?
> The somehow may be thishow.   (I. 705-6)

A reaction against the literalism of Judge Gest's and Mrs. Russell's criticisms was inevitable, and this found expression in a fine essay, "The 'Donna Angelicata' in *The Ring and the Book*," by J. E. Shaw, *PMLA,* 1926. Mr. Shaw recognizes the validity of the arguments that Browning's poem cannot be regarded as a transcript of fact. He calls it "a glorious misinterpretation," and he even adds weight to its factual inaccuracies in one particular. As an expert Italian scholar, Professor Shaw is able to show, beyond the possibility of reasonable doubt, that the love letters of Pompilia were genuine, not forgeries as the poet regarded them. But, having proved this, he proceeds to stress the right of Browning to idealize and transfigure his source material. In this connection, he dwells upon the primary motive which led Browning to glorify Pompilia and to be predisposed to disregard any evidence discreditable to her: the poet's heroine had become inseparably linked in his mind with the cherished memory of his dead wife. This association had been indicated by Herford and other writers, but Shaw enlarges upon it. He emphasizes the "keen chivalrous instinct" of Browning which is revealed in many of his poems. He points out how the analogy between Caponsacchi's rescue of Pompilia and the poet's rescue of Elizabeth Barrett, at the time of their elopement, from her invalid life under the domination of an unreasoning and autocratic father, would colour Browning's thought. Shaw also thinks that another analogy, the love of Dante for Beatrice, which he believes was blended in Browning's mind with his own love for Elizabeth, entered into his portraiture of the ideal and spiritual love of Caponsacchi for Pompilia as depicted in *The Ring and the Book*.

Despite his insistence on the glorification of Pompilia, Shaw's estimate of her as depicted in the Old Yellow Book is favourable. His reaction is that of Cook rather than of Judge Gest. "It is evident, I think, that Browning's Pompilia is not the Francesca of the *Old Yellow Book*—she is 'another guess' lady—but it is also evident that she is not merely a white-washed Francesca, she is not a bad girl made into a good girl; the testimony of Fra Celestino Angelo, in the *Book*, represents her as innocent, modest, and forgiving, dying like a saint."

Professor W. C. DeVane, in his article "The Virgin and the Dragon," printed in the *Yale Review*, 1947, reinforces Mr. Shaw's emphasis on a chivalric motif in the account of the relations between Caponsacchi and Pompilia. DeVane points out that the rescue of an innocent woman in distress is the theme of a number of Browning's poems, as for instance *Count Gismond* and *The Flight of the Duchess*. This motif is frequently symbolized by the poet through references to the Perseus-Andromeda myth and the cognate legend of St. George slaying the dragon.

There are at least thirty allusions to these tales in *The Ring and the Book*. In his youth Browning kept on his desk the picture of Caravaggio's Andromeda, and references to this myth, beginning as early as *Pauline,* are interspersed throughout his poetry. Caponsacchi, a heaven-sent rescuer, plays the role of a Perseus saving an Andromeda, Pompilia, from the clutches of a monster, Guido. He is also compared to St. George the dragon-slayer. Browning's imagination is kindled not only by the analogy between Caponsacchi's rescue of Pompilia and his own rescue of Elizabeth Barrett, but also by his long-cherished romantic ideal of the hero saviour who in the extreme hour of need slays the powers of evil and delivers a woman from deadly peril.

The unique narrative and dramatic structure of *The Ring and the Book* has interested recent writers. Professors DeVane and McElderry have I feel successfully refuted Santayana's criticism that Browning's "long poems have no structure—for that name cannot be given to the singular mechanical division of 'The Ring and the Book.' "[13] In *A Browning Handbook,* 1935, DeVane refers to the poet's artistry in the composition of his great work as "final and consummate." Certain elements of the poem he regards as probably part of Browning's original plan. These are: the series of interrelated monologues in which many people view the same event differently; the symbolism of the Ring as an emblem of central truth; and the allotment of the divisions of the twelve books to the spectators, principal characters, lawyers, and the poet himself. "The great form," what might be defined as the dramatic movement of *The Ring and the Book,* was evolved, DeVane conjectures, in the actual composition of the poem. This he defines as: "the steady great rise to the height, culminating in Pompilia's speech (Book VII), and then the deliberate dropping into anticlimax in the speeches of the opposing lawyers, and then the sharp rise to the Pope's great utterance in the second peak of the poem."[14]

"The Narrative Structure of Browning's *The Ring and the Book*," by B. R. McElderry, Jr., *RSSCW,* 1943, is an excellent study of the architectonic of the work. McElderry shows that, while the plan of *The Ring and the Book* is unique, the poem is a "psychological unity." So far from being, as Santayana asserts, without structure, it reveals "an extraordinary organizing power." "The story is told not only with richness of detail and interpretation, but with surprising lack of pointless repetition and digression." McElderry comments on the skill of Browning's use of balance and contrast, the variety of individual views which give a different perspective to each speaker's account of the same events. The fertility of the poet's resource, and the remarkable way in which repetition is reduced to a minimum are illustrated through a detailed tabular analysis of the twelve books. The method of this analysis is to set down the chronological sequence of episodes; and then to indicate the number of lines devoted to each in the various books. A column is also left for lines classified as miscellaneous. A scrutiny of these tables reveals the avoidance of undue repetition through the shifting of emphasis on this or that incident of the story from book to book in accordance with the predilection or bias of the individual speaker. Variety is also secured through freshness of approach, each speaker's recital being coloured by his own personality.

In summing up his findings, Professor McElderry points out that his chart shows how episodes prior to the murder trial are developed more fully in the early books and subordinated afterwards. He, therefore, concludes that "Browning's master-plan was to make the murder trial progressively dominant."

A somewhat different conception of the poet's master-plan is set forth in Henry James's address delivered before the Academic Committee of the Royal Society of Literature in 1912, subsequently printed in his *Notes on Novelists,* 1914, under the title, "The Novel in 'The Ring and the Book.'" James feels that the artistic and spiritual centre of Browning's poem lies in "the embracing consciousness of Caponsacchi." "He *is* the soul of man at its finest—having passed through the smoky fires of life and emerging clear and high." Since "the direct relation" of Caponsacchi is "always to Pompilia," it is their intertwined story and the bond of ideal love between them which is the core of

The Ring and the Book. "What comes out clearest, comes out as straightest and strongest and finest, from Browning's genius" is, according to James, "the exhibition of the great constringent relation between man and woman at once at its maximum and as the relation most worth while in life for either party; an exhibition forming quite the main substance of our author's message."

As was to be expected, an enthralling element of *The Ring and the Book* for Henry James is the intimacy of the poet's contact with Italy. Browning, as he puts it, "stirs up, to my vision, a perfect cloud of gold-dust"; and in eloquent prose the great American novelist comments on the saturation of the atmosphere of the poem with local colour, "those wonderful dreadful beautiful particulars of the Italy of the eve of the eighteenth century."

Louise Snitslaar's *Sidelights on Robert Browning's "The Ring and the Book,"* 1934, centres on the minor characters of the poem—those who voice the opinions of the streets in "Half-Rome," "The Other Half-Rome," "Tertium Quid," and, as another grouping, the lawyers. The theme of her book is summed up in the Introduction: "In our subsequent chapters we wish to write a vindication of these minor characters. It is our intention to point out how they, as well as the main figures have a right to their place in Browning's great work; how they even enhance the beauty of the work as a whole; how they give proof of Browning's untiring and incessant efforts to look at so important a thing as the truth from as many sides as possible."

In the hue and cry of criticism attacking the prolixity and crabbedness of Browning's *magnum opus,* the books containing the speeches of the minor characters have been a special target. On the other hand, their legitimate and necessary place in the plan and economy of the poem has been ably defended in A. K. Cook's *Commentary* and elsewhere. Louise Snitslaar's work is an expansion of Cook's argument. She emphasizes the importance of the books voicing the opinions of the Roman streets in creating an atmosphere for the dramatic tale and preparing the way for the introduction of the principal figures, Guido, Caponsacchi, and Pompilia. The pleas of the opposing lawyers supply relief, realism, and comedy; and, since the story is based on the murder trial, to leave them out would disembowel the legal fabric of the poem, and sever its intrinsic connection with the Old Yellow Book.

One of the most interesting and original sections of Miss Snitslaar's work is that in which she takes issue with Judge Gest's criticism of Browning's representation of the lawyers. She admits that they are, in a sense, parodies, but then proceeds to analyse the deeper motives that lay back of the poet's treatment of them. *The Ring and the Book* is to be evaluated as a poem, not as an historical record. The lawyers stand for that dry-as-dust rationalism of the head severed from the heart which Browning always mistrusted. "For them this murder is but one out of many cases, a lawsuit which by means of their more or less close reasoning they will either win or lose."[15] They serve as a foil for the impassioned pleading of Caponsacchi and Pompilia, in which human sympathies, the emotions of the heart, and imaginative intuitions are deeply involved. They serve also as a foil for the higher insights of the saintly Innocent XII. "The Pope, an old man on the verge of death, sheds the benevolent light of his wisdom and philosophy upon the unfortunate participants in the tragedy enacted before our eyes."[16]

Paul E. Beichner's "Fra Celestino's Affidavit and *The Ring and the Book*," *MLN*, 1943, is a brief but significant article from an historical point of view. The attestation of Fra Celestino has been regarded by Browning himself and many later readers of the Old Yellow Book as convincing proof of Pompilia's innocence in her relations with Caponsacchi. Beichner, however, points out the obligation the priest was under not to reveal what had been told him in confession, and stresses what he considers to be the deliberate ambiguity of the phrase in which Fra Celestino refers to Pompilia as "a good, modest, and honourable girl." He sums up his conclusions as follows:

The affidavits, I think, should not be accepted as an indication of Pompilia's character nor of her guilt or innocence, because any or all of these things—the Seal of Confession, the professional secret, the natural secret, and the right of a person to keep his own conscience secret from the public—make them questionable. The writers of the affidavits could not have spoken otherwise if Pompilia had been guilty; a refusal to speak in any case would have been interpreted as an admission of her guilt.

Beichner and Gest are in essential agreement with regard to this matter, but it may be maintained that to delve minutely into the frailties of an unfortunate Italian peasant girl, whose conduct under terrible duress evokes compassion rather than condemnation, is to inquire too curiously. The important thing is not what the historical Francesca was, but the Pompilia that Browning made of her.

Amongst the numerous writings since 1910 on individual poems of Browning other than *The Ring and the Book,* one work may be singled out as of especial importance. This is, W. C. De Vane's volume, published in 1927, *Browning's Parleyings: The Autobiography of a Mind.* Although the way for a critical commentary on *Parleyings with Certain People of Importance in Their Day* had been paved by Griffin and Minchin's account of the early reading of the poet and its influence on this work, the larger aspects of its autobiographical significance escaped them. With the exception of occasional passages of sheer poetry, the *Parleyings* share the limitations of Browning's later verse, but they are a unique record of his mental history. Here, as Professor DeVane has shown, may be traced the literary origin of central artistic, philosophical, and political ideas and convictions of the poet. The growth of these throughout the course of years is also indicated and, finally, their present application at the time of the composition of the poem. The seven "mute spirits" whom Browning summons up in the *Parleyings* are, with one exception, men whose works had been familiar to the poet from boyhood. DeVane stresses the fact that they represent seven major interests of Browning's life—philosophy, history, poetry, politics, painting, the classics (Greek), and music. As the poet comments and reflects on the works of the various characters he has selected, the development of these interests in his own life is suggested.

In practically every instance his consideration of "certain people of importance in their day" becomes a *point d'appui* for contemporary reference. Browning uses them as stalking horses not only to set forth his own ideas in the spheres of major interest represented, but also to criticize or confute different ideas held by some of his Victorian compeers. Amongst these are Carlyle, Disraeli, Swinburne, and possibly Matthew Arnold. In connection with the contemporary allusions, DeVane has drawn attention to the influence of several incidents of an intimate personal nature. Browning's defence of his son's paintings of the nude is indirectly reflected in the Parleying with "Francis Furini." The unhappy episode of his unfortunate courtship of Lady Ashburton is responsible for an outburst of passionate invective in the Parleying with "Daniel Bartoli."

While DeVane's book is technically a critical review of an individual poem, the nature of his subject-matter enables him to give a somewhat sweeping vista of the poet's intellectual and artistic horizons. His work has therefore a larger reference, and is a valuable contribution to the study of Browning's thought and cardinal interests as a whole.

A. J. Whyte's edition of *Sordello,* 1913, deserves mention for its excellent introduction to the various books of the poem, and its scholarly critical and historical annotations. In his general introduction the author, while recognizing the peculiar difficulties of *Sordello,* emphasizes "the great and undeniable beauties" of the poem and regrets that these have been neglected. He illustrates through citation the lyrical loveliness of individual lines and passages, and the poet's gift of rapid and vivid characterization.

Articles on the numerous poems of Browning, as distinct from books, have flowed from prolific pens, "thick as autumnal leaves that strow the brooks in Vallombrosa." All I can attempt to do is to review briefly a few of those written since 1910, without pretence to include everything of worth.

W. C. DeVane's *"Sordello's* Story Retold," *SP,* 1930, is an important contribution. His able and painstaking study of the evolution of a poem which has become a byword for obscurity does much to clarify a reader's understanding of this difficult and complex work. He distinguishes four periods of composition between 1833 and 1840 in which like geological strata later layers of interpretation are superimposed upon the original sketch of Sordello's character. In the first Sordello is envisaged as the poet; in the second as the lover and the warrior; in the third the objective historical background of the hero's career is stressed; in the fourth the humanitarian element becomes paramount. Sordello finally elects to side with the people and to become the champion of the masses. "The final result," as DeVane writes in his *Handbook,* "may be said to be a conglomeration of all these conceptions."[17] He calls *Sordello* "a bewildering potpourri of poetry, psychology, love, romance, humanitarianism, philosophy, fiction, and history."[18] Yet, like Whyte, he is keenly appreciative of the strength as well as the weakness of the poem. He comments on its magnificent descriptions of the landscapes of northern Italy, and the excellence of its character sketching, culminating in the portrait of the veteran warrior Salinguerra.

Harold Gloder's article, "Browning's 'Childe Roland,'" *PMLA,* 1924, contains the best account of the way in which the poet's subconscious mind made use of various sources in folk lore, fairy tales, and medieval romances in the weaving of this imaginative work of fantasy. His essay should be linked with DeVane's "The Landscape of Browning's *Childe Roland,*" *PMLA,* 1925. DeVane points out the genesis of the descriptions of the grotesque and ugly aspects of nature in the poet's early reading of Gérard de Lairesse's *The Art of Painting in All Its Branches.* In chapter XVII of this work, "Of Things Deformed and Broken, Falsely Called Painter-like," the origin of numerous touches in Browning's poem may be traced. "Here the old cripple, the pathless field, the desperate vegetation, the spiteful little river, the killing of the water-rat, the enclosing mountains, the leering sunset, and many other details of *Childe Roland* are to be found."[19]

Some competent essays and critical articles on the plays of Browning have been written since 1910. Shortly before this date,

however, in "'A Blot in the 'Scutcheon' (An Appreciation),"
Canadian Magazine, 1908, George Herbert Clarke protests
against undue depreciation of this drama. He stresses the beauty
of its poetry and the "freedom and flexibility" of its language.
He feels that critics have exaggerated the flaws of improbability
of dramatic situation and stage motivation. This article should
be read in conjunction with Ethel Colburn Mayne's discriminating analysis of the character of Mildred Tresham in her charming
book, *Browning's Heroines,* 1913.

The review of *Strafford* in D. C. Somervell's "An Early Victorian Tragedy," *London Mercury,* 1927, contains an account of
the poet's studies in preparation for the writing of this drama,
and shows how they helped to develop and crystallize his own
political views. Elmer E. Stoll's "Browning's *In a Balcony,*" to
be found in *From Shakespeare to Joyce,* 1944, is a vivaciously
written critical analysis of a play whose conclusion has been a
subject of controversy.

The enigmatical *Fifine at the Fair* has been somewhat clarified
by a realization of its connection with the unhappy personal incident of Browning's proposal of marriage to Lady Ashburton
around 1871. The bitterness of the aftermath of this unfortunate
happening found indirect expression in the Parleying with "Daniel
Bartoli" and in *St. Martin's Summer,* but in *Fifine at the Fair* it
colours the whole poem. Its pervasive influence throughout this
work, independently noted by Professor DeVane and myself, is
fully discussed in my article, "Browning's Dark Mood: A Study
of *Fifine at the Fair*" (see pages 105-28 of this book). The poem
may also include some echoes of the feud between Dante Gabriel
Rossetti and Robert Buchanan, as DeVane maintains in his
article, "The Harlot and the Thoughtful Young Man: A Study
of the Relation between Rossetti's 'Jenny' and Browning's 'Fifine
at the Fair,'" *SP,* 1932.

A natural consequence of the discovery of Elizabeth Barrett's
eleven pages of notes suggesting revisions in the manuscript of
The Flight of the Duchess (previously referred to in this survey)
has been conjecture regarding a possible element of autobiography in this poem. Although *The Flight of the Duchess* was

published nearly a year before the marriage and elopement of Elizabeth, the theme of it suggests an analogy to these coming events. In 1845 Elizabeth Barrett anticipated a voyage to Italy, whither Browning would have followed her. Professor Fred Manning Smith has argued cogently that there is a symbolic connection between the life and character of Miss Barrett as well as the situation in which she was placed, and the evolution of Browning's poem. His point of view is set forth in two articles printed in *SP,* 1942.

C. R. Tracy's articles, "Browning's Heresies," *SP,* 1936; "Caliban upon Setebos," *SP,* 1938; "Bishop Blougram," *MLR,* 1939, contain some pertinent reflections on the poet's religious and philosophical views, with particular reference to his attitude towards rationalism. These articles are somewhat along the lines of my own essay, "Browning's Casuists," *SP,* 1940 (see pages 129-55 of this book).

Fresh light has been thrown on the sources of individual poems in such studies as Arthur Dickson's "Browning's Source for *The Pied Piper of Hamelin,*" *SP,* 1926; John D. Rea's "My Last Duchess," *SP,* 1932; Frederic E. Faverty's "The Source of the Jules-Phene Episode in *Pippa Passes,*" *SP,* 1941; and many others. As has been stated, my review of articles on single poems must of necessity be selective rather than inclusive on account of the plethora of material.

It would be a serious omission to conclude any survey of this nature without mention of the two-volume *Concordance to the Poems of Robert Browning* by Leslie N. Broughton and Benjamin F. Stelter, 1924-25. This work of faithful and laborious scholarship is an indispensable tool for the student of Browning's poetry.

Check-List of Titles

Armstrong, A. J., ed. "The Diary of Miss Evelyn Barclay"; *Intimate Glimpses from Browning's Letter File; Letters of Robert Browning to Miss Isa Blagden;* Letters written by Landor to Browning, printed in *Baylor Bulletin.*

Beichner, P. E. "Fra Celestino's Affidavit and *The Ring and the Book.*"

England and America, 1910-1949

BONNELL, J. K. "Touch Images in the Poetry of Robert Browning."
BROUGHTON, L. N. and STELTER, B. F. *Concordance to the Poems of Robert Browning.*
BROWNING, FANNIE (Mrs. R. W. B.) *Some Memories of Robert Browning.*
BURDETT, OSBERT. *The Brownings.*
CHARLTON, H. B. "Browning as Poet of Religion"; "Browning's Ethical Poetry."
CLARKE, G. H. " 'A Blot in the 'Scutcheon' (An Appreciation)."
COOK, A. K. *A Commentary upon Browning's The Ring and the Book.*
CRAMER, M. B. "Browning's Friendships and Fame before Marriage (1833-1846)"; "Browning's Literary Reputation at Oxford, 1855-1859"; "What Browning's Literary Reputation Owed to the Pre-Raphaelites, 1847-1856."
CRESSMAN, E. D. "The Classical Poems of Robert Browning."
CUNDIFF, P. A. "The Dating of Browning's Conception of the Plan of *The Ring and the Book.*"
CURLE, RICHARD, ed. *Robert Browning and Julia Wedgwood.*
DEVANE, W. C. *A Browning Handbook; Browning's Parleyings: The Autobiography of a Mind;* "The Harlot and the Thoughtful Young Man"; "The Landscape of Browning's *Childe Roland*"; "*Sordello*'s Story Retold"; "The Virgin and the Dragon."
DICKSON, ARTHUR. "Browning's Source for *The Pied Piper of Hamelin.*"
DUCKWORTH, F. R. G. *Browning: Background and Conflict.*
ELTON, Sir OLIVER. "The Brownings."
FAVERTY, F. E. "The Source of the Jules-Phene Episode in *Pippa Passes.*"
GEST, J. M. *The Old Yellow Book, Source of Browning's The Ring and the Book.*
GLODER, HAROLD. "Browning's 'Childe Roland.' "
HARLAN, AURELIA BROOKS and J. LEE, Jr., eds. *Letters from Owen Meredith to Robert and Elizabeth Barrett Browning.*
HATCHER, H. H. *The Versification of Robert Browning.*
HODELL, C. W. *The Old Yellow Book.*
HOOD, T. L. "Browning's Ancient Classical Sources"; ed., *Letters of Robert Browning,* collected by Thomas J. Wise.
HUTTON, J. A. *Further Guidance from Robert Browning in Matters of Faith.*

HUXLEY, LEONARD, ed. *Elizabeth Barrett Browning: Letters to Her Sister, 1846-1859.*
JAMES, HENRY. "The Novel in 'The Ring and the Book.'"
JONES, Sir HENRY. "Robert Browning and Elizabeth Barrett Browning."
KENYON, Sir F. G., ed. *New Poems by Robert Browning and Elizabeth Barrett Browning; The Works of Robert Browning,* with Introductions.
LOUNSBURY, T. R. *The Early Literary Career of Robert Browning.*
MCELDERRY, B. R., Jr. "Browning and the Victorian Public in 1868-69"; "The Narrative Structure of Browning's *The Ring and the Book*"; "Victorian Evaluation of *The Ring and the Book.*"
MINCHIN, H. C. *Walter Savage Landor.*
PALMER, G. H. "The Monologue of Browning."
PETTIGREW, HELEN P. "The Early Vogue of 'The Ring and the Book.'"
PHELPS, W. L. *Robert Browning.*
POTTLE, F. A. *Shelley and Browning: A Myth and Some Facts.*
REA, J. D. "My Last Duchess."
RUSSELL, FRANCES THERESA. *One Word More on Browning.*
SHAW, J. E. "The 'Donna Angelicata' in *The Ring and the Book.*"
SMALLEY, DONALD. *Browning's Essay on Chatterton;* "A Parleying with Aristophanes."
SMITH, C. W. *Browning's Star-Imagery.*
SMITH, F. M. Elizabeth Barrett and Browning's *The Flight of the Duchess*"; "More Light on 'Elizabeth Barrett and Browning's *The Flight of the Duchess.*'"
SNITSLAAR, LOUISE. *Sidelights on Robert Browning's "The Ring and the Book."*
SNYDER, EDWARD and PALMER, FREDERICK, Jr. "New Light on the Brownings."
SOMERVELL, D. C. "An Early Victorian Tragedy"; "The Reputation of Robert Browning."
STOLL, E. E. "Browning's *In a Balcony.*"
TISDEL, F. M. "Browning's *Aristophanes' Apology.*"
TOYNBEE, WILLIAM. *The Diaries of William Charles Macready, 1833-1851.*
TRACY, C. R. "Bishop Blougram"; "Browning's Heresies"; "Caliban upon Setebos."

TREVES, Sir FREDERICK. *The Country of "The Ring and the Book."*
Twenty-two Unpublished Letters of Elizabeth Barrett Browning and Robert Browning, Addressed to Henrietta and Arabella Moulton-Barrett.
WANN, LOUIS. "Browning's Theory of Love."
WENGER, C. N. *The Aesthetics of Robert Browning.*
WHITING, LILIAN. *The Brownings: Their Life and Art.*
WHYTE, A. J., ed. *Sordello.*

Notes

ESSAY 1:

1. William Clyde DeVane, *A Browning Handbook* (New York, 1935), p. 79.
2. *The Letters of Robert Browning and Elizabeth Barrett Barrett, 1845-1846* (London, 1899), I, 17.
3. A. M. Terhune, *The Life of Edward FitzGerald* (New Haven, 1947), p. 254.
4. From *Interpretations of Poetry and Religion* (New York, 1900), p. 189.
5. *Ibid.*, p. 206.
6. F. L. Lucas, *Ten Victorian Poets* (Cambridge, 1948), pp. 36; 23.
7. Cf. Browning's letter to Isabella Blagden, cited in *Letters of Robert Browning*, collected by Thomas J. Wise and ed. by Thurman L. Hood (New Haven, 1933), p. 82. See also F. R. G. Duckworth, *Browning: Background and Conflict* (London, 1931), p. 121.
8. *The Works of John Ruskin*, ed. by E. T. Cook and Alexander Wedderburn, XXXVI (London, 1909), xxxiv.
9. *An Introduction to the Study of Browning* (London, 1916), p. 27.
10. *Lady Geraldine's Courtship*, stanza 41.
11. G. K. Chesterton, *Robert Browning* (New York, 1903), p. 149.
12. *By the Fire-side*, ll. 244-45.
13. *The Brownings* (London, 1928), p. 338.
14. *Old Pictures in Florence*, ll. 149-52.

ESSAY 2:

1. Cf. John Theodore Merz, *A History of European Thought in the Nineteenth Century* (Edinburgh and London, 1914), IV, 360-63. In a note on page 363, Merz stresses the importance of the contribution of the great English poets of the nineteenth century to religious thought, pointing to "imaginative writers, such notably as Tennyson and Robert Browning, who have, together with Wordsworth, perhaps more than any other writers, not only supplied thoughtful minds in this country with as much philosophy of religion as they required or could assimilate, but exhibit more than any others those specific characteristics of British thought which are so difficult for the foreigner to get hold of."
2. *A Writer's Recollections* (London, 1919), pp. 224-25.
3. From a letter dated May 11, 1876. This was printed in the *Nonconformist*, 1890; see *Letters of Robert Browning*, collected by Thomas J. Wise and ed. by Thurman L. Hood (New Haven, 1933), pp. 171-72. Cf. also Mrs. Sutherland Orr's statement with regard to Browning: "He has repeatedly written or declared in the words of Charles Lamb: 'If Christ

entered the room I should fall on my knees'; and again, in those of Napoleon: 'I am an understander of men, and *He* was no man.' He has even added: 'If he had been, he would have been an impostor.' " *Life and Letters of Robert Browning* (London, 1891), p. 318.

4. Arthur Penrhyn Stanley, *The Life and Correspondence of Thomas Arnold* (5th ed., London, 1845), I, 404.

5. From a letter of 1841 in *Letters, Literary and Theological,* ed. by J. J. S. Perowne and Louis Stokes (London, 1881), p. 175.

6. John William Burgon, *Inspiration and Interpretation* (London, 1861), p. 89.

7. Cited as quoted in R. M. Wenley's "Some Lights on the British Idealistic Movement in the Nineteenth Century," *AJT,* July, 1901.

8. Arthur Penrhyn Stanley, *Life and Correspondence,* II, 175.

9. Frederick Maurice, *The Life of Frederick Denison Maurice* (London, 1884), II, 423.

10. See Matthew Arnold's strictures on Colenso in two articles in *Macmillan's Magazine,* Jan. and Feb., 1863, and in his essay on "The Function of Criticism at the Present Time," 1865.

11. Otto Pfleiderer, *The Development of Theology in Germany since Kant, and Its Progress in Great Britain since 1825,* trans. by J. F. Smith (London, 1890), p. 387.

12. "Robert Browning's 'Christmas-Eve and Easter-Day' und 'Das Leben Jesu' von D. F. Strauss," *Archiv,* CXLVII (1924), 203.

13. See *The Letters of Robert Browning and Elizabeth Barrett Barrett, 1845-1846* (London, 1899), I, 145-46, 147; II, 429-30, 436-37. Cf. "Mrs. Browning's Religious Opinions as Expressed in Three Letters" cited in *Literary Anecdotes of the Nineteenth Century,* ed. by W. R. Nicoll and T. J. Wise (London, 1896), II, 123-42.

14. Browning's own religious observance was in keeping with this declaration. In 1885, he wrote to W. G. Kingsland: "I frequently attended the service at Mr. Jones' Chapel about twenty years ago." The place of worship referred to is Bedford Chapel, London. In Normandy, the poet went to a French Reformed service, with Milsand. In Venice he often attended a chapel of the Waldensians. His son was baptized in the church of the French Lutherans at Florence.

15. Cited from *QR,* CLXX (1890), 493.

16. Thomas Carlyle, *The Life of John Sterling* (London, 1851), p. 271.

17. *Ibid.,* p. 243.

18. *The Ideal of a Christian Church* (London, 1843), p. 266.

19. Mrs. Orr, *Life and Letters,* p. 108. See also the statement in Mrs. Orr's *A Handbook to the Works of Robert Browning* (London, 1899), p. 4, that Browning "has no bond of union with German philosophers, but the natural tendencies of his own mind," and "resembles Hegel, Fichte, or Schelling . . . by the purely creative impulse which has met their thought."

20. *Robert Browning and Alfred Domett,* ed. by Frederic G. Kenyon (London, 1906), p. 52.

21. *Ibid.,* p. 57.

22. Cited from George Eliot's translation of Strauss's *Das Leben Jesu* (6th ed., London, 1913), p. xxx.

23. Fräulein Käthe Göritz (see note 12) draws attention to an interesting parallel between these lines and the following passage from Coleridge's *Aids to Reflection*: "Did Christ come from Heaven, did the Son of God

leave the Glory which he had with his Father before the World began, only to *show* us a way to life, to *teach* truths, to *tell* us of a resurrection? Or saith he not, I *am* the way—I *am* the truth—I *am* the Resurrection and the Life?" See edition of Thomas Fenby (Edinburgh, 1905), Aphorism CXVII. 2.

In view of the seminal influence of *Aids to Reflection* on the religious thought of minds as various as those of John Sterling, Frederick Maurice, Cardinal Newman, and John Stuart Mill, it is possible that Browning may have been directly indebted to Coleridge's work. On the other hand, Mrs. Orr has stated that he "was emphatic in his assertion that he knew neither the German philosophers nor their reflection in Coleridge. . . ." (See note 19.) In any event, since the argument for Christ's divinity based on his life as the essence of his revelation is as frequently used by Tractarian and Evangelical writers as by Coleridge and Maurice, it does little to support Fräulein Göritz's contention: "Aus dem Geiste der Broad Church Movement ist Browning's 'Christmas-Eve and Easter-Day' geboren." Perhaps the most elaborate example in English theology of a vein of thought similar to that in which Browning contrasts "mere morality," with "the God in Christ" is to be found in the Bampton Lectures for 1866 of the High Churchman Canon Henry Parry Liddon, *The Divinity of Our Lord and Saviour, Jesus Christ,* and in his lectures of 1870, *Some Elements of Religion.*

24. Cf. *Bishop Blougram's Apology,* ll. 577-95.

25. See pp. 23-4.

26. *Browning Society Papers,* vol. II, pt. III. Cited from the Abstract of the Forty-Eighth Meeting.

27. References in the letters of Browning make it evident that a number of the poems printed in *Dramatis Personae* were composed in the later part of his Italian period before the death of his wife in 1861. On the other hand, Edmund Gosse is of the opinion that the greater part of *Dramatis Personae* was written at the village of Ste Marie, near Pornic, Brittany, where the poet spent the summers of 1862, 1863. Passages in Browning's letters to Isabella Blagden allude to the composition of various pieces at Ste Marie which were to be included in "the new poems" (i.e., *Dramatis Personae*). Of the few poems in the first edition of *Dramatis Personae* whose dates of writing can be approximately determined by internal evidence, *Prospice, James Lee's Wife, Gold Hair, Apparent Failure,* and the *Epilogue* were written after Mrs. Browning's death, and several of these as late as 1863.

28. *Letters of Robert Browning to Miss Isa Blagden,* arranged for publication by A. Joseph Armstrong (Waco, Tex., 1923), pp. 100-1.

29. As Chapman and Hall's advertisement of the first edition of *Dramatis Personae* appeared on May 28, 1864, *A Death in the Desert* was published six months after Browning's reading of Renan's *La Vie de Jésus.*

The contemporary notices of *Dramatis Personae* in English literary journals generally assume that the poet had Renan's book in mind when composing *A Death in the Desert.* For example, the *Athenaeum* review of June 4, 1864, discussing the religious import of the poem, states: "It embodies the death of St. John in the Desert, and has the piquancy of making the beloved apostle reply with last words, in far-off ghostly tones, which come, weirdly impressive, from that cave in the wilderness, to the Frenchman's 'Life of Jesus.' It is done simply and naturally; but could any sensation-novelist contrive anything half so striking?" In like fashion, *QR* of July, 1865 comments as follows: "After M. Renan's 'Life of Jesus,' and the prelections of the Strasbourg school of theological thought, it should be welcome as it is worthy." But, in *David Gray, and Other Essays* (London, 1868), p. 33, Robert Buchanan regards *A Death in the Desert* as being aimed at Strauss: "The second extract is from 'A Death in the Desert,' in which John the Evangelist is supposed to detail his opinions of his contemporaries, and, in a spirit impossibly prophetic, to review the arguments, in the 'Leben Jesu,' against miracles."

30. *Contemporary Review*, LX (1891), 879.

31. The lack of consistency that characterizes the poet's thought in this respect has been ably discussed by A. C. Pigou in his valuable and discriminating Burney Essay for 1900, *Robert Browning as a Religious Teacher*.

32. It is of interest to note that this is the identical argument used by Browning in the course of his conversation with Mrs. Orr in 1869. See p. 39.

33. *Ferishtah's Fancies*, "A Pillar at Sebzevar," ll. 134-35.

34. *Ibid.*, "The Sun," ll. 138-43.

35. *Bishop Blougram's Apology*, ll. 621-27.

36. *Ibid.*, ll. 206-7.

37. *The Ring and the Book*, X. 1643-58.

38. *Saul*, XVIII. 307-12. It is a strange travesty of Browning's thought in *Saul* to infer, as Gilbert Chesterton has done, that he regarded the Incarnation as proceeding from an envious desire of the Almighty to surpass his creature in sorrow and self-denial and read into the Crucifixion the "tremendous story of a Divine jealousy." Were it not for the weight given to such a statement by the imprimatur of Mr. Chesterton, it would hardly seem needful to point out that the poet has no such monstrous paradox in mind. Rather, he is simply voicing a fundamental Christian idea connected with the Incarnation, that, since love at its highest contains an element of suffering and self-sacrifice, God's love must exceed man's in the manifestation of these qualities. Equally surprising is Mr. Chesterton's assertion that one of Browning's two great theories of the universe is what may be called "the hope that lies in the imperfection of God." This is to caricature the poet's view and invert its true perspective. So far from basing his argument for the necessity of the Incarnation on "the hope that lies in the imperfection of God," Browning bases it on the hope, or rather the assurance, that lies in the perfection of God and the infinite resources of his love. The conception of God which Chesterton represents Browning as holding is that which the poet himself ascribed to Caliban. Cf. G. K. Chesterton, *Robert Browning* (New York, 1903), p. 178.

39. The Pope, in *The Ring and the Book*, voices the complement of this faith, from the human side, when he avows that man's perception of God must be conditioned by the finiteness of his faculties.

> O Thou,—as represented here to me
> In such conception as my soul allows,—
> Under Thy measureless, my atom width!—
> Man's mind, what is it but a convex glass
> Wherein are gathered all the scattered points
> Picked out of the immensity of sky,
> To re-unite there, be our heaven for earth,

> Our known unknown, our God revealed to man?
> Existent somewhere, somehow, as a whole;
> Here, as a whole proportioned to our sense,—
> There, (which is nowhere, speech must babble thus!)
> In the absolute immensity, the whole
> Appreciable solely by Thyself,—
> Here, by the little mind of man, reduced
> To littleness that suits his faculty,
> In the degree appreciable too;
> Between Thee and ourselves. . . .   (X. 1308-24)

40. *The Ring and the Book*, XII. 775-78. Innocent XII became Pope in 1691; Voltaire was born in 1694.

41. *MLN*, XLI (1926), 213-19.

42. Cited from Mrs. Orr's article, "The Religious Opinions of Robert Browning," p. 880.

ESSAY 3:

1. Henry James, *William Wetmore Story and His Friends* (Edinburgh and London, 1903), II, 94.

2. *Poems by the Late Isa Blagden,* with a Memoir by Alfred Austin (Edinburgh and London, 1873), p. ix.

3. *Letters from Owen Meredith to Robert and Elizabeth Barrett Browning,* ed. by Aurelia Brooks Harlan and J. Lee Harlan Jr. (Baylor University, 1936), p. 9.

4. *Letters of Robert Browning to Miss Isa Blagden,* arranged for publication by A. Joseph Armstrong (Waco, Tex., 1923), p. viii.

5. Thomas Adolphus Trollope, *What I Remember* (London, 1887), II, 173.

6. *The Florence of Landor* (Boston, 1905), p. 138.

7. W. H. Griffin and H. C. Minchin, *The Life of Robert Browning* (London, 1910), p. 171.

8. *Letters from Owen Meredith to Robert and Elizabeth Barrett Browning,* p. 123.

9. *The Letters of Elizabeth Barrett Browning,* ed. by Frederic G. Kenyon (London, 1897), II, 270.

10. MS is in the New York Public Library.

11. From an unpublished letter of Mrs. Browning's, the typescript of which is in the British Museum.

12. *Letters of Browning to Isa Blagden,* p. 99.

13. *Letters of Anna Jameson to Ottilie von Goethe,* ed. by G. H. Needler (London, New York, Toronto, 1939), p. 217.

14. The reader may consult Miss Whiting's *Kate Field: A Record* (Boston, 1899).

15. *Atlantic Monthly,* Dec., 1864.

16. *Ibid.*

17. *Life of Frances Power Cobbe,* by Herself (Boston, 1894), II, 342.

18. *The Letters of Elizabeth Barrett Browning,* II, 341.

19. *Letters of Robert Browning,* collected by Thomas J. Wise and ed. by Thurman L. Hood (New Haven, 1933), p. 64.

20. *Letters of Browning to Isa Blagden,* pp. vii-viii.

21. *Ibid.*, p. 179.

22. Thomas Adolphus Trollope, *What I Remember*, II, 173.
23. From an unpublished letter. Cited in Miss E. Walton's unpublished MS. on Isabella Blagden.
24. *Poems by the Late Isa Blagden*, p. xiv.
25. *Letters of Browning to Isa Blagden*, p. 207.
26. *William Wetmore Story and His Friends*, II, 94-96.
27. *Poems by the Late Isa Blagden*, p. xi.
28. *Ibid.*, p. xiii.
29. *Elizabeth Barrett Browning: Letters to Her Sister, 1846-1859* (London, 1929), p. 196.
30. *The Letters of Elizabeth Barrett Browning*, II, 290-91.
31. *Letters of Browning to Isa Blagden*, p. 82.
32. *Ibid.*, p. 155.
33. Cited in Miss Walton's MS.
34. *Letters of Browning to Isa Blagden*, p. 179.

ESSAY 4:

1. Mrs. Sutherland Orr, *Life and Letters of Robert Browning* (London, 1891), pp. 259-60.
2. That is, up till 1928, when this article was first printed.
3. *Letters of Robert Browning to Miss Isa Blagden*, arranged for publication by A. Joseph Armstrong (Waco, Tex., 1923), pp. 59-67.
4. Mrs. Orr, *Life and Letters*, p. 266.
5. *Letters of Browning to Isa Blagden*, pp. 59-62.
6. Abbé J. Dominique, in "Le Poète Browning à Sainte-Marie-de-Pornic," *Revue de Bretagne, de Vendée & d'Anjou*, XXII (1899), 329-48, has preserved several reminiscences of old inhabitants concerning his stay in this Breton village. Since these traditions were collected by the Abbé during a visit to the neighbourhood around the time of the publication of his article in November, 1899, they have no bearing on the dates of the poet's residences in Brittany. In placing Browning at Pornic in 1863, 1864, and 1865, it is clear that Abbé Dominique is simply following Mrs. Orr's account. For example, he cites, from Mrs. Orr's *Life*, the letter in which the poet describes his first arrival at Ste Marie, and accepts the date of 1863 she assigns to it. But the correct date, as the *Letters of Browning to Isa Blagden* prove, is August 18, 1862.
7. *Letters of Browning to Isa Blagden*, p. 71.
8. *Ibid.*, p. 94.
9. Henry James, *William Wetmore Story and His Friends* (Edinburgh and London, 1903), II, 138.
10. For further evidence, a letter of Browning's to Robert Lytton, see the Addendum.
11. Edward Dowden, *Robert Browning* (London, 1904), p. 230 n.
12. W. H. Griffin and H. C. Minchin, *The Life of Robert Browning* (London, 1910), p. 235.
13. This letter is printed, in full, in *Letters of Browning to Isa Blagden*, pp. 103-5.
14. This letter is printed, in full, by Henry James in *William Wetmore Story and His Friends*, II, 153-56.
15. Cited from *Alfred Lord Tennyson, a Memoir by His Son* (New York, 1911), II, 16.

16. From a letter printed by G. F. Palgrave in *Francis Turner Palgrave* (London, 1899), pp. 94-95.
17. *Letters of Browning to Isa Blagden,* p. 104.
18. Henry James, *William Wetmore Story and His Friends,* II, 154.
19. *Ibid.,* p. 155.
20. *Ibid.*
21. Mrs. Orr, *Life and Letters,* p. 259.
22. See citation in the Addendum of letters to Isabella Blagden and Julia Wedgwood written by Browning which prove that Browning was in Biarritz in September, 1864.
23. *Rossetti Papers 1862 to 1870,* compiled by William Michael Rossetti (London, 1903), p. 302.
24. *Tennyson, a Memoir,* II, 16.
25. Henry James, *William Wetmore Story and His Friends,* II, 154-55.
26. See the Addendum for quotation of a passage from a letter to Julia Wedgwood which confirms the accuracy of this date.
27. Professor C. H. Herford, *Robert Browning* (Edinburgh and London, 1905), p. 171 n., sensed the fact that the laying out of the plan of *The Ring and the Book* at Roland's Pass and Browning's mention of the Roman murder story in the Biarritz letter are closely related in time. It is not, however, Rossetti's reminiscence, as Professor Herford conjectures, but the Biarritz letter that is misdated. See the Addendum for a statement of Browning's which proves that *The Ring and the Book* was begun in 1864.
28. Mrs. Orr, *Life and Letters,* p. 284.
29. *Ibid.,* p. 260.
30. *Letters of Robert Browning,* collected by Thomas J. Wise and ed. by Thurman L. Hood (New Haven, 1933), pp. 80-82.
31. *Ibid.,* pp. 93-94.
32. *Letters from Owen Meredith to Robert and Elizabeth Barrett Browning,* ed. by Aurelia Brooks Harlan and J. Lee Harlan Jr. (Baylor University, 1936), pp. 202-3.
33. *Robert Browning and Julia Wedgwood,* ed. by Richard Curle (London, 1937), p. 63.
34. *Ibid.,* pp. 85-86.

ESSAY 5:

1. It was Miss Blagden's practice to write to Browning on the 12th of each month, while he replied on the 19th. This explains the frequent recurrence of the latter date in the correspondence cited.
2. *Letters of Robert Browning to Miss Isa Blagden,* arranged for publication by A. Joseph Armstrong (Waco, Tex., 1923), p. 65.
3. *Ibid.,* pp. 68-69.
4. Mrs. Sutherland Orr, *A Handbook to the Works of Robert Browning* (London, 1899), p. 83 n.
5. See the preface to Professor Hodell's English translation of the Secondary Source (Everyman's Library, 1911), p. 258.
6. W. H. Griffin and H. C. Minchin, *The Life of Robert Browning* (London, 1910), p. 230.
7. Arthur K. Cook, *A Commentary upon Browning's The Ring and the Book* (London, 1920), p. 277.
8. *Letters of Browning to Isa Blagden,* pp. 68-69.

9. Pp. 259-66.

ESSAY 7:

1. Mrs. Sutherland Orr, *Life and Letters of Robert Browning* (London, 1891), pp. 294-97.
2. Cf. extract from Alfred Domett's diary, cited in W. H. Griffin and H. C. Minchin, *The Life of Robert Browning* (London, 1910), pp. 248-49.
3. Mrs. Orr, *Life and Letters*, pp. 295-96.
4. Cited in Griffin and Minchin, *Life*, p. 258.
5. *Ibid.*
6. Cited in Edward Dowden, *Robert Browning* (London, 1904), p. 303.
7. Cited from *The Works of Robert Browning*, with Introductions by F. G. Kenyon (London, 1912), VII, xiii.
8. Osbert Burdett, *The Brownings* (New York, 1929), pp. 310-11.
9. George Santayana, *Interpretations of Poetry and Religion* (New York, 1900), p. 209.
10. For this essay see *Peacock's Four Ages of Poetry, etc.*, ed. by H. F. B. Brett-Smith (Oxford, 1923). Cf. with Browning's analysis of Shelley's poetry the statement of his own poetic aims in the original Advertisement to *Paracelsus*.
11. *SP*, XXIX (1932), 463-84.
12. Cf. William Clyde DeVane, *Browning's Parleyings* (New Haven, 1927), pp. 232-34.
13. *Robert Browning*, p. 301.
14. Mrs. Orr, *Life and Letters*, p. 297.
15. G. K. Chesterton, *Robert Browning* (New York, 1903), p. 125.
16. *The Poetry of Robert Browning* (London, 1920), p. 423.
17. See Griffin and Minchin, *Life*, p. 224.
18. See DeVane, *Browning's Parleyings*, pp. 79-91.
19. *Letters of Robert Browning*, collected by Thomas J. Wise and ed. by Thurman L. Hood (New Haven, 1933), pp. 325-38.
20. Henry James, *William Wetmore Story and His Friends* (Edinburgh and London, 1903), II, 196-97.
21. These dates are determined by references in Browning's letters and also, as pointed out by Mr. DeVane, by the manuscript of *Fifine* in the library of Balliol College.
22. Wise and Hood, *Letters of Browning*, pp. 152-54.
23. *Ibid.*, pp. 154-56.
24. Cf. "Daniel Bartoli," xviii.
25. *The Poetry of Robert Browning*, p. 425.
26. *Robert Browning*, p. 305.
27. Though the character of Fifine was suggested to Browning by a handsome gipsy-woman, a member of a circus troupe whom he had seen in Pornic at St. Giles Fair, it is evident that she is but a figure for his imagination to play about.
28. In writing of Browning's allegorical representation of the Lady Ashburton incident in "Daniel Bartoli," Professor DeVane has drawn attention of the temporary inconstancy of her husband to her memory after her *Husband* (1855), a poem dealing, in a general way, with a wife's anticipation of the temporary inconstancy of her husband to her memory after her death. It is of interest, in this connection, to note certain striking corre-

spondences between the imagery of this poem and the illustrations of *Fifine at the Fair*. Cf. the allusions to the fen-fire and the painting by Raphael in *Fifine* with the following stanzas from *Any Wife to Any Husband*.

> "So, what if in the dusk of life that's left,
> I, a tired traveller of my sun bereft,
> Look from my path when, mimicking the same,
> The fire-fly glimpses past me, come and gone?
> —Where was it till the sunset? Where anon
> It will be at the sunrise! What's to blame?" . . .

> "It cannot change the love still kept for Her,
> More than if such a picture I prefer
> Passing a day with, to a room's bare side:
> The painted form takes nothing she possessed,
> Yet, while the Titian's Venus lies at rest,
> A man looks. Once more, what is there to chide?"

29. *Letters of Robert Browning to Miss Isa Blagden,* arranged for publication by A. Joseph Armstrong (Waco, Tex., 1923), p. 191.
30. *Ferishtah's Fancies,* "A Pillar at Sebzevar," ll. 22-26.
31. *Ibid.,* ll. 134-35.

ESSAY 8:

1. *Ferishtah's Fancies,* "A Pillar at Sebzevar," ll. 64-66.
2. Browning's ethical and religious ideas have been amply expounded in Henry Jones's *Browning as a Philosophical and Religious Teacher* and A. C. Pigou's *Robert Browning as a Religious Teacher*. I merely allude to these in order to emphasize the poet's antithesis of love versus reason, ending in intellectual agnosticism, which has a vital bearing on his casuistic monologues.
3. *Lectures on the Present Position of Catholics in England* (London, 1851), pp. 410-11.
4. See his article, "Browning's Casuistry," *National Review,* XL (1902), 534-52.
5. See Louise Snitslaar, *Sidelights on Robert Browning's "The Ring and the Book"* (Amsterdam, 1934).
6. Sir Charles Gavan Duffy, *My Life in Two Hemispheres* (London, 1898), II, 157.
7. For fuller consideration of his religious background see pp. 24-27.
8. *QR,* CLXX (1890), 493.
9. *The Ring and the Book,* I. 442-44.
10. See Duffy, *My Life in Two Hemispheres*.
11. *Rambler,* V (1856), 54-71.
12. *The Works of John Ruskin,* ed. by E. T. Cook and Alexander Wedderburn, XXXVI (London, 1909), xxxiv.
13. Mr. C. R. Tracy has drawn attention to close correspondences between allusions in *Bishop Blougram's Apology* and passages in Newman's writings. See "Bishop Blougram," *MLR,* XXXIV (1939), 422-25.
14. See "Browning and Higher Criticism," above, where I have fully discussed the poet's attitude towards the evidences of Christianity. In his

earlier writings his intellectual theories vacillate, but in *La Saisiaz, Ferishtah's Fancies,* and the Parleying with "Bernard de Mandeville," his position is that of complete distrust in the capacity of reason to verify the historicity of the gospels, or to solve the metaphysical paradox of the doctrine of the Incarnation, that "God once assumed on earth a human shape."

15. "Browning's Casuistry," p. 542.

16. Horace Wyndham, *Mr. Sludge, the Medium* (London, 1937). Additional material on the seances of Home and the attitudes of the Brownings and their friends towards spiritualism has been made available through the publication of *Letters from Owen Meredith to Robert and Elizabeth Barrett Browning,* ed. by Aurelia Brooks Harlan and J. Lee Harlan Jr. (Baylor University, 1936).

17. C. H. Herford, *Robert Browning* (Edinburgh and London, 1905), pp. 165-66.

18. *Letters of Robert Browning to Miss Isa Blagden,* arranged for publication by A. Joseph Armstrong (Waco, Tex., 1923), p. 196.

19. *Letters of Robert Browning,* collected by Thomas J. Wise and ed. by Thurman L. Hood (New Haven, 1933), p. 152.

20. *The Statue and the Bust,* ll. 220-23.

21. See p. 121.

22. "A Pillar at Sebzevar," ll. 22-26.

ESSAY 9:

1. Stopford Brooke, *The Poetry of Robert Browning* (London, 1920), pp. 14-15. In a similar vein Hugh Walker writes of *Paracelsus,* in *The Greater Victorian Poets* (London, 1895), p. 37: ". . . that wonderful poem is so near the front of its author's writings, that we may almost say he appears in it complete and perfect."

2. Edward Dowden, *Robert Browning* (London, 1904), p. 27.

3. *The Boston Browning Society Papers* (New York, 1897), pp. 221-48.

4. For a careful consideration of the weight to be attached to the historical element in *Paracelsus,* see *The Life of Robert Browning,* by W. H. Griffin and H. C. Minchin (London, 1910), pp. 65-72. The following citations represent the conclusions reached in this biography regarding the point in question:

"Browning's research was not vast: the erudition, seen especially in his notes [i.e. in *Paracelsus*], is more apparent than real . . ." (p. 69).

". . . the so-called 'sources' of his poem are practically contained in a few pages of Bitiskius, sundry passages in the works of Paracelsus himself, and in that interesting little octavo of 1620, the *Vitae Germanorum Medicorum* of Melchior Adam. But the most important source of all is Robert Browning." (p. 72)

"The record of aspiration, defeat and attainment—all that really constitutes the spiritual history of the poem—is of Browning's creation, it is his 'commentary' . . ." (p. 70).

5. *The Works of John Ruskin,* ed. by E. T. Cook and Alexander Wedderburn, XXXVI (London, 1909), xxxiv.

6. *Reverie,* ll. 201-5.

7. Cited from an article on Robert Browning in *Littell's Living Age,* CLXXXV (1890), 668.

8. Cf. Plato's *Symposium* (Shelley's translation): "He who aspires to love rightly, ought from his earliest youth to seek an intercourse with beautiful forms, and first to make a single form the object of his love. . . . He ought, then, to consider that beauty in whatever form it resides is the brother of that beauty which subsists in another form; and if he ought to pursue that which is beautiful in form, it would be absurd to imagine that beauty is not one and the same thing in all forms, and would therefore remit much of his ardent preference towards one, through his perception of the multitude of claims upon his love." *The Complete Works of Percy Bysshe Shelley*, ed. by Roger Ingpen and W. E. Peck, VII (London, 1930), 205.

9. W. F. Alexander, *An Introduction to the Poetry of Robert Browning* (Boston, 1899), p. 54.

10. C. H. Herford, *Robert Browning* (Edinburgh and London, 1905), p. 308.

11. Elizabeth Barrett Browning, *Lady Geraldine's Courtship*, stanza 41.

12. *Saul*, xviii. 308-9.

13. *An Epistle of Karshish*, ll. 304-11.

ESSAY 10:

1. *Letters of Thomas J. Wise to John Henry Wrenn*, ed. by Fannie E. Ratchford (New York, 1944), p. 547.

2. See *Atlantic Monthly*, Feb., 1945, pp. 96-97.

3. Randall, Carter, and Pollard all refuse to believe that the word in question, *mangoes*, is in Gosse's handwriting. Pollard in a cable to Carter goes so far as to declare: "Mangoes hand unascribable but more like Wise than Gosse stop letters not Gosse type." See *ibid.*, p. 98, for a discussion of this point.

4. This letter is cited by Miss Ratchford in *Letters of Wise to Wrenn*, pp. 86-87.

5. *Ibid.*, p. 82.

6. *Literary Anecdotes of the Nineteenth Century*, ed. by W. R. Nicoll and T. J. Wise (London, 1896), II, 96.

7. My conclusion that Gosse was unacquainted with the Reading edition of the *Sonnets from the Portuguese* when he published his catalogue must be corrected in the light of a letter of Gosse to Wise of June 21, 1893, printed in Wilfred Partington's *Thomas J. Wise in the Original Cloth* (London, 1947) which was published after the first printing of my article. In this letter, Gosse, who has evidently just been informed by Wise of the purported discovery of the Reading edition, promises that he will chronicle its existence. Although the letter shows that Wise planted the story of the forgery upon Gosse a few months earlier than I had conjectured, it in no way invalidates my arguments. In addition the contents of this letter reveal that Gosse himself did not possess a copy of the Reading edition in June, 1893, which would be incredible if he had been a collaborator in the forgery.

8. Given in Furnivall's corrections to Sharp's *Life of Browning* (1890), p. 3. See John Carter and Graham Pollard, *An Enquiry into the Nature of Certain Nineteenth Century Pamphlets* (London and New York, 1934), pp. 33.

Notes

9. For Gosse's narrative, to which frequent allusion is made in this essay, see *Critical Kit-Kats* (London, 1896), pp. 1-3 from the essay "The Sonnets from the Portuguese."

10. *An Enquiry into the Nature of Certain Nineteenth Century Pamphlets*, pp. 33-34.

11. *Robert Browning and Julia Wedgwood*, ed. by Richard Curle (London, 1937), p. 114.

12. *Life of Robert Browning* (London, 1890), pp. 147-48.

13. The date of the printing of the Reading edition cannot be determined with certainty, but Furnivall knew nothing about it in 1890, nor Gosse before 1893. The earliest provenance of a copy of this forgery does not go back beyond 1897.

Wise's career as a forger probably began sometime between 1886 and 1888. From his correspondence with Browning and Swinburne we know that the spurious editions of *The Runaway Slave* and *Cleopatra* were fabricated in 1888. Wilfred Partington in his book, *Forging Ahead* (New York, 1939), cites the following extract, dated January 11, 1888, from the diary of an English man of letters. ". . . Went to Shelley Society meeting. At this gathering Wise, Forman, Tegetmeier, Furnivall, Rossetti, &c were there, but not Dr. Salt, whom I had expected to see. Wise is still proceeding on his wild career of reprinting or pirating Browning, Shelley, Swinburne, &c." Partington comments: "It is unfortunate that for the time being the writer of this diary must remain under the anonymity of Mr. Y. Z. His identity would reveal with what authority it speaks." In view of the present controversy, it is regrettable that Mr. Partington has been pledged not to disclose the name of the writer of this important entry.

14. *The Letters of Robert Browning and Elizabeth Barrett Barrett*, 1845-1846 (London, 1899), II, 355.

15. *The Life and Letters of Sir Edmund Gosse* (London, 1931), pp. 198-99.

16. *Forging Ahead*, p. 167.

17. *Letters of Wise to Wrenn*, p. 176.

ESSAY 11:

1. F. R. G. Duckworth, *Browning: Background and Conflict* (London, 1931), pp. 7-8.

2. *The Works of John Ruskin*, ed. by E. T. Cook and Alexander Wedderburn, XXXVI (London, 1909), xxxiv.

3. *The Letters of Robert Browning and Elizabeth Barrett Barrett, 1845-1846* (London, 1899), I, 6.

4. *Robert Browning and Julia Wedgwood*, ed. by Richard Curle (London, 1937), p. 171.

5. *Ibid.*, p. 176.

6. William Clyde DeVane, *A Browning Handbook* (New York, 1935), p. 300.

7. Charles W. Hodell, *The Old Yellow Book* (Washington, 1908), p. 255.

8. *Ibid.*, p. 283.

9. A. K. Cook, *A Commentary upon Browning's The Ring and the Book* (London, 1920), Appendix V.

10. *Ibid.*, pp. 285-86.
11. John Marshall Gest, *The Old Yellow Book, Source of Browning's The Ring and the Book* (Boston, 1925), p. 15.
12. *Ibid.*, p. 624.
13. *Interpretations of Poetry and Religion* (New York, 1900), p. 208.
14. DeVane, *A Browning Handbook*, p. 286.
15. Louise Snitslaar, *Sidelights on Robert Browning's "The Ring and the Book"* (Amsterdam, 1934), p. 82.
16. *Ibid.*, p. 87.
17. DeVane, *A Browning Handbook*, p. 68.
18. *Ibid.*, p. 79.
19. *Ibid.*, p. 206.

Index

ALEXANDER, Louisa, 69
Alexander, W. H., 167
Armstrong, A. J., 64, 76, 97, 195 ff.
Arnold, Matthew, 23, 26, 30, 36, 64, 109, 130 f., 225, 232
Arnold, Thomas, 21 ff., 26
Ashburton, Lady Louisa, 115–28, 135, 151, 196, 225, 227, 238–39
Austin, Alfred, 53 f., 65, 68, 196

BABBITT, Irving, 8
Bagehot, Walter, 8
Baker, Mrs., 90 ff., 95
Barclay, Evelyn, 202
Barrett, Arabella, 197
Barrett, Edward, 202
Barrett, Henrietta, 69, 195 ff.
Baur, F. C., 35
Beichner, P. E., 223–24
Blagden, Isabella, 52–74, 92, 198; letters from Browning, 34 f., 55, 59, 63–64, 66, 69, 70–71, 75–84, 86 ff., 89–90, 93, 127, 148, 195–96, 198, 231, 233, 237
Bonnell, J. K., 208
Brooke, Stopford, 114, 120, 156, 204, 209
Brooks, Van Wyck, 53
Broughton, L. N., 228
Browning, Elizabeth Barrett, autograph notes of 1845 on Browning's poems, 198–99, 227–28; Browning's memory of her, 114–16, 117–19, 121 f., 124–27, 155, 201, 219 f.; correspondence, 7, 24, 56–58, 59, 63, 69, 187, 195 ff., 199, 201, 205; death, 61 ff., 66, 72, 114, 233; friendship with Isabella Blagden, 56–58, 62 ff., 66, 69; religious affiliations, 24, 201;
views on Napoleon III, 147, on spiritualism, 62, 142, 198, 240
Aurora Leigh, 59, 61, 198
Lady Geraldine's Courtship, 15, 174, 229
The Runaway Slave, 183, 242
Sonnets from the Portuguese, 177, 181, 183–90, 201 f., 241 f.
Browning, Fannie, 196, 200, 201–2
Browning, Robert
Abt Vogler, 13
Andrea del Sarto, 134
Any Wife to Any Husband, 238–39
Apparent Failure, 233
Aristophanes' Apology, 5, 108, 134, 206–7
Bishop Blougram's Apology, 5, 27, 31–32, 42 f., 109, 129, 132–41, 142, 145, 155, 228, 233
The Bishop Orders His Tomb, 129
A Blot in the 'Scutcheon, 227
By the Fire-side, 13 f., 17
Caliban upon Setebos, 134, 228, 234
Childe Roland, 226
Christmas-Eve and Easter-Day, 19, 24–25, 27–31, 33, 44, 109, 136, 146–47, 165
Cleon, 27, 31, 109, 134
Confessions, 11, 15
Count Gismond, 219
Cristina, 165
A Death in the Desert, 27, 32–38, 40, 43–45, 50–51, 109, 175, 233–34
De Gustibus, 14
Dramatic Lyrics, 11
Dramatic Romances, 6, 11
Dramatic Romances and Lyrics, 198–99

Dramatis Personae, 23, 32 f., 86, 134, 231, 233–34; *Epilogue* to, 27, 32 f., 35, 49–51, 233
Epilogue to Asolando, 207
An Epistle of Karshish, 27, 31, 35, 46, 175
Ferishtah's Fancies, 5, 27, 41–42, 43, 47, 127 f., 131, 155, 174–75, 207, 240
Fifine at the Fair, 5, 105–28, 129, 133, 135, 151–55, 227, 238
The Flight of the Duchess, 15 f., 121, 199, 227–28
Fra Lippo Lippi, 17, 102, 134
Gold Hair, 23–24, 27, 32, 233
In a Balcony, 227
In a Gondola, 7
James Lee's Wife, 15, 233
La Saisiaz, 240
Luria, 198
Men and Women, 6, 11, 134
Mr. Sludge, "the Medium," 5, 109, 129, 135, 141–47
My Last Duchess, 129, 228
New Poems, 194, 199
Numpholeptos, 205
Old Pictures in Florence, 11, 16, 18
Pacchiarotto, 16, 65
Paracelsus, 130, 134, 138, 156–75, 200, 238
Parleyings with Certain People of Importance, 27, 43, 47–48, 109, 112, 115 f., 119, 134, 147, 224–25, 238–39, 240
Pauline, 138, 160, 162, 163, 165 f., 220
The Pied Piper of Hamelin, 12, 228
Pippa Passes, 4, 10 f., 14 f., 228
Popularity, 6, 12 f.
Prince Hohenstiel-Schwangau, 5, 108, 109, 129 f., 134 f., 142, 147–50
Prospice, 233
Rabbi Ben Ezra, 13
Red Cotton Night-Cap Country, 5, 108
Reverie, 159, 161
The Ring and the Book, 3 ff., 14, 17, 27, 32, 36, 38–39, 40–41, 43–46, 48–49, 64, 75 ff., 78, 81, 84–87, 89–94, 95–104, 130, 134, 136 f., 145–46, 147, 177, 193 ff., 197, 201, 203, 207, 209–24, 234–35
Saul, 15, 27, 31, 44, 46–47, 131, 142, 175
Sibrandus Schnafnaburgensis, 6, 16
Sordello, 5, 10 f., 45, 105, 134, 138, 160, 163, 166, 168, 200, 206, 225–26
A Soul's Tragedy, 134, 147, 198
St. Martin's Summer, 227
The Statue and the Bust, 12, 106, 150
Strafford, 200, 206, 227
Browning, Robert W. (Penini), 63, 80, 196, 200 ff.
Browning, Sarianna, 196
Buchanan, Robert, 110, 227, 234
Burdett, Osbert, 17 f., 107–8, 200 f.
Burgon, J. W., 21
Burton, J. R., 183 f., 188
Byron, Lord, 64, 106, 151, 161

CARLYLE, Thomas, 17, 28 f., 64, 109, 196, 225
Carter, John, 176 ff., 181 f., 186, 191, 201, 241
Charlton, H. B., 207
Charteris, Evan, 188–89
Chatterton, Thomas, 176, 195
Chesterton, Gilbert, 8, 16, 113, 193, 203 f., 234
Clarke, G. H., 226–27
Clough, A. H., 28
Cobbe, Frances, 54, 61–62, 72
Colenso, J. W., 21–23, 32
Coleridge, S. T., 22, 29, 232-33
Comte, Auguste, 30, 132
Cook, A. K., 91–92, 215–17, 219, 222
Copleston, Edward, 26
Corrigan, Beatrice, 96, 210
Cramer, M. B., 205–6
Crawford, Thomas, 54
Cundiff, P. A., 210
Curle, Richard, 195, 210
Cushman, Charlotte, 54, 65–66, 72

DARWIN, C. R., 132
Davies, J. L., 23, 33–35

Index

DeVane, W. C., 5, 75, 110-12, 115 f., 194, 213 f., 219-20, 224-27, 238-39
Dickens, Charles, 54, 177
Dickson, Arthur, 228
Disraeli, Benjamin, 109, 134, 147, 225
Domett, Alfred, 29, 105
Dominique, Abbé J., 236
Dowden, Edward, 78-79, 112-13, 120, 158, 193, 204, 209
Duckworth, F. R. G., 204-5, 231
Duffy, Sir C. G., 135 f.

ELIOT, George, 28, 36, 54, 62, 177
Eliot, T. S., 7 f.
Elton, Sir Oliver, 205
Emerson, R. W., 54, 143
Essays and Reviews, 21, 23, 26, 32, 36, 46

FAVERTY, F. E., 228
Field, Kate, 52, 54, 60-61, 62, 64, 67, 70, 72, 200
FitzGerald, Edward, 7, 196
Forman, Buxton, 178, 182 f., 185, 242
Forster, John, 136
Froude, J. A., 28
Fuller, Margaret, 54
Furnivall, F. J., 106, 185 f., 196, 224, 242

GEST, J. M., 215, 216-17, 219, 223 f.
Gladstone, W. E., 22
Glazebrook, Mrs. M. G., 33, 35
Gloder, Harold, 226
Göritz, Käthe, 23, 232-33
Gosse, Sir Edmund, 22, 177 f., 180, 182-92, 193, 196, 204, 209, 213, 233, 241
Gosse, Philip, 132
Greg, W. R., 28
Griffin, W. H., 75, 78-79, 91 f., 193, 196, 204, 213, 224, 239, 240

HAMPDEN, R. D., 26
Harlan, Aurelia and J. Lee, Jr., 57, 88, 198, 240
Hatcher, H. H., 206

Hawthorne, Nathaniel, 54, 61, 72
Hennell, Charles, 28
Herford, C. H., 36, 120, 142, 167, 193, 204, 209, 219, 237
Hodell, C. W., 90 ff., 204, 213-14, 215
Home, Daniel, 54, 109, 135, 141-42, 147, 240
Hood, T. L., 64, 87, 195 f., 206
Hosmer, Harriet, 54, 62, 72
Hunt, Leigh, 20, 186, 196, 202
Hutton, J. A., 207
Huxley, Leonard, 195 f.
Huxley, T. H., 132

JAMES, Henry, 52-53, 54 f., 67-68, 72, 116, 221-22
Jameson, Mrs. Anna, 54, 60
Jarves, J. J., 54
Jones, Sir Henry, 38, 134, 204 f., 208 f., 239
Jowett, Benjamin, 26, 64

KEATS, John, 66, 161 f.
Keble, John, 26
Kenyon, Sir F. G., 33, 93, 107, 194, 196, 199
Kingsley, Charles, 132
Kipling, Rudyard, 73-74, 177
Kirkconnell, Watson, 49
Kirkup, G. S., 54

LAIRESSE, Gérard de, 226
Lamb, Charles, 19-20, 231
Landor, W. S., 54, 60 f., 66, 72, 197-98
Leighton, Sir Frederic, 54, 86, 91-92, 196
Liddon, H. P., 233
Longfellow, H. W., 54
Lounsbury, T. R., 200, 206
Lowell, J. R., 54
Lucas, F. L., 8-9
Lytton, Robert (Owen Meredith), 54 f., 56-60, 72, 88, 198

MCALEER, E. C., 57-58, 59
McElderry, B. R., 211-13, 220-21
Macready, W. C., 200
Manning, H. E., 64
Marks, Jeannette, 202
Maurice, F. D., 22-23, 233

Mayne, Ethel, 227
Mertz, J. T., 231
Mill, J. S., 233
Minchin, H. C., 75, 193, 196, 197–98, 209, 213, 224, 240
Mitford, Miss, 184 f., 190
Morris, William, 177

NAPOLEON I, 20, 232
Napoleon III, 64, 109, 134 f., 147–50
Newman, Francis, 28
Newman, J. H., 22, 26, 131 f., 136 f., 139, 233
Norton, C. E., 54

ORIEL NOETICS, 22, 26
Orr, Mrs. Sutherland, 29, 39, 51, 63, 75–88, 91, 93, 105–6, 107, 112–13, 116, 193, 202 f., 210, 231 ff., 236
Oxford Declaration, 21, 32
Oxford Movement, 26, 49

PALGRAVE, Francis, 78, 81, 84
Palmer, Frederick, Jr., 199
Palmer, G. H., 207
Partington, Wilfred, 176 f., 190–91, 241 f.
Pettigrew, Helen, 211–12
Pfleiderer, Otto, 23
Phelps, W. L., 203
Pigou, A. C., 204, 234, 239
Pollard, Graham, 176 ff., 181, 186, 201, 241
Pottle, F. A., 202
Powers, Hiram, 54

RANDALL, David, 182
Ratchford, Fannie, 176, 177–78, 180, 181–92
Rea, J. D., 228
Renan, J. E., 21–23, 32–35, 50, 64, 109, 132, 233–34
Rossetti, D. G., 110–12, 227
Rossetti, W. M., 85
Royce, Josiah, 158–60, 164
Ruskin, John, 10, 111, 138, 160, 191, 205
Russell, Frances, 203, 215, 217–18

SAND, George, 58–59

Santayana, George, 7 f., 108, 220 f.
Scott, Sir Walter, 17
Sharp, William, 186–87, 189, 202, 241
Shaw, J. E., 218–19
Shelley, P. B., 66, 106, 108, 161–65, 167, 173, 195, 202, 238, 241 f.
Smalley, Donald, 194–95, 206 f.
Smith, C. W., 208–9
Smith, F. M., 228
Smith, Robertson, 22
Snitslaar, Louise, 222–23, 239
Snyder, Edward, 199
Somervell, D. C., 205, 227
Spencer, Herbert, 132
Stelter, B. F., 228
Stephen, Sir Leslie, 120, 133–34, 141
Sterling, John, 28, 233
Stevenson, R. L., 177
Stoll, E. E., 227
Story, Edith, 117, 148, 196, 200
Story, Emelyn, letters to, from Browning, 78–85, 196
Story, W. W., 54, 62, 72, 78 f., 114, 116, 196, 208
Stowe, Harriet, 54
Strachey, Lytton, 9
Strauss, D. F., 21–23, 28–30, 32–36, 43, 109, 132
Swinburne, Algernon, 17, 106, 110, 177, 179 f., 190, 225, 242
Symons, Arthur, 15, 209

TENNYSON, Alfred, 3, 11, 36, 42, 45, 78 f., 81, 84 f., 112, 131, 137, 177, 196, 231
Tennyson, Frederick, 54
Thackeray, W. M., 54, 177
Thirlwall, Connop, 21
Tisdel, F. M., 206–7
Toynbee, William, 200
Tracts for the Times, 26
Tracy, C. R., 228, 239
Treves, Sir Frederick, 103, 214–15
Trollope, Anthony, 54, 62, 65, 95
Trollope, Frances, 54
Trollope, Theodosia, 52, 57, 64–65, 66, 69, 72
Trollope, Thomas Adolphus, 52, 54 f., 61 f., 64–65, 66 f., 72, 90, 92, 95

Index

Tübingen School, 22 f., 33, 35 f., 43

VILLARI, Mme Pasquale, 66, 200

WALKER, Hugh, 240
Walton, E., 236
Wann, Louis, 208
Ward, Mrs. Humphry, 19 f., 24
Ward, W. G., 29
Watts-Dunton, W. T., 180
Wedgwood, Julia, correspondence with Browning, 64, 88, 186, 195, 197, 202, 210–11
Wenger, C. N., 207
Whately, Richard, 26
Whiting, Lilian, 55, 60, 200–1, 202
Whitman, Walt, 7
Whyte, A. J., 225 f.
Wise, Thomas, collection of Browning letters, 64, 87, 116, 195, 196–97, 201; forgeries, 176–92, 201, 241 f.
Wiseman, N. P. S., 32, 109, 135–37
Woodward, W. H., 96–97, 99
Wordsworth, William, 161, 177, 231
Wrenn, J. H., 177–78, 179
Wyndham, Horace, 141

YARRILL, E. H., 95, 210